❦ INDONESIA'S ELITE

Political Culture and Cultural Politics

INDONESIA'S ELITE:

Political Culture and Cultural Politics

DONALD K. EMMERSON
///

Cornell University Press   ITHACA AND LONDON

International Standard Book Number 0-8014-0917-9
Library of Congress Catalog Card Number 75-36525
Printed in the United States of America by York Composition Co.
Librarians: Library of Congress cataloging information appears on the last page of the book.

To my parents,
John K. and Dorothy M. Emmerson,
with love and gratitude

CONTENTS

8   CONTENTS

TABLES

ACKNOWLEDGMENTS

I first became attracted to Indonesia as a graduate student at Yale University in 1966–1967. A Foreign Area Fellowship from the Ford Foundation enabled me to spend two years in the country from 1967 through 1969, when the interviews that form the core of this book were completed. I wrote a first draft during 1970–1973 while teaching at the University of Wisconsin in Madison. A Faculty Research Abroad Award from the U.S. Office of Education, a Southeast Asia Fellowship from the Ford Foundation, and a grant from the Graduate Research Committee of the University of Wisconsin brought me back to Indonesia in 1974 for more research and to write the final draft. A Visiting Fellowship at the Australian National University in 1975 gave me time to prepare the printer's copy. For this institutional assistance, I am grateful.

Persons who were unusually helpful to me include Partomo Alibazah, S. M. Ardan, Harsja Bachtiar, Musaffa Basjyr, the late Harry Benda, John Bresnan, Koen de Heer, Djaelani, Barry Gaberman, Bambang Gunardjo, Ismid Hadad, Fuad Hasan, Aristides Katoppo, Roger Long, Nono Makarim, Suhadi Mangkusuwondo, Frank Miller, Goenawan Muhamad, Niels Mulder, G. J. Resink, Ki Rijasudibyaprana, Joel Rocamora, Paul Samadiono, Allan Samson, Selosoemardjan, Thomas Sherburne, Sabam and Toenggoel Siagian, Aurora Simadjuntak, the late Soe Hok Gie, Daniel Sullivan, Kapto Sunoto, Edy Tedjasukmana, Robert Tilman, Ibu Tobing, and Judy Williams. And they are merely in the foreground of a Balinese painting crammed with generous friends and acquaintances.

For criticizing the manuscript, I thank Benedict Anderson,

Charles Anderson, Willard Barber, Dwight King, Robert Lane, Daniel Lev, William Liddle, Karl Pelzer, James Scott, and Frank Weinstein. Interviewing is convivial fun, but writing is lonely discipline, and these colleagues were doubly sustaining in the latter phase. Intellectually they refreshed my perspective, while personally they made it easier for me to believe in academe as a community of people of ideas rather than an industry of idea people. I am also grateful to John Collis and Dorothy L. Emmerson for help in preparing the bibliography and in proofreading.

My wife, Carolyn, shared the adventure and the ordeal. She went with me twice to Indonesia, learned the language, and wrote a thesis on an Indonesian topic. When my writing turned voracious, devouring my time, she protested. When I needed her help in improving the beast—criticizing, indexing, proofreading it—she was unstinting. From her loving resistance and assistance, both family and manuscript gained.

As for the forty men whose voices you are about to hear, but for their cooperation and forbearance, this book could not have been written. May they recognize themselves.

Finally, my gratitude does not lessen my responsibility. Without all these people, this book would have been much less than it is. With them, I should have made it more.

DONALD K. EMMERSON

Madison, Wisconsin

ORTHOGRAPHICAL NOTE

All Indonesian words, including names of places, organizations, and legendary figures, are spelled according to the new orthography introduced in 1972. Names of real people, however, are spelled the way their owners signed them or as printed in historical accounts or contemporary local media—many Indonesians continue to write their names the old way—with the exception that, for ease of recognition by readers whose native tongue is English, "oe" is rendered "u"; to preserve verisimilitude, pseudonyms are spelled the old way, but also with "u" instead of "oe". To help in finding the literature cited, the spelling of authors' and publishers' names and untranslated titles has not been altered at all. Aside from "oe" = "u" (both pronounced "oo" as in the English word "zoo"), equivalences between the old and new spellings, respectively, and their unchanged pronunciations include "j" = "y" (pronounced "y" as in "yes"), "dj" = "j" (pronounced "j" as in "jar"), "sj" = "sy" (pronounced "sh" as in "she"), "tj" = "c" (pronounced "ch" as in "chat"), and "ch" = "kh" (pronounced about like "ch" in the German word "ach"). For the further convenience of readers, the plural form of Indonesian words is given, following English usage, by adding "s".

ABBREVIATIONS

ABRI: Angkatan Bersenjata Republik Indonesia (Armed Forces of the Indonesian Republic)

Ampera: Amanat Penderitaan Rakyat (Message of the People's Suffering)

BPKI: Badan Penyelidik Kemerdekaan Indonesia (Body for the Investigation of Indonesian Independence)

CSI: Chuo Sangi In (Central Advisory Council)

DPR: Dewan Perwakilan Rakyat (People's Representative Council) or, in 1960–1971, Dewan Perwakilan Rakyat Gotong Royong ("Mutual Help" People's Representative Council)

Golkar: Golongan Karya (Functional Groups)

HIS: Hollandsch Inlandsche School (Dutch Native [Primary] School)

Masyumi: Majelis Syuro Muslimin Indonesia (Consultative Assembly of Indonesian Muslims)

MPR: Majelis Permusyawaratan Rakyat (People's Consultative Assembly), first convened in 1972

MPRS: Majelis Permusyawaratan Rakyat Sementara (Provisional People's Consultative Assembly), last convened in 1968

NU: Nahdlatul Ulama (Muslim Teachers' Party)

Parindra: Partai Indonesia Raya (Greater Indonesia Party)

Parkindo: Partai Keristen Indonesian (Indonesian Christian [Protestant] Party)

Parmusi: Partai Muslimin Indonesia (Indonesian Muslims' Party)

PKI: Partai Komunis Indonesia (Indonesian Communist Party)

PNI: Partai Nasional Indonesia (Indonesian National Party)

PPBB: Perhimpunan Pegawai Bestuur Bumiputera (Association of Native Administrative Employees)

PPKI: Panitia Persiapan Kemerdekaan Indonesia (Committee for the Preparation of Indonesian Independence)

PSII: Partai Sarekat Islam Indonesia (Party of the Indonesian Islamic Union)

RUUP: Rancangan Undang-Undang tentang Perkawinan (Draft Law on Marriage)

TKR: Tentara Keamanan Rakyat (People's Security Army)

❀ INDONESIA'S ELITE

Political Culture and Cultural Politics

POLITICAL CULTURE AND CULTURAL POLITICS

All of us are forever trapped at the pivot between what we have been and what we might become, and upon the discrepancy between the two depends the ease of our transition. For many, the times are out of joint. Some find refuge in a cherished, obsolescent past from a future that past cannot justify; others struggle to remain forever contemporary by shunning permanent commitment or belief. But most of us, quixotically and in a patchwork sort of way, try to change and yet remain the same, rationalizing what we might become in terms of what we like to think we have always been.

Political elites in large, multicultural nations find themselves in a potentially explosive version of this predicament. Beyond their own personal search for consistency between yesterday and tomorrow, they have a capacity to influence that search in the lives of millions of others. What would be introspective contemplation in the individual is, in the culturally plural polity, a contest for larger stakes. Abiding collectivities of shared experience and outlook become overtly political; the unorganized are organized, the intuited is made explicit, and boundaries and doctrines arise to define pre-emptive claims to a future that threatens to belong to another group. Change is no mere chronology but is measured in terms of power gained and lost.

In the extreme case, politics itself becomes a purely intercultural struggle. Leaders of ethnic groups, religious communities, and secular associations clash, coalesce, and clash again as they strive to implement the images of the future that favor their respective clienteles. In the competition for power, parochial loyalties count for more than the rhetoric of national unity, which is reduced to whatever is so vague or trivial as to be acceptable to all. The elite's subnational origins triumph over its national position. Society splits the state.

But the opposite is also possible: that by virtue of their shared high status and exposure to a secularizing "world culture,"[1] the national elite prefigures a truly national future to which ethnic and religious forces can creatively contribute even as they are demobilized from the political arena into private life. The elite's position integrates its origins. The state unites society.

This book explores these and other more nuanced perspectives on multicultural Indonesia. Depending on the criteria used to distinguish them, there are between ninety and over three hundred ethnic groups in this largest archipelagic nation in the world, and all the great religions are represented there. What makes these identities fascinating for the student of political culture, however, is less their diversity than their skewed distribution and their unequal access to political power. The latter facts are of central concern in this study.

In the Indonesian mosaic, some pieces are much bigger than others. Ethnically, the Javanese overshadow the rest. Although no one knows exactly, they account for perhaps half the total population. The second largest group, the Sundanese, represent less than a fifth; the many other groups are much smaller. The homeland of the Javanese is the island of Java, where some two-thirds of all Indonesians live, and where the Javanese elaborated over centuries a rich culture that has become the single greatest source of Indonesian identity. Although cabinets have been recruited to include minority groups, most of the powerful men in government are Javanese.[2]

1. See Lucian W. Pye, *Aspects of Political Development* (Boston: Little, Brown, 1966), pp. 9–10 and 199–200.
2. Population estimates are based on M. A. Jaspan, *Daftar Sementara dari Sukubangsa-bangsa di Indonesia* (Yogyakarta: Gadjah Mada University, Social Research Committee, 1958), cited by Hildred Geertz, "Indonesian Cultures and Communities," in Ruth T. McVey, ed., *Indonesia* (rev. ed., New Haven: Yale University Southeast Asia Studies, 1967), p. 24; Frank M. Lebar, ed. and comp., *Ethnic Groups of Insular Southeast Asia* (New Haven: Human Relations Area Files Press, 1972), Part III; and 1971 Indonesian census returns provided through the courtesy of Gordon Temple. For ethnic patterns in three cities (Jakarta, Bandung, and Medan), see Lance Castles, "The Ethnic Profile of Djakarta," *Indonesia*, 1 (April 1967),

Among Indonesia's religions, Islam is numerically by far the strongest. In the past, Muslim political leaders have proudly referred to Indonesia as "ninety per cent Muslim." Even official estimates in 1969–1970 identified at least 89 per cent of the total population as Muslims, compared to only 5 per cent or less as Protestants, 2 per cent or less as Catholics, about 2 per cent as Hindus (mainly Balinese), and less than half of one per cent as Buddhists. But these figures underestimate the size of non-Muslim communities, which burgeoned after the attempted coup and countercoup of 1965. The 1971 census showed a decline in Islam's share of the population to 87 per cent; the true figure could be lower.[3] Even so, non-Muslim communities are dwarfed by the Islamic statistic.

Given Islam's preponderance, one might expect elite political culture in Indonesia to be not only heavily Javanese, which it is, but piously Muslim too. This is not the case, however, for although the Muslim Javanese include a core who are serious and exclusive about their faith, a much larger periphery take Islam's obligations lightly and leave room for other beliefs.

This contrast between practicing (*santri*) and lax (*abangan*) Javanese Muslims is a favorite topic among students of Indonesian political life.[4] It has led to acrimony and violence among Indo-

153–204, and Edward M. Bruner, "The Expression of Ethnicity in Indonesia," in Abner Cohen, ed., *Urban Ethnicity* (London: Tavistock, 1974), pp. 251–280.

3. The official estimates in 1969–1970 were made by the Central Statistical Bureau as cited by Anwar Harjono, "The Future of Islamic Law in Indonesia," *South East Asia Journal of Theology*, 14, 2 (1973), 57, and by the Department of Religion as cited in *Statistik Indonesia 1970 & 1971* (Jakarta: Biro Pusat Statistik, 1972), p. 42. The 1971 percentage was calculated from figures in *Penduduk Indonesia*, Sensus Penduduk 1971, Seri D (Jakarta: Biro Pusat Statistik, 1975), p. 90. An example of the 90 per cent statistic being used to describe Indonesia as "Muslim" is Kasman Singodimedjo's speech reported in *Abadi*, Aug. 30, 1969. Figures on Christian expansion can be found in T. B. Simatupang, "The Situation and Challenge of the Christian Mission in Indonesia Today," *South East Asia Journal of Theology*, 10, 4 (April 1969), 21–24. Work in progress by M. Polak documents the also striking growth of the Hindu community. The claim of a Buddhist spokesman, quoted in *Sinar Harapan*, May 10, 1974, that up to 8 per cent of Indonesia's 127 million people belonged to his faith is interesting not for its accuracy—it appears exaggerated—but for the fact that he felt justified in making it.

4. For example: Bruce Cruikshank, "Abangan, Santri, and Prijaji: A Critique," *Journal of Southeast Asian Studies*, 3 (March 1972), 39–43; Ruth

nesians. In the period of conflict politics that began when the colonial order collapsed in the early 1940's, as political organizations mobilized supporters either among pious or among perfunctory Muslims, including non-Javanese, the religious cleavage grew and cut more deeply into national politics. Militantly sincere Muslims struggled to realize if not an Islamic state then at least an Islamic presence in the nation-state that could safeguard their community against a feared secular or even Christianizing future. Their utopia, in turn, has been repeatedly frustrated by a shifting coalition of communist and nationalist movements with abangan followings on Java and Christian organizations based in enclave communities on the outer islands.

Among the elite, the problem of incorporating Islamic demands and allowing for Islamic sensitivities within a nonconfessional state preoccupied a constitutional convention in 1945, stalemated a constituent assembly in 1959, and in 1968 prevented a consultative assembly from writing a substantive mandate to accompany its acclamation of General Suharto as president. At the mass level, in West Java, Aceh, and South Sulawesi in the 1950's, Muslim movements rose against the central authority, hoping in vain to create a future out of their own distant past: a House of Islam in twentieth-century Indonesia in the image of the Prophet's theocracy in seventh-century Medina. In East Java in the mid-1960's, Muslim leaders cooperated with the army in anticommunist purges to destroy the rival utopia of the secular, collectivist left. Although its strength varied, politically creative Islam never commanded a majority, and so could never enact its plans; it could only hope to

---

T. McVey, "Nationalism, Islam, and Marxism: The Management of Ideological Conflict in Indonesia," an introduction to Sukarno, *Nationalism, Islam and Marxism*, trans. Karel H. Warouw and Peter D. Weldon (Ithaca: Cornell University Modern Indonesia Project, 1970), pp. 1–33; Donald Hindley, "Alirans and the Fall of the Old Order," *Indonesia*, 9 (April 1970), 23–66; W. F. Wertheim, "From Aliran towards Class Struggle in the Countryside of Java," *Pacific Viewpoint*, 10, 2 (1969), 1–17; Clifford Geertz, *The Social History of an Indonesian Town* (Cambridge, Mass.: MIT Press, 1965), pp. 153–208; Robert R. Jay, *Religion and Politics in Rural Central Java* (New Haven: Yale University Southeast Asia Studies, 1963); Clifford Geertz, "The Javanese Village," in G. William Skinner, ed., *Local, Ethnic, and National Loyalties in Village Indonesia* (New Haven: Yale University Southeast Asia Studies, 1959), pp. 34–41. An interesting attempt to operationalize the santri-abangan distinction is M. M. Billah's "Beberapa Masalah Metodologis di Seputar Pengusahaan Penelitian Lapangan," *Cakrawala*, 6 (March-April 1974), 407–456.

thwart what it saw as the inimical designs of others. In the late 1960's and early 1970's, Indonesia's military, technocratic, and bureaucratic regime could be called Muslim neither in name nor in practice.

Had ethnic and religious distinctions coincided, Indonesia could not possibly have survived as one nation; the struggle for power and other resources would have blown her apart. Instead, the abangan-santri contrast divided the Javanese and prevented their presence in politics from becoming monolithic, while the ethnic contrast between Javanese and non-Javanese mitigated religious conflict by cutting through core and periphery in the community of Islam. The impact of political Islam was further vitiated by competition within, notably between that fundamentalist minority of reformers in the cities who would return to the Koran and the sayings of the Prophet and the easier-going custodians of evolved Muslim custom in the countryside. Of these two groups, the second, being larger and politically stronger, will merit more attention here.

In his classic study, *The Religion of Java,* Clifford Geertz defined abangan and santri and an additional term, *priyayi,* by juxtaposing substructure and superstructure. At the substructural level, he identified "three main social-structural nuclei in Java today: the village, the market, and the government bureaucracy." Typically (though not exclusively), Geertz wrote, abangan describes peasants in the village sphere, santris are traders in the market sphere, and priyayis are officials in the bureaucratic sphere. Superstructurally, in terms of religious belief, the world views of the three types according to Geertz are, respectively, animist, Islamic, and Indianized: the abangan religious tradition is centered in a ritual sharing of food (*selamatan*) and the complex of spirit beliefs surrounding it; the santri tradition upholds the faithful performance of the rituals of Islam; and the priyayis are heirs to a third, Indianized variant of Javanese religion elaborated and refined over centuries in the inland courts.[5]

The difficulty with Geertz' trichotomy is that it combines two dimensions, status and religion, which the Javanese keep separate. To the Javanese, the priyayis are a social class. Beneath the priyayis are not abangan individuals but the "little people" (*wong*

5. Clifford Geertz, *The Religion of Java* (New York: Free Press, 1960), pp. 4–7.

cilik), the lower classes. Abangan refers to the Hindu-Buddhist-animist (not just animist) religious views and practices of many Javanese; in contrast the santris are proper Muslims. In religious matters, many priyayis are abangan, but some are secular or even santri.[6]

Following Geertz, I use the term santri to describe a pious or practicing Javanese Muslim (and sometimes, more narrowly, a pupil in a traditional Muslim learning center or *pesantren,* literally, a place for santris). But I call abangan those nominally Muslim Javanese in whose religious beliefs and practices animist, Islamic, and Hindu-Buddhist elements mix or coexist. The term priyayi I reserve for members of the Javanese bureaucratic elite. Because this book is about the elite, the "little people" will hardly appear in it at all.

I define "the elite" as the members of the higher central bureaucracy and the national legislature. The politically and culturally relevant orientations of these individuals constitute "elite political culture." Defining the elite by institutional membership rather than by possession and exercise of power at once limits and expands the inquiry. The question of who "really counts" in decision-making (which is in any case short-term, personality-centered, and hard for an outsider to answer) is abandoned at the start. Instead, the focus is on enduring patterns of conflict and adaptation that are more likely to matter for the larger system in the long run. Today's ins may be tomorrow's outs, but bureaucracies and even legislatures are permanent fixtures of the modern state. A focus on them should reveal some important institutional and organizational dimensions of elite political culture.

I use the term "cultural politics" to refer to what happens when cultural differences are politicized and political differences are cast

6. Four Indonesian scholars have already corrected Geertz along these lines: Harsja W. Bachtiar, "The Religion of Java: A Commentary," written in 1964 and published in *Madjalah Ilmu-ilmu Sastra Indonesia,* 5, 1 (Jan. 1973), 85–118; Koentjaraningrat, "The Javanese of South Central Java," in George Peter Murdock, ed., *Social Structure in Southeast Asia* (Chicago: Quadrangle Books, 1960), pp. 89–93, and "Tjelapar: A Village in South Central Java," in Koentjaraningrat, ed., *Villages in Indonesia* (Ithaca: Cornell University Press, 1967), pp. 245–246; Soedjito Sosrodihardjo, "Religious Life in Java," *Monografi Sosiologi Indonesia dan Hukum Adat,* Special Issue (1963), 24; Sartono Kartodirdjo, *The Peasants' Revolt of Banten in 1888: Its Conditions, Course and Sequel* (The Hague: Martinus Nijhoff, 1966), p. 50, n. 84.

in cultural terms. In cultural politics there can be as many goals as actors, but one possible overarching goal is a dynamic relationship between community and change in which each symbiotically nurtures the other. In such an ideal political culture, upholders of the old ways would not rail against the future but would help make it less alienating by giving it indigenous meaning, just as its partisans would not forsake their origins for the individual comforts and ulcers of a merely Western model. Departures would be moored, anchors portable. The nation-state would be as solicitous of its citizens as they would be willing to cooperate to make it work; system and subsystem would be mutually enriching. Cultural politics would become a dynamic process of appreciation, criticism, and learning among disparate groups aware of their shared interests.

While this hope has guided my interest in the subject, I have tried not to read it into the evidence. I have tried to discover actual patterns of cleavage and convergence—between religious and ethnic groups, political organizations and institutions, and personal experiences and orientations. Among the questions asked are: In the national elite, to what degree and in what ways do cultural and institutional differences cut across one another or coincide? Are bureaucrats and legislators culturally similar or different, and how? Depending upon these patterns of cleavage and reinforcement, is elite political culture an asset or a liability to a dynamically integrative cultural politics? My assumption, which is also my justification for asking these questions, is that cultural patterns of elite identity will continue deeply to affect the prospect for creative balance and synthesis in the ongoing political experiment that is Indonesia.

Cultural politics is never the unmediated expression of cultural differences in political terms. Mixes of issues develop; other differences, especially economic and status grievances, acquire cultural overtones. And the motivations of the elites who interpret and use the resulting blends are also mixed; they act, not as unalloyed ethnics or believers, but as incumbents in bureaucratic or parliamentary institutions or as members of military or party organizations that themselves range in cultural heterogeneity from monoliths to mosaics. Any assessment of the potential in elite political culture for conflict and its resolution must take into account these political dimensions.

The basic institutional contrast drawn in this book is between administrators and legislators. Several studies of elite political culture elsewhere in the Third World have spotlighted this difference,[7] but among students of Indonesia it has been largely ignored. The Indonesian Parliament is easily seen as a fragile ornament imported from the West to decorate a much older and more influential culturally authoritarian bureaucratic system.[8] But if this is so, it is not an argument against studying Parliament. On the contrary, it underscores the importance of asking what cultural differences or similarities, if any, exist between administrators and politicians. The more dominant, Javanese, and abangan is the bureaucracy, and the weaker, more multi-ethnic, and devoutly Muslim is the legislature—that is, the more political and cultural imbalances are reinforcing—the poorer the prospects for constructive interplay between representative and executive institutions in Indonesia's cultural politics.

Politically relevant orientations have been widely studied in the Third World—the literature is already too vast to summarize—but the tool of survey research has often been used to disembody

7. The literature on politicians and administrators includes: on Burma, Lucian W. Pye, *Politics, Personality, and Nation Building* (Cambridge, Mass.: MIT Press, 1962), ch. 7 and pp. 15–18; on the Philippines, Jose V. Abueva, "Social Backgrounds and Recruitment of Legislators and Administrators in the Philippines," *Philippine Journal of Public Administration,* 9 (Jan. 1965), 10–29; on India, Shanti Kothari and Ramashray Roy, *Relations between Politicians and Administrators at the District Level* (New Delhi: Indian Institute of Public Administration, 1969); on Nigeria, Victor Adeola Olorunsola, "The Relationship between Bureaucratic and Political Leadership in the Nigerian Polity" (Ph.D. dissertation, Indiana University, 1967); on Tanzania, Raymond F. Hopkins, *Political Roles in a New State* (New Haven: Yale University Press, 1971). Also see P. Merkl and J. E. Moore, "Beamtentum oder parteien: Rivalisierende eliten des modernisierungsprozesses," *Politische Vierteljahresschrift,* 11 (Dec. 1970), 607–622.

8. This view is best represented in the writings of Harry J. Benda and Ann Ruth Willner. See Benda's "Democracy in Indonesia," *Journal of Asian Studies,* 23 (1963–1964), 449–456, and "Modern Indonesia under the Historian's Looking Glass," in *Japan's Future in Southeast Asia* (Kyoto: Kyoto University Center for Southeast Asian Studies, 1966), and Willner's *The Neotraditional Accommodation to Political Independence: The Case of Indonesia* (Princeton: Princeton University Center of International Studies, 1966), revised and updated in Lucian W. Pye, ed., *Cases in Comparative Politics: Asia* (Boston: Little, Brown, 1970). Compare Herbert Feith's *The Decline of Constitutional Democracy in Indonesia* (Ithaca: Cornell University Press, 1962) and his rejoinder to Benda, "History, Theory, and Indonesian Politics," *Journal of Asian Studies,* 24 (1964–1965), 305–312.

opinions rather than situate them. Too much stress has been laid on the content of what people believe—how authoritarian or how achievement-oriented they are—and too little on the reasons why they believe what they do. Subnational differences within the elite have been slighted in the search for a modal personality or a national character; so too has the intervening medium of personal experience through which cultural and political contexts influence elite outlooks.[9] These weaknesses partly justify the choice of Indonesia, whose cultural diversity is a natural stimulus to intranational comparison and where interviews in depth can recapture the past experiences that sustain present attitudes.

In short, for all the attention paid by scholars to the contrasts between Javanese and non-Javanese, Muslim and non-Muslim, santri and abangan, no systematic effort has been made to link those differences with politically relevant orientations of the bureaucratic and legislative elite. Without such an attempt, the elite can plausibly be pictured as either culturally integrated and secularized, like-minded in their lofty, cosmopolitan, national position, harbingers of the eventual end of cultural politics, or as riven by coinciding cultural and attitudinal differences that have been revalidated in political struggle—the extreme portraits sketched earlier—or as the product of some intermediate combination of cleavage and convergence. By specifying a prevailing pattern, I hope to resolve the ambiguity.

9. This was the thrust of Stein Rokkan's critique, in the *American Political Science Review*, 58 (1964), 676–679, of the most influential of the political culture studies to appear in the 1960's, Gabriel A. Almond and Sidney Verba's *The Civic Culture: Political Attitudes and Democracy in Five Nations* (Princeton: Princeton University Press, 1963). Philip H. Melanson and Lauriston R. King made the same point in their "Theory in Comparative Politics: A Critical Appraisal," *Comparative Political Studies,* 4 (July 1971), 214, as did Dennis Kavanagh, *Political Culture* (London: Macmillan, 1972), p. 64. Kavanagh recommended the study of culture variation within nations as a useful corrective to generalizations about system characteristics made directly from attitudinal survey data. The same logic can be used to argue for studying differences between institutions in one nation. In "The Comparative Study of Elite Socialization," *Comparative Political Studies,* 1 (1969), 484–486, 491, Donald D. Searing found that standard social background variables helpful in forecasting elite attitudes in one country were likely to be completely inadequate in another; a variable such as "level of education" probably referred to very different socialization experiences in different cultures. He concluded that such broad categories "need to be refined by moving closer to relevant experiences."

In this study, then, cultural and political contexts are given concrete ethnic and religious, institutional and organizational meaning.
But what specific outlooks are included in the content of elite political culture? Politically relevant orientations are, in theory, infinite.
Those explored here were chosen because of their importance to
cultural politics.

One obviously relevant pair of orientations is eclectic religious
tolerance (the belief that truth is not the monopoly of any one
religion) and support for empathy (the belief that society needs
people who can view matters from perspectives other than their
own). If low tolerance and low support for empathy are concen-
trated in a strongly religious and mainly non-Javanese Muslim
minority, and if that minority is stronger in Parliament than in the
bureaucracy, and if in addition bureaucrats as a group are more
tolerant and supporting of empathy than are legislators, then leaders who wish to promote an atmosphere of tolerance and empathy
will be justifiably wary of non-Javanese, nonbureaucratic, intensely
committed Muslims in the elite. This hypothetical combination—
many others are logically possible—is selected for mention because
it represents an elite-level version of the spectre of fanatic, populist, anti-abangan Islam that haunted colonial elites on Java and
continued to plague their successors after independence. One reason why in Indonesia today political Islam is so weak, and the
representative body so penetrated by executive authority, is that
influential abangan military leaders have acted as if this spectre
were real.

Is it? The question is crucial, for if piety and closed-mindedness
are inseparable in the nation's major religion, then secularization
may be a prerequisite to cultural democracy. As for political democracy, if the dominant bureaucratic elite is strikingly more
empathic and generous toward other religions than are the people's
representatives, shifting power from the first to the second may
only divide the nation.

The question also requires knowledge of the orientations of
different cultural groups toward leaders and authority and toward
central authority in particular. Compared with the representatives
of santri- or abangan-based parties, for example, how deferential
are the members of the ruling military-technocratic alliance in
Parliament? Do abangan Javanese leaders in the elite expect defer-

ence, trust, and obedience more than, say, non-Javanese practicing Muslims do? When applied to high Javanese bureaucrats, how accurate is the common claim that Javanese culture is authoritarian? The answers to these questions should illuminate the prospects for intercultural harmony in politics.

These questions in turn require an understanding of two more elite orientations: the sense of fit between a more or less effective self and a more or less benign social environment (perceived anomie) and the appreciation of conflict as something contingent and creative (nonzerosum) or, conversely, unavoidable and win-or-lose (zerosum). How dark or bright are the pictures of interpersonal integration and conflict in the outlook of a cultural minority compared with those of a cultural majority, and how do any observed differences relate to the groups' differing experiences and power positions? If cultural minorities and majorities are both markedly optimistic, the case for an orientationally homogenized elite will be strengthened. If elite minorities are consistently less optimistic than majorities, the opposite will follow: that cultural cleavages are politically exacerbated. From the latter result one might argue, for example, the need for adjustment between the culture of a dominant majority (say, nominally Muslim) and that of an isolated minority (passionately Islamic) to relieve the latter's siege mentality.

The choice of method was difficult. Asking the same questions to large numbers of randomly chosen people raises confidence that their answers are typical of a still larger population. But the larger the sample, the greater the risk that its members will be approached in quick, artificial interviews that serve the researcher's opinions more than the respondent's. That risk is acute when the researcher comes from another culture.

In the end, I chose forty people. Twenty higher officials in the central administration made up one sample, twenty members of Parliament the other. Both samples were drawn randomly using quotas to ensure proportional representation of military officers and, in the legislative case, of party and nonparty groups. In this way institutional and organizational affiliations could be related to identities, experiences, and orientations, and the resulting patterns compared. Intensively interviewed over many months, these forty men gave most of the evidence on which this study rests. Most of them also completed a questionnaire in which they were asked what they thought about various statements of opinion on the key themes of tolerance, empathy, leadership, authority, anomie, and conflict.

The aim of the first three chapters of the book is mainly descriptive: to place the administrative and legislative elite in the perspective of colonial history, to contrast the experiences and orientations of an abangan bureaucrat and a santri politician, and to describe briefly the samples and how they were chosen. The comparisons drawn between institutions and between individuals are intended to yield some tentative hypotheses that can guide the inquiry in the fourth and fifth chapters, where the experiences and orientations of the two samples will be presented and related to each other and to institutional, organizational, religious, and ethnic cleavages in order to map and interpret elite political culture. That interpretation will be used in a case-focused concluding chapter to evaluate the elite's approach to problems of cultural politics in Indonesia and the prospects for creative future solutions.

To summarize, elite political culture is here conceived as a politically relevant set of outlooks flowing from a constant interplay between patterns of belonging and meaning—here specified as ethnic and religious, institutional and organizational—as they give rise to and are interpreted through experience. So complex is that interplay that to aspire to portray it through the lives and ideas of only forty people may seem naive. A few final comments should clarify my intentions.

This book is not about mass behavior. My informants did react to statements about behavior (and belief)—for example, "A leader's orders must always be obeyed." But one who agreed enthusiastically with this opinion might not always obey the orders of someone he recognized as a leader, nor invariably demand blanket obedience from persons who so recognized him; people may say one thing and do another. Rather, the book sets out to discover, for the elite, whether those who agree on a matter of political importance also share some cultural or political affiliation or experience in contrast to others who disagree; how these linkages between the content and context of belief actually operate; and what potentials they reveal for elite behavior in cultural politics.

Psychoanalytic explanations are avoided, for I doubt the cross-cultural validity of the assumptions about human nature which they require.[10] The questionnaire was intended not to catch the external signs of unconscious drives but to tap internalized norms at a conscious level. (The failure to make this distinction bedevils the literature on political culture.[11]) The statements to which my informants were asked to respond were written in the third person, not the first. Yet I have tried not to stray too far from my subject matter, which is human beings. Chapter 2 is mainly an essay in microbiography; and personal anecdotes are used freely throughout the study to tie down abstractions, such as "eclectic religious tolerance" or "perceived anomie," and to restore some of the detail lost in statistical displays.

Finally, beyond finding empirical patterns, the book addresses an ultimately moral question: whether elite political culture can foster a balance between cultural communities and political institutions such that the latter do not repress the former in the national interest, yet are themselves not colonized by the former to sectarian ends. For only then will political change imply an empathic building upon the good in what people already are to realize the better in what they could become.

10. For a good critique of Freudian theory as culture-bound, incomplete, and inaccurate, see Morton Deutsch and Robert M. Krauss, *Theories in Social Psychology* (New York: Basic Books, 1965), pp. 155–158. The leading exponent of a psychocultural approach in comparative politics is Lucian Pye. His 1962 study, *Politics, Personality, and Nation Building*, is brilliantly original and suggestive; but it has been fairly criticized—for example, by Clifford Geertz in *Economic Development and Cultural Change*, 12 (1964), 205–209—for its ahistorical assumption that only a certain kind of political culture will permit a nation to modernize. In *The Spirit of Chinese Politics: A Psychocultural Study* (Cambridge, Mass.: MIT Press, 1968), p. 19, Pye characterized Chinese political culture as obsessive, fearful, and mistrusting, and described the Chinese as needing to identify enemies and to picture themselves as mistreated. "The Chinese, in their politics," concluded Pye, "have been giving expression to some deep and disturbing personality problem." In the same vein, in his *Mao's Revolution and the Chinese Political Culture* (Berkeley: University of California Press, 1971), pp. 520–521, Richard Solomon pictured Mao Tse-tung as an "anal" leader trying to transform an "oral" society. Such generalizations are hard to prove or disprove. At worst they recklessly project beyond time and place the psychic burdens of Victorian Vienna's sexually repressed middle class.

11. For a good critique, see Robert R. Alford, *Bureaucracy and Participation: Political Cultures in Four Wisconsin Cities* (Chicago: Rand McNally, 1969), pp. 5–7.

CHAPTER 1

INSTITUTIONS

In a multicultural polity, cultural groups are more or less well represented in a government that more or less decisively affects them. The problem of cultural politics is to fashion a future that benefits all of these groups but belongs exclusively to none of them. If the problem is to be solved along the lines of the Western democratic model, some balance must be worked out between two institutions: a parliament where popular grievances and aspirations can be freely voiced, compared, and accommodated in law and an administration that effectively, impartially implements the law. That this formula is so rarely achieved in practice in the Third World—to say nothing of the West itself—is a short-run consequence of the rise to power of political armies and mobilizing parties that span and penetrate both institutions. But the earlier history of these institutions has already affected their legitimacy and therefore the ease with which they can be overwhelmed and the distinctions between them obliterated. If one cultural group has been overrepresented in one institution, and if that institution has grown disproportionately powerful, then the ideal of separate branches of government reciprocally checking and facilitating each other's assigned part in the political process may already be a dispensable fiction. To place the two institutions in their own historical time and cultural place is, therefore, to begin to understand how they shape and are shaped by cultural politics.

Kingdom and Bureaucracy on Java

The Indonesian bureaucracy is a Janus-faced institution. As an agency of change entrusted with tasks of social and economic betterment, it belongs to a future its leaders are attempting to create.

As a preserver of continuity, it embodies a tradition with origins in the Javanese past.

The Department of Trade building in Jakarta displays this contrast dramatically. In its offices, Western-trained economists try to predict and influence domestic and international trade patterns for the future material benefit of Indonesia. But the murals decorating its downstairs walls depict traditional Javanese myths. One shows Bima, mighty mainstay of the Pandawa brothers in the Mahabharata epic, grappling with a giant snake in the sea. Bima's childhood mentor, Durna, has instructed Bima to seek the water of life at the bottom of the ocean. In his struggle against the snake who guards the deep, Bima is a model of fidelity to his former teacher's instructions. And his perseverance is rewarded when he reaches his goal and acquires true wisdom.

High officials of the second empire of Mataram, the last of the great sacral states of Java, used this story to inculcate in their apprentices the devotion and loyalty to the king that, ideally, characterized his officials (*punggawa*) and the priyayi class in general.[1] The Pandawa hero has survived the intervening periods of colonialism, occupation, revolution, and independence. In 1968, in a Javanese shadow play (*wayang kulit*) performance held in Jakarta to mark the inauguration of President Suharto's first Development Cabinet, Bima appeared once again before the appointed officials of the realm, persevering in his appointed task, ever the exemplar of the ideal servant of the king. The Javanese puppeteer, a young air force officer with an engineering degree, presented the ancient figure of Bima as a model of conduct to inspire the ministers as they faced the challenge of Indonesia's development in the twentieth century.[2]

Another mural in the Trade building shows the evil giant Rahwana being destroyed by the forces of the good ruler Rama, hero of the Ramayana epic. If Bima's qualities are worth emulating, so too are Rama's; the "eight statesman's virtues" associated with

1. Prijohoetomo, *Nawaruci* (Groningen, 1934), p. 177, as cited by Soemarsaid Moertono, *State and Statecraft in Old Java: A Study of the Later Mataram Period, 16th to 19th Century* (Ithaca: Cornell University Modern Indonesia Project, 1968), p. 97.

2. Interview with Sri Muljono, Jakarta, June 8, 1968. On Bima, see William F. Stutterheim, *Studies in Indonesian Archaeology* (The Hague: Martinus Nijhoff, 1956), pp. 107–143.

Rama constitute a ruler's paragon.[3] Several shadow plays performed in 1967 pursued this theme of the statesman's virtues, as spokesmen and well-wishers of the new regime tried to associate Rama's strengths with Suharto's in the public mind. Of one of these plays, a journalist wrote that it was "famous because every Javanese cabinet minister or high official seems to have [initial] good intentions to behave well," following Rama's example.[4]

Although the Indian Mahabharata and Ramayana epics have been adapted to Javanese tastes, and even, to a degree, to Muslim sensibilities, they rarely attract santris; Rama's status as a reincarnation of the Hindu god Vishnu, for example, is denied by monotheistic Islam. These models of the Indonesian bureaucracy are largely the cultural property of a single ethnic group, the Javanese (although the myths are also known among the Sundanese and Balinese), and a single religious strain, the abangan.

Aside from being associated with abangan culture, the bureaucracy has come virtually to define priyayi status. The origins of Indonesia's modern administrative elite can be traced back, past the colonial era, to the retinues of Javanese royalty; although its earlier aristocratic and Javanese image has been democratized and nationalized to accord with the notion of a civil service working in the public interest, the old legacy remains. As Harry Benda pointed out, the Dutch did not destroy the existing political order; they cut off its head and replaced it with their own.

What is socially important is that it was members of the decapitated political system, the Javanese bureaucratic aristocracy, who served as

3. Rama is said to be benevolent in providing for his people (as one "who showers the earth with scent"), relentless in eradicating evil ("all dirt of the state, he tries to sweep away"), patient and kind toward his officials (for "even if a man is not sharp of mind his heart can always be reached"), lovingly peaceful ("never showing any strain," a feeling of "intrinsic peace towards humanity" in his heart), vigilantly aware (so that his officials "cannot make a move which [the king] will not see clearly"), generous and trusting toward his officials ("in their efforts to do no wrong"), carrying a weapon in his hand and the power of magic in his heart (so that, "excelling in insight and full of caution," he may wipe away all the crooked men of bad living), and, finally, brutal in combat ("blown away will the enemy be, overwhelmed and ground down"). Jasadipoera, *Serat Rama* (Semarang, 1919), pp. 432ff., as translated by Moertono, *State and Statecraft*, appendix 3.

4. Sumantri Mertodipuro, "The Astabrata: The Eight Duties of a King," *Indonesian Observer*, Oct. 27, 1967.

officials for the new masters. Indeed, if we scan the entire colonial period in Java we can observe one striking fact of continuity: in the course of two centuries the Javanese elite did not move out of its traditional moorings, its bureaucratic habitat. . . . Its world view remained basically aristocratic and bureaucratic.

Later, Benda also suggested that the period of occupation and revolution (1942–1949) could be seen as a mere interruption in a bureaucratic style and structure that were resilient enough to re-emerge and flourish, modified but not transformed, in independent Indonesia.[5]

In the first half of the present millennium, however, Javanese officials were not bureaucrats in the modern meaning of the term. They were the king's servants, appended to and partly coterminous with the royal family-in-court. They had great organizing potential, realized in such achievements as the massive Borobudur stupa or the Prambanan burial temples; but their geographic scope, functional range, and daily impact upon the lives of the common people were limited and weak. In times of war, for example, no general mobilizations seem to have been undertaken; and the regional governors were more often than not only nominally under the king's purview.

For most royal officials, service at the court was probably only a part-time activity. Numbers of them might take turns filling an office, each devoting only a portion of his time to the affairs of his king. Although secular and sacred officials were distinguished from one another, and although the division of the realm and its officials mirrored certain cosmic classifications, administrative specialization in the modern sense was unknown. The king's men were in his service in a personal, not a functional capacity; they were not even clearly separated into military and nonmilitary components. An

5. Harry J. Benda, "Decolonization in Indonesia: The Problem of Continuity and Change," *American Historical Review,* 70 (July 1965), 1065, and "The Pattern of Administrative Reforms in the Closing Years of Dutch Rule in Indonesia," *Journal of Asian Studies,* 25 (Aug. 1966), 604–605. Also see Willner, *Neotraditional Accommodation,* pp. 20–21. For a view of the contemporary bureaucracy that departs from this literature, see my "The Bureaucracy in Political Context: Weakness in Strength," in Karl D. Jackson and Lucian W. Pye, eds., *Communication and Power in Indonesia* (forthcoming).

individual's duties depended mainly on the current interests of the king.[6]

The administrative structure of the sixteenth-to-nineteenth century kingdom of Mataram differed from its predecessors more in degree than kind;[7] cultural conditions, however, had changed, for the disintegration of the previous (thirteenth-through-fifteenth century) Majapahit empire coincided with the rise of Islam on Java's northern coast. Very gradually, through a remarkable process of conflict and acculturation, Islam was incorporated into the Hindu-Javanese state. The chief official of the central mosque took his place in the royal palace (*kraton*), while around him developed an office of Islamic affairs whose functions continued to find organized expression under the Dutch and the Japanese and ultimately in Indonesia's present Department of Religion. In the eighteenth century, the Mataram kings finally appropriated the title of *Khalifah Allah,* representative of Allah on earth. In Yogyakarta still, on the Prophet's birthday, a ritual procession of the king's officials moves from the kraton to the mosque, symbolically re-enacting the link between the two cultures.

The forerunner of the present Indonesian bureaucracy, then, was a functionally unspecialized corps of retainers, more Indianized than Islamic, appointed on grounds of birth or appearance rather than talent, and serving a culturally exemplary but politically far from all-powerful center.

The economic interest of the Dutch East India Company was to tap and drain off the surplus in agriculture; political control was needed only insofar as the supply was insufficient or endangered by a rebellious prince. At first content with a coastal trading presence, the Company in the course of the eighteenth century became ever more inextricably involved in coercing the indigenous administration to assure and expand the supply of coffee, spices, and other crops. The point at which the Company sank its tap and

6. This summary is based on Theodore G. Th. Pigeaud, *Java in the 14th Century: A Study in Cultural History* [The Nagarakertagama], IV (3d ed., The Hague: Martinus Nijhoff, 1962), pp. 521–546. Pigeaud wrote about Majapahit; the political order of earlier centuries was probably even less complex.

7. See B. Schrieke, *Indonesian Sociological Studies,* Part II: *Ruler and Realm in Early Java* (The Hague: Van Hoeve, 1957), pp. 207–211.

exerted the greatest pressure was the office of the regent (*bupati*), Mataram's version of the Majapahit provincial governor (*adipati*). The "decapitated" native administration became a tributary satellite of the Company. Under monopoly conditions, underpaid Company officials coerced, maneuvered, and coopted the Javanese nobility. Abuses were rife.

Toward the end of the eighteenth century, the Company, by then bankrupt, was abolished; its debts were taken over by the Dutch state. In a brief period of experimentation, conducted (as a consequence of Napoleonic warfare in Europe) first under French and then under British auspices, the colonial authority sought to undercut the position of the regents, not only to moderate their abuse of the population but also, in the aim of Sir Stamford Raffles, to change the character of colonial exploitation from that of an extractive feudalizing monopoly to a system based on "free labor, free cultivation, and free trade." Although the accomplishments of this period fell far short of such antifeudal ideals, segments of the nobility remained sensitive to any attempt to curtail their income or position. Further irritation came a decade later, when the restored Dutch authority took steps to check the use of forced labor by Dutch- and Chinese-managed estates, steps that threatened not only the foreigners but also the nobility who owned and leased the land to them. A prince of Yogyakarta, Diponegoro, rallied a substantial following under the twin banners of Mataram and Islam, and a costly five-year war ensued.

Reacting to these events, the colonial regime in 1830 initiated a system more invidious, because more effective, than that of the Company; the latter's forced deliveries were replaced by the obligatory cultivation and sale of specified crops, especially sugar, and the colonial impress sank yet deeper into the wet-rice fields of Java. Once again the indispensable link in the chain tying the peasant to the markets of Europe was the regent; his authority was restored and his office made hereditary by fiat of the colonial regime.

This "culture" system gave way first to a "liberal" period and ultimately, in the early twentieth century, to an "ethical" policy— each phase in some way misnamed and all recapitulating a basically exploitative relationship. To implement colonial directives, a body of native officials worked beneath the regent and in direct contact with the linchpin of the system, the Dutch local government adviser (*controleur*). The Dutch, as they raised their expectations of profit from the colony and later their pretensions to minister to the needs of its people, trained and employed these officials as a professional, specialized, and centralized administrative corps. The population was penetrated and regulated more thoroughly than ever before.

"From the top of the structure of Government," wrote one high Dutch official,

an innumerable number of wires reach down to the population. . . . This top rests mainly upon the vertical steel structure of the administrative corps. Without the latter, the Government would be unable to govern, the population could not express itself. . . . Hide-bound anarchy would take the place of the beautiful regularity that now characterizes this great clockwork.[8]

Even discounting his hyperbole, the loose arrangements of the precolonial era had been transformed. As a status group, the Javanese administrative or priyayi elite had become integrated into an institution that possessed unprecedented physical power and applied it more effectively than ever before. At the same time, however, the legitimacy of the priyayis had been eroded as they became more dependent upon the Dutch, more a fixture of the colonial status quo, and thus more an obstacle than an ally in the eyes of santri Muslims and populist nationalists. The priyayis were simultaneously empowered and isolated.

Prince Diponegoro had used Islamic symbols in his revolt against colonial authority early in the nineteenth century. Later, in the 1880's, an incident occurred in the Cilegon area of West Java that illustrates well the imbalance in the triangle of forces that Dutch and native administrators and Islamic elites came to em-

8. A. D. A. de Kat Angelino, *Colonial Policy*, II, ed. and trans. G. J. Reiner in collaboration with de Kat Angelino (Chicago: University of Chicago Press, 1931), p. 357. More balanced is Schrieke's observation that while the members of the nobility were being transformed into a modern administrative corps, they were also bringing into the new service "elements of the old feudal tradition"; acculturation worked both ways. B. Schrieke, "Native Society in the Transformation Period," in Schrieke, ed., *The Effect of Western Influence on Native Civilisations in the Malay Archipelago*, trans. H. J. Bridge (Batavia: Kolff, 1929), pp. 246–247. Also see Sartono Kartodirdjo, "Bureaucracy and Aristocracy: The Indonesian Experience in the XIXth Century," *Archipel*, 7 (1974), 151–168.

body. His sleep being disturbed by the regular call to prayer issuing from a nearby minaret, a Dutch official asked the local *patih* (one rank below the regent) to do something about it. The patih ordered the minaret destroyed and circulated a memorandum among his subordinates instructing them to enforce a ban on noise emanating from Muslim places of worship. (After all, he wrote, God is not deaf.) These lesser officials in turn circulated the prohibition among the populace. A local *kiyai,* or Islamic teacher, concluding that Muslims had been forbidden to pray, led a brief revolt against the government that cost several lives, including his own.[9]

This incident—others could be cited—encouraged Dutch and native administrators to view "fanatic Islam" as a threat to stability and their own position. In the 1910's, the fact that the colony's first mass nationalist movement took shape and prospered under Muslim auspices—it was called the Islamic Union (Sarekat Islam) —confirmed these fears. At about this time, the regent Djajadiningrat, whose account of the Cilegon affair has already been cited, publicly voiced his disdain for the rural kiyais. Anyone, he said, who had tried, as he had, to introduce new ideas into village life and apply new regulations on the villagers' behalf would realize that these Islamic teachers were a block to social progress; even though the colonial administration had done much to curtail their activities, he continued, the authority of the kiyai was regrettably still intact among the unenlightened peasantry. By the same token, he might have added, the legitimacy of the administrative elite was insecure.

A cultural distinction had acquired political force. Insofar as Islam was considered anticolonial, the priyayi elite was more likely to cultivate an abangan-secular rather than a santri outlook. Dutch fears of rampaging Islam shaped the structure of opportunity in the native civil service; when a patih who had reportedly ridiculed Islam was promoted by the Dutch to the position of regent, the lesson was not lost on his colleagues.[10]

Critics of the regime who did not speak in the name of Islam were also suspect. In the administrative schools—outgrowths of an

9. Achmad Djajadiningrat, *Kenang-kenangan Pangeran Aria Djajadiningrat,* trans. from Dutch by the Balai Pustaka (Batavia: Kolff-Buning, 1936), pp. 49–71. For a full scholarly study, see Sartono Kartodirdjo, *Peasants' Revolt.*

10. Djajadiningrat, *Kenang-kenangan,* pp. 78 and 389–390.

1848 decision to train the sons of regents—Dutch principals tried to insulate their pupils from politics, especially anything that smacked of nationalism. Years afterward, a civil servant recalled how, in Bandung, the director of a boarding school for native officials in which he was enrolled in the 1920's had told him and his classmates to kick the word "politics" out of their vocabulary and confined them to the school grounds for two weeks for reading a pamphlet satirizing the government.[11] These efforts did not prevent the eventual recruitment into the nationalist movement of large numbers of priyayis, but they did help to limit the appeal of nationalism mainly to lower-ranking employees in less traditional services—railroad workers, for example—whose jobs were least directly tied to the "vertical steel structure of the administrative corps."

In sum, the Dutch simultaneously reinforced and undermined the priyayi class. By incorporating the regent and his sons into the administrative state, the Dutch at once gave them Western bureaucratic standing and authority and detached them from the patrimonial system in which they played an integral ruling part. A group once linked to both the santri and abangan strains of Javanese society found itself in the artificial climate of a colonial hothouse state, culturally and politically insulated from Islam as a source of primary self-definition or political organization. In 1944, on the eve of the revolution, well over four-fifths of the central administrative corps had graduated from schools of native administration like the one whose pupils had been told to delete the word "politics" from their vocabulary; not one had received an Islamic education.[12]

This colonially fostered bureaucratic elite survived the Japanese occupation. By reinforcing on Java the centralized administrative elitism of the colonial era, the Japanese contributed to its survival, not only through the occupation but beyond independence.[13] And

11. Soelaeman Soemardi, "Regional Politicians and Administrators in West Java (1956): Social Backgrounds and Career Patterns" (M.A. thesis, Cornell University, 1961), p. 104.

12. This conclusion is based on an examination of the educational backgrounds of the 638 members of the corps (*pangreh praja*) whose biographic data were included in *Orang Indonesia Jang Terkemoeka di Djawa* (Jakarta: Gunseikanbu, 1944), a who's who of prominent Indonesians in Java compiled by the Japanese.

13. On Japanese cooperation with the priyayis, see William H. Frederick's

by encouraging separate organizations for abangan and santri elites to further the war effort, they probably deepened the tension between the two.

Parliament and the Administrative State

Compared to the bureaucracy, with its roots deep in precolonial soil, Indonesia's Parliament is a shallow plant. The models for the present People's Representative Council are two twentieth-century creations: the colonial People's Council (Volksraad) and the wartime Central Advisory Council. Although differing significantly in other respects, these three bodies have been generally subordinated to and incorporated into the executive power.

Indonesia is not unique in having a relatively impotent legislative forum; the principle of separate and mutually balancing branches of government is at least partly fictive even in systems that give it constitutional recognition. But Indonesia has never had a completely elected legislature—the one installed in 1955 came close, but it had three appointed members—and the overshadowing of the ostensibly rule-making by the ostensibly rule-applying branch has been especially marked. The 1945 constitution, which was reintroduced by President Sukarno in 1959 as the basis for his Guided Democracy, and which remains in force, allows for a strong executive. President Suharto's government is well within this tradition of executive dominance; in the 1971 parliamentary elections, only the second to be held since Indonesia became an independent republic in 1950, 100 of the 460 seats in the legislature were reserved for official appointees.

Penetration has also taken place in the opposite direction, from the

introduction to his translation of Mohammad Hatta, *The Putera Reports: Problems in Indonesian-Japanese Wartime Cooperation* (Ithaca: Cornell University Modern Indonesia Project, 1971), pp. 22–26. Compare Bernard Dahm, *Sukarno and the Struggle for Indonesian Independence* (Ithaca: Cornell University Press, 1969), p. 265; B. R. O'G. Anderson, "Japan: 'The Light of Asia,'" in Josef Silverstein, ed., *Southeast Asia in World War II: Four Essays* (New Haven: Yale University Southeast Asia Studies, 1966), p. 18; and Harry J. Benda, *The Crescent and the Rising Sun: Indonesian Islam under the Japanese Occupation* (The Hague: Van Hoeve, 1958), pp. 154–157. On Japanese support for Islamic organizations, compare Benda; Dahm; and Anthony J. S. Reid, *Indonesian National Revolution 1945–1950* (Hawthorn, Vic.: Longman, 1974), pp. 14–16, and "The Japanese Occupation and Rival Indonesian Elites: Northern Sumatra in 1942," *Journal of Asian Studies*, 35 (November 1975), 49–61.

party-political into the administrative realm. The colonial apparatus, which had been more or less successfully protected against the shocks of partisan politics in the Indies, was deeply affected by the repercussions of postindependence political conflict. From being an instrument of policy, the bureaucracy changed in time into a prize of politics. An elite administrative corps grew haphazardly into a ramshackle assemblage of overstaffed agencies and under-salaried officials.[14] Survival superseded performance as the civil servant's concern, and survival was a matter of economics and politics, of moonlighting and bandwagoning and dodging the occasional purge. As the bureaucratic pie expanded, so did the size of the slices carved and kept as sinecure ministries for the party faithful. The abangan-based Indonesian National Party (Partai Nasional Indonesia, PNI) became well entrenched in the Ministries of Information and Home Affairs, while the santri-based Muslim Teachers' Party (Nahdlatul Ulama, NU) gained control of the Ministry of Religion. Under the emergency conditions of the late 1950's in which officers took over nationalized Dutch enterprises and put down revolts in Sumatra and Sulawesi, the armed forces too acquired political position and administrative influence.

But if administration became political, the origins of Parliament were administrative. First authorized in 1916, the Volksraad represented a reform from above designed to accommodate and coopt the Indonesian national awakening of the preceding decade; the new Council was not a legislative power but an advisory adjunct of the colonial government. The chairman was appointed by the Dutch Crown and half the members by the Dutch governor general; the other half were selected in a complex system of indirect elections that assured Dutch control. Indonesians were never a majority in the Council, nor were those favoring independence ever a majority among Indonesian members.[15]

A contemporary French observer was not impressed with the powers of the Volksraad; the three Dutch governors of Java, he felt, probably had more political influence between them than all

14. The characterization is Herbert Feith's in his "Suharto's Search for a Political Format," *Indonesia*, 6 (Oct. 1968), 104.
15. Bureau for Decentralization, "De Regeling van de verkiezingen voor den Volksraad," *Koloniale Studien*, Extra politiek nummer, 1 (Oct. 1917), 162–168; S. L. van der Wal, *De Volksraad en de staatkundige ontwikkeling van Nederlands-Indië* (Groningen: Wolters, 1964–1965), II, pp. 690–694.

the Council members combined. He saw the Volksraad as an outlet for a few nationalists to blow off steam, an opportunity for the government to keep itself informed about the views of various groups, and above all an exercise in cooptation whereby certain members of the indigenous elite gained prestige and perquisites and the government gained a loyal opposition.[16]

One way in which the Dutch tried to limit the Volksraad's horizons to ameliorating the status quo was by drawing heavily on colonial officialdom, both European and indigenous, for members. Of the seventy-five or so native East Indians who ever sat on the Council, approximately two-thirds were civil servants, even if government-paid teachers and railway employees are not counted. Regents formed the largest group, followed by district heads and other officials. Patihs and the staffs of the royal kratons in Yogyakarta and Solo were also represented; about two-thirds of the seventy-five claimed, not always plausibly, noble birth. Nor did the weight of the administrative elite in the Volksraad decline in later years; in its final session in 1939–1941, twenty of the thirty native members were active or pensioned government officials.[17]

Doubtless repeating the rationale used at the time, another observer wrote that, despite many objections, "something may be said for officials as members of the legislative body in a colonial society. The natives are not yet politically conscious, and the only counterweight to bureaucracy is freedom of criticism within a bureaucracy. Officials are among the few persons who can intelligently discuss government problems."[18] But in light of the radical talk outside the Volksraad by noncooperating politicians like Sukarno, many of whom came from liberal and technical professional backgrounds, the colonial elite was probably at least as interested in the harmlessness of the discussion as in its sophistication.

The administrative state's practice of drawing upon its own ranks even for its critics guaranteed the strong representation of

16. G. H. Bousquet, *La politique musulmane et coloniale des Pays-Bas* (Paris: Paul Hartmann, 1939), pp. 88–96 and 104–107. For a different view, see J. S. Furnivall, *Netherlands India: A Study of Plural Economy* (Cambridge, Eng.: Cambridge University Press, 1944), pp. 275–276.

17. Van der Wal, *Volksraad*, II, pp. 707–727; Central Statistical Bureau, *Indisch Verslag*, II (Batavia: Landsdrukkerij, 1941), p. 540.

18. Amry Vandenbosch, *The Dutch East Indies: Its Government, Problems, and Politics* (2d ed., Berkeley: University of California Press, 1941), p. 122.

aristocratic-bureaucratic backgrounds among native Indonesian members of the Volksraad. This bias in recruitment is illustrated by the importance of the Association of Native Administrative Employees (Perhimpunan Pegawai Bestuur Bumiputera, PPBB)[19]— founded in 1929 by R. A. A. Wiranatakusuma, regent of Bandung and a long-standing Council member. By the late 1930's, this organization had as members some 15,000 public officials, from clerks up to patihs and regents, and a share of those Volksraad seats reserved for Indonesians roughly equal to that of the cooperating nationalists. In the cultural conservatism of the leaders of the Association, the Dutch saw a useful counterbalance to the nationalists; the PPBB members indirectly elected to the 1931–1935 session, for example, were all regents or patihs. Javanese accounted for a disproportionate two-thirds of this group, compared to one-third Sundanese, and none had ethnic origins outside Java; in contrast, a majority of the indirectly elected cooperating nationalists did. Insofar as the colonial regime sought loyal critics among its native employees, it found them mainly among higher priyayi Javanese.

The PPBB and several cross-racial groups made up what the government in its more liberal moods hoped to develop into a base of centrist support for official policy between Indonesian nationalists on the left and Dutch settlers on the right.[20] In the early 1930's, the Dutch colonial official for Volksraad affairs urged that this "middle group" in the Council be bolstered by adding someone from the "native right," that is, a regent, to the PPBB delegation. By enlarging the PPBB contingent, greater "balance" could be achieved in the Council's native representation and the government could reward the regents for their loyal service and prepare them for a possible future role as "responsible" politicians. Implicit in the latter remark was the hope that the regents could some day successfully compete with the nationalists in the political arena. The official also justified appointment of another regent as a token

19. On the PPBB, see J. M. Pluvier, *Overzicht van de ontwikkeling der nationalistische beweging in Indonesië in de jaren 1930 tot 1942* (The Hague: Van Hoeve, 1953), pp. 160–161.

20. This was not always the view of Dutch officials. One who covered Volksraad affairs called the right and left wings in the Council "worthwhile" and "worthless," respectively. Even he, however, put the PPBB in the middle. Van der Wal, *Volksraad*, II, p. 191.

of appreciation to the native administrative service for its cooperation in the work of the Volksraad.[21]

Despite this cooperation, however, and despite the prevalence
among Indonesian members of men with aristocratic backgrounds
and civil service careers, the Volksraad and the native administrative corps were not the same thing. In the first place, beyond the
reality of the Volksraad as a mere bureaucratic concession lay the
theoretical goal of a fully empowered representative assembly.
Radical socialists who denounced the Council in 1918–1919 as a
capitalist trick and its Indonesian members as imperialist tools
envisioned a bicameral "true Volksraad" of proletarian party delegates that would implement the transition to socialism. In more
moderate vein, Sukarno in 1921 could hope for "a parliament of
our own, truly representative of the people." Unrealized, the vision
persisted. In 1939, some ninety different organizations, brought
together in an Indonesian People's Congress (Kongres Rakyat
Indonesia), found a common rallying ground in the slogan "A
Parliament for Indonesia!"—by which they meant a Volksraad
transformed into a democratic, popular body to which the government would be responsible. By the very fact of its name and existence as a potentially sovereign representative legislature, the
People's Council was a politicizing force.[22]

21. Van der Wal, *Volksraad,* II, pp. 102–114 and 234.
22. Sources for this paragraph are, in order, Robert Van Niel, *The Emergence of the Modern Indonesian Elite* (The Hague: Van Hoeve, 1960), pp.
130 and 141; Ruth McVey, *The Rise of Indonesian Communism* (Ithaca:
Cornell University Press, 1965), p. 44; *Utusan Hindia,* May 6, 1921 (*Inlandsche persoverzichten 1921,* 19, p. 263), cited by Dahm, *Sukarno,* p. 42;
George McT. Kahin, *Nationalism and Revolution in Indonesia* (Ithaca:
Cornell University Press, 1952), pp. 97–98; Pluvier, *Overzicht,* pp. 178–183;
van der Wal, *Volksraad,* II, pp. 492–535.

In September 1941, the Indonesian People's Congress gave way to an Indonesian People's Assembly (Majelis Rakyat Indonesia), also outside the
Volksraad. Although the Japanese invasion soon ended the Assembly, the
make-up of its short-lived executive committee was significant in that it
brought together priyayi elements in a working association with the two political forces from which the Dutch had tried to quarantine them: nationalism and Islam. The executive committee was a tripartite alliance between
nationalist parties, Muslim organizations, and the Federation of Civil Servants' Unions (Persatuan Vakbonden Pegawai Negeri, PVPN). The revend-
icative PVPN, formed in the 1920's under the leadership of a priyayi Volksraad member, R. P. Suroso, had by the outbreak of World War II gained a
following estimated at 42,000—rather an improvement on the PPBB, to say
nothing of the still smaller, older, and bluer-blooded Union of Regents (Re-

In the second place, whereas the native administration was relatively homogeneous, being heavily Javanese and abangan and centralized on Java, the Volksraad brought together Indonesians of disparate ethnic, religious, and regional origins. The names of many of the Council's parliamentary groups identified their members as Muslims, Protestants, or Catholics, as Sundanese, Ambonese, or Minahassans, as Sumatrans or Jakartans. Regent and Volksraad member Djajadiningrat later recalled the inauguration of the People's Council in glowing terms: "Divergent in their interests and points of view, coming from various different parts of far-flung Insulinde [a poetic term for the Indies], thirty-nine individuals of various races and social positions, each in his national dress, sat together in the meeting-hall." He went on to relate how, after that opening ceremony, the native members "instinctively" came together to develop a united position across the cultural and status gaps that separated them. At that first native caucus, one of the oldest among the Indonesian members spoke first, and then "they understood one another."[23]

The prior existence of a native National Committee[24] and Djajadiningrat's own recollections notwithstanding, the Indonesian Volksraad contingent was never more than a loose and easily

gentenbond). As the priyayis were politicized they were differentiated, socially along status lines and politically over questions of cooperation with the state. On the Majelis Rakyat Indonesia, see A. K. Pringgodigdo, *Sedjarah Pergerakan Rakjat Indonesia* (6th print. [Jakarta]: Dian Rakjat, 1967), p. 148; on the PVPN, see *Zeven jaar Republik Indonesia* (The Hague: Information Service Indonesia [1952]), p. 81.

23. For a photograph of the occasion, see Muhammad Yamin, comp., *Lukisan Sedjarah* (Jakarta: Djambatan [1956]), p. 33. Lieutenant Governor General H. J. van Mook, writing later from his own perspective, characterized "the friendly and intimate relations" between members of different races in the Volksraad, which he called "the only really mixed club in the Orient," as probably unique in an otherwise racially exclusive colonial establishment (*The Stakes of Democracy in South-East Asia* [London: George Allen and Unwin, 1950], p. 196, n. 4). Djajadiningrat also cited the remark of a fellow Volksraad member, Prince Prangwadana, later monarch of the House of Mangkunegara in Solo, that "the native nobility and the people have for centuries been bound together in a blood-tie" (A. Djajadiningrat, "Vorst en volk," *Djawa*, Mangkoenagoro-nummer, 4 [1924], 62–63).

24. The committee was mainly Javanese. Formed in 1917 on the initiative of the abangan cultural organization Budi Utomo (Noble Endeavor), it included representatives of the Islamic Union, the Union of Regents, an association of native teachers, and the four courts of central Java. See J. Th. Petrus Blumberger, *De Nationalistische beweging in Nederlandsch-Indië* (Haarlem: Tjeenk Willink, 1931), p. 25.

fragmented coalition. Not until July 1941 was a National Indonesian Group (Fraksi Nasional Indonesia) formally established, and even then, although it included Minahassans, Sundanese, nationalists, independents, and regents, only seventeen of the thirty Indonesian members of the Council belonged. The Volksraad, however, did serve as a meeting ground for sustained contact among various indigenous elites. As a parliamentary minority in their own land, Indonesians in the Council did develop some self-consciousness and solidarity.[25]

A third distinguishing feature of the Volksraad compared to the civil service was that Council members could and did openly criticize the government. Much of this criticism came from Europeans demanding greater autonomy from the metropole, but indigenous voices could be heard as well. During the Council's first session, a proposal to cable an expression of loyalty to the Queen in Holland was defeated. Contrary to the wishes of the government, the members voted to allow the use of Malay (Indonesian) as a language of debate. Antigovernment sentiments subsequently voiced in the Volksraad debates led H. Colijn, future minister of the colonies, to describe the Council as a rotten tree, unfruitful for the Indonesians because it could grant them no real control over their own affairs and intolerable for the colonial power because it was a nesting-place for irresponsible critics. Colijn saw clearly the contradiction between the goal of responsibility and the reality of dependence, and his proposed solution was at least consistent: to uproot the rotting tree.[26]

Nearly a decade later, in 1936, observing the same contradiction, five Indonesian members of the Volksraad put forward the

25. Kahin, *Nationalism and Revolution,* p. 39, reached a parallel conclusion. An index of this growing Indonesian solidarity is the percentage of all Indonesian members affiliated with racially mixed parliamentary groups. This figure rose from 40 per cent in the 1918–1921 session to 76 per cent in 1924–1927—across a comparatively relaxed decade that gave way to the uprisings of 1926–1927 and the harsher period of the 1930's. By the Volksraad's final session in 1939–1942, the figure had plunged to 13 per cent. Conversely, the proportion of Indonesian members belonging to exclusively Indonesian groups dropped from 27 to 14 per cent between 1918 and 1924 but then rose sharply to 63 per cent in 1942. A. K. Pringgodigdo, who made these calculations (*Sedjarah Pergerakan,* p. 148), finds in them clear evidence of a shift in stance from colonial association toward Indonesian nationalism.

26. Furnivall, *Netherlands India,* pp. 228–229 and 276–277; van der Wal, *Volksraad,* I, p. 227; Dahm, *Sukarno,* p. 89.

other solution: to allow the tree to flower. The suggestion of Sutardjo Kartohadikusumo and his four colleagues, all to the right of the nationalist group, was moderate enough. The Dutch government would be asked to convene a conference of delegates from Holland and the Indies, who, meeting as equals, would plan a gradual devolution of power to the colony, still within the framework of the Kingdom of the Netherlands, over the next ten years. The Sutardjo Petition, as it was known, passed the Council by a vote of twenty-six to twenty, but two years later the Dutch government formally rejected it, calling it a "drastic top-to-bottom reform."[27]

Sutardjo was a Javanese patih, "an intelligent priyayi" in the words of one Dutch report, who had replaced Wiranatakusuma as chairman of the PPBB. At a meeting in Batavia (Jakarta) held to enlist public support for his resolution, Sutardjo declared that as a public official he had introduced the motion because he believed the civil service to be a bridge between ruler and ruled.[28] Although his motion was political, in presenting it he reaffirmed his commitment to the priyayi role.

If Sutardjo reasserted his administrative identity in a political act, still hoping somehow to preserve the link between governors and governed, he could not bridge the cleavage between cooperating civil servants like himself and radical nationalist politicians who disdained his motion as a plea for too little too late.[29] The latter wanted Indonesian independence pure and simple. But what the government thought of this notion was clear. In November 1940, more than six months after the mother country had fallen to the Germans, a government spokesman in the Volksraad could still declare that if the nationalist opposition desired a fully empowered legislature as a means to independence, agreement "would be impossible and, in that case, the Government would take the necessary measures."[30] This proved a meaningless intransigence; by March 1942 the Japanese had entered Java and ended the colonial era.

27. Pluvier, *Overzicht*, p. 126, citing *Bijlagen Tweede Kamer*, 1937–1938, II, 4, document 7.
28. Van der Wal, *Volksraad*, II, p. 234; Pluvier, *Overzicht*, p. 124.
29. Van der Wal, *Volksraad*, II, pp. 378–382.
30. Bernard H. M. Vlekke, *Nusantara: A History of Indonesia* (rev. ed., Chicago: Quadrangle Books, 1960), p. 396.

In their own draft principles for administering the "occupied Southern Areas," the Japanese decided to avoid the "premature encouragement of native independence movements."[31] But in the ensuing three and a half years, as Japanese hopes of victory over the Allies grew more and more illusory, Indonesian independence finally became an explicit official goal. This transition—from wartime subjugation and mobilization to the prospect of independence —was reflected in two successive forms of pseudolegislative organization: the Central Advisory Council and the Committee for the Preparation of Indonesian Independence.

The Japanese military administration on Java set up the Central Advisory Council (Chuo Sangi In, CSI) to enlist selected indigenous leaders on behalf of Japan's war aims and to serve as a wing of the military government in "expeditiously furthering" its policies. The CSI met in the old Volksraad building in Jakarta, had about as many members as the Volksraad, and, like the earlier institution, was composed of both appointed and indirectly elected members.[32] But behind these formal similarities lay important differences.[33]

31. Harry J. Benda, James K. Irikura, and Koichi Kishi, comps. and trans., *Japanese Military Administration in Indonesia: Selected Documents* (New Haven: Yale University Southeast Asia Studies, 1965), p. 2.

32. A predecessor body was apparently formed in the summer of 1942, but little is known about it. See Mitsuo Nakamura, "General Imamura and the Early Period of Japanese Occupation," *Indonesia,* 10 (Oct. 1970), 20–21. On the origin and membership of the CSI, see Benda, *Crescent,* p. 137; I. J. Brugmans, et al., *Nederlandsch-Indië onder Japanse bezetting: Gegevens en documenten over de jaren 1942–1945* (Franeker: Wever, 1960), p. 53; O. D. P. Sihombing, *Pemuda Indonesia Menantang Fasisme Djepang* (Jakarta: Sinar Djaya [1962]), p. 159; Soebekti, *Sketsa Revolusi Indonesia 1940–1945* (Surabaya: GRIP, 1966), p. 46. However, Soebekti gives the date of the opening ceremony as August 15, 1943, which is clearly incorrect; the Council was not even officially decreed until September 5.
In its lifetime (1918–1942), the Volksraad expanded from 38 to 60 members; in its far shorter span (1943–1945), the CSI grew from 43 to 60. The first Volksraad was half elected and half appointed, whereas the CSI started out with an appointed majority (23 out of 43). And whereas the Volksraad wound up with an elected majority (37 out of 60), the CSI ended with an even more decisive preponderance of appointed members (40 of 60) than it began with. Appointed members were not necessarily docile—the Sarekat Islam leader, Tjokroaminoto, was appointed by the Dutch in 1918, Sukarno by the Japanese in 1943—but the difference in the proportions of appointees initially and the changes in those proportions during the lifetimes of the two bodies suggest that far greater control was exercised over the CSI.

33. That these similarities and differences were cause for concern on the

Whereas the Volksraad had withheld a pledge of loyalty to Queen Wilhelmina, the first session of the CSI expressed the members' deeply felt gratitude that the Japanese commander-in-chief had come to attend the ceremony in person "to give us noble advice and point out the path that we shall take."[34] More important was the difference in where the power to raise issues lay. Whereas the government had answered questions posed by the Volksraad, the CSI answered questions posed by the government. During the first session, for example, CSI members had to stand and listen to the Japanese commander ask how the local population could give practical help to the Japanese army, a question later restated in terms at once sweeping and precise: "How can we utilize all sources of energy on Java, both human and inanimate, to further the war effort?" One such source, the authorities pointed out, was the rice that certain peasants were refusing to surrender to the government. The Council had four days to answer.[35]

---

part of the Japanese military authorities is clear from their early statements about the CSI. They argued that the right of Volksraad members to express themselves had been meaningless, part of a farcical "democracy" camouflaging colonial oppression. Any association in the public mind between the CSI and the Volksraad had to be broken, for the more thoroughly subordinated CSI would disappoint expectations built on the tradition of vocal criticism in the earlier body; at the same time those who considered the Volksraad to have been an instrument of oppression had to be convinced that the new Council was not. That suspicions on this score existed is evident from official assurances made to the Jakarta press corps that the CSI was not, in the words of the Japanese proverb, a piece of dog meat being sold as veal. *Asia Raya,* Aug. 3, 2605 [1945]; "De Central Adviesraad vergeleken bij de Volksraad," in Brugmans, et al., *Nederlandsch-Indië,* pp. 577–578. (In references to occupation publications, the Christian calendar will be used henceforth in preference to Japanese chronology.)

34. This became a standard oath read out at the opening of each session; *Asia Raya,* Oct. 17, 1943, Jan. 30, May 8, Nov. 13, 1944, and June 18, 1945.

35. *Asia Raya,* Oct. 18, 1943; Dahm, *Sukarno,* p. 254. Essentially the same question was put to the CSI at its second session early the following year in a tone more critical and urgent, as the Pacific war intensified and victory remained out of sight (*Asia Raya,* Jan. 19, 30, and 31, 1944). This time the Japanese commander-in-chief urged members to set an example by their own actions, to make sure that not even the land around their houses went unplanted, to toil themselves in the fields—for "one good deed is worth more than a thousand words!" (*Asia Raya,* Feb. 3, 1944). For other questions asked the CSI, all of them elaborations on this how-best-to-mobilize theme, see *Asia Raya,* April 25, Oct. 31, 1944, and Feb. 12 and June 8, 1945.

Unlike the Volksraad debates, CSI deliberations were not a matter of public record. In the Japanese-sponsored body, members who wanted the floor had first to obtain the chairman's permission, whereas government officials had only to inform him that they would speak. The rules of order required the silencing of any member who might make trouble and allowed the authorities to deprive him of his seat. The Japanese could censor members' speeches in advance and attended Council meetings in force to hear them given.[36] Finally, unlike the Volksraad, the CSI's purview was limited to Java.

In creating the CSI, the Japanese had exaggerated into a caricature the colonial tradition of administrative dominance over the legislature. In another sense, however, they had broken with that same colonial past. In 1942, the Volksraad had been 50 per cent native Indonesian; a year later, in the CSI, the figure soared to 93 per cent. The chairman of the Volksraad had always been a Dutchman; Sukarno chaired the CSI.[37]

Although the indigenous memberships of the two bodies did overlap—among those who ever sat in the CSI, 17 per cent had served in the Volksraad[38]—the composition of the two groups was fundamentally different. Radical nationalists and the spokesmen of

36. *Asia Raya,* Oct. 17, 1943. One member later illustrated the innocuousness of these speeches by recalling one he had made before the CSI in which he had appealed for programs of physical education for Indonesian schoolchildren. "Not only was the speech altogether harmless," he later wrote, "but in giving it I was only knocking on an open door, inasmuch as physical education already occupied an important place in the curriculum of all educational institutions" (Margono Djojohadikusumo, *Herinneringen uit 3 tijdperken* [Amsterdam: Nabrink, 1970], pp. 126–127). Although Margono exaggerated the innocence of his speech—the text as reported in *Asia Raya,* Nov. 14, 1944, shows him urging that the Indonesian people be given not only training but leadership in various fields—the margin of dissent in the CSI was undoubtedly thin.

37. Dahm's statement (*Sukarno,* p. 225) that the CSI was "composed exclusively of Indonesians" is true if the three members of Chinese origin are so classified. The members are listed in John O. Sutter, *Indonesianisasi: Politics in a Changing Economy, 1944–1955,* IV (Ithaca: Cornell University Southeast Asia Program, 1959), appendix B. Sukarno proudly pointed out the difference in chairmen in his first speech as CSI head; *Asia Raya,* Oct. 17, 1945.

38. *Asia Raya,* Oct. 17, 1945; van der Wal, *Volksraad,* II, pp. 707–727. Sihombing's observation (*Pemuda,* p. 160) that "many" CSI members had been members of the Volksraad appears unwarranted.

organized Islam had been conspicuous by their virtual absence from the People's Council; they were neither welcome in nor attracted to an expressly evolutionary body. Only one representative of Islam sat in the Volksraad in 1918; in 1942, despite a near tripling of seats, there was still only one. Even cooperating nationalists were always a minority.

In contrast, in 1943, a much larger minority of CSI members (six of forty-three) were prominent Muslims. A nationalist contingent, larger still, included Sukarno (chairman), Mohammad Hatta (later a vice-chairman), and Ki Hadjar Dewantoro, all three of whom had been exiled by the Dutch and the last of whom was the author of the satirical pamphlet that the civil service trainees in Bandung in the 1920's had been punished for reading. Representatives of the old administrative tradition also sat in the 1943 Council, among them a former regent (later vice-chairman and adviser to the CSI secretariat) and two delegates from the royal houses of central Java. In sum, compared to the Volksraad, the CSI was politically more representative but less powerful.[39]

The Dutch had tried to protect the priyayi mainspring in their "clockwork" regime from the shock of Islamic or nationalist organization; the Japanese retained the basic mechanism and enlisted these previously suspect clienteles in separate organizations to promote "greater East Asian" cooperation against the Allies. Santri leaders were channeled into a Consultative Assembly of Indonesian Muslims (Majelis Syuro Muslimin Indonesia, or Masyumi), while abangan and secular nationalists found a platform first in a Center of the People's Strength (Pusat Tenaga Rakyat) and later, under tighter Japanese rein, in a Java People's Service Association (Jawa Hokokai). Unwilling to erect a national front for fear that its strength might be used against its sponsor, the Japanese preferred a policy of cultural divide and political rule.

39. Benda, *Crescent,* p. 137; Sutter, *Indonesianisasi,* IV, appendix B; and George S. Kanahele, "The Japanese Occupation of Indonesia: Prelude to Independence" (Ph.D. dissertation, Cornell University, 1967), pp. 99–104. Dahm's conclusion (*Sukarno,* pp. 254–255) that in the CSI "the opportunity to set up roadblocks against oppression was never to be ignored" seems overgenerous. The representative character of the CSI is also a matter of degree; the Indonesian Communist Party (Partai Komunis Indonesia, PKI) was not represented in either the Volksraad, the CSI, or the BPKI and PPKI (see below).

Islamic and nationalist leaders, sharing generally anticolonial political credentials, were distinguished mainly by religious ideology. According to the Muslim militants, the nation could only be approached through belief in Allah as the creator of all things; true patriotism was the expression of a still higher, necessarily Islamic faith. The nationalists needed no such justification. In their mainly abangan, secular, and even Christian view, the claims of the "majority" religion were, if not suspect in their own right, at least secondary to the need for national unity. These two groups also held competing visions of the future. In nationalist eyes, independence would allow Indonesia to enter the "race toward progress" alongside other nations of the world, and "progress" was to them a strictly nonconfessional condition. The Islamic militants saw the future in the past, in the Prophet's experience in Medina, where, with the cooperation of non-Muslims, Muhammad first established an Islamic state and went on to win a holy war (*jihad*) against the unbelievers. The desire expressed by several Islamic spokesmen that this history should be repeated in Indonesia disquieted the nationalists, for although the Dutch and their allies were unbelievers so, to varying degrees, were many Indonesians. Even the etiquette of the two groups differed: nationalists often hailed one another with the cry "Merdeka!" (Freedom!) but committed Muslims continued to use the Arabic "Assalamualaikum" (Peace be with you).[40]

The difference between the administrative and nationalist elites (many of them abangan or secular in outlook), on the other hand, was mainly one of political position. In 1943, one nationalist argued (unsuccessfully) before the Japanese authorities that since the regents had been used as tools of Dutch colonial oppression they should be abolished entirely and forever. In 1944, a speaker at a rally to promote unity between the civil service and the nationalist movement recalled the days when a member of the central

40. Muhammad Isa Anshary was among those who expressed the militant Muslim viewpoint; see his "Tjinta Tanah Air," *Indonesia Merdeka,* June 25, 1945, and "Rasa Tanggoeng Djawab," *Asia Raya,* July 17, 1945. Also see the Islamic sermon by Zain Zambek, *Asia Raya,* Sept. 21, 1944. Typical of the nationalist side of the argument is the editorial [by Sukardjo Wirjopranoto?] in *Asia Raya,* June 2, 1945. The statements by A. K. Muzakkir and Ki Bagus Hadikusumo and the editorial in *Asia Raya,* Sept. 18, 1944, June 22 and June 2, 1945, respectively, provide further contrasts; also see *Asia Raya,* Sept. 6, 1945.

administrative corps (*pangreh praja,* later *pamong praja*) had been afraid to provide overnight shelter for a relative who might be a nationalist leader or to stand up at a meeting when the nationalist (later the national) anthem was played. In Dutch times, said Sukarno in 1945, the administrative corps had been "a favorite son lulled to sleep on a soft pillow." The regents and the pamong praja, of course, were mainly Javanese and Sundanese, while several of their nationalist critics came from the outer islands. And the paternalism of the administrative corps contrasted with the antifeudal cast of the nationalists' vision. Sukarno's call for a "modern" civil service in a "modern" state, for example, appeared to conflict with the view of one Javanese official who understood the term pamong praja to derive from the Javanese *ngemong* and thus to imply a corps of symbolic fathers benevolently tutoring the population. The word priyayi itself, argued this administrator, was a compound of *priya,* meaning person, and *yi,* love—that is, a person who loves and looks after the common people in his charge and upon whose mercy they depend.[41] However, a truly egalitarian ideology was notably absent from the rhetoric of either of these elites.

Sukarno and others argued during the occupation that the Dutch had turned Indonesia's three elite groups—Muslim, nationalist, and administrative—against each other. By the same logic, anticolonialism and, eventually, independence became reasons to unite. At its third session, in May 1944, the CSI suggested, in answer to the standard how-to-mobilize question, that civil servants, Muslim kiyais, and the "people's representatives" (including the CSI and the nationalist Jawa Hokokai) should be brought together. The proposal was made in the context of furthering Japan's war effort, but when in September 1944 Tokyo announced that Indonesia

41. Sources are, in order: J. Latuharhary, "The Development of the Position of the Regents on Java," Jakarta, June 1, 1943 (typescript, Wason film 905, reel 3, Cornell University); speech by R. Susanto Tirtoprodjo, *Asia Raya,* Nov. 7, 1944; speech by Sukarno on June 23, 1945, as reported in *Asia Raya.* On the regents and the pangreh praja generally, see Heather Sutherland, "Notes on Java's Regent Families," *Indonesia,* 16 (Oct. 1973), 113–148, and 17 (April 1974), 1–42, and her "Pangreh Pradja: Java's Indigenous Administrative Corps and Its Role in the Last Decades of Dutch Colonial Rule" (Ph.D. dissertation, Yale University, 1973). The terms pamong praja and priyayi were interpreted by R. P. Singgih, *Asia Raya,* Aug. 4, 1945; compare Sutherland, "The Priyayi," *Indonesia,* 19 (April 1975), 57–58.

would someday be granted independence the idea of unity acquired new meaning. At its February 1945 session, the Council urged that Masyumi and the Jawa Hokokai engage in joint actions to promote full unity and unanimously adopted the slogan "Freedom or Death" amid passionate statements that independence could be achieved only by Indonesians willing to shed blood and sweat on their own behalf.[42]

Cross-cultural political unity depends in part on the adequate representation in political institutions of important cultural groups. In the progression from the Volksraad to the CSI, to put it simply, although the majority changed, the minority did not. The Volksraad had been mainly administrative in conception and composition; in the CSI, by contrast, Sukarno and his fellow nationalists were the leading group. The Islamic elite, despite some gains under the occupation, remained the weakest side of the triangle.

The pressure of unrest on Java and Japan's deteriorating position in the Pacific led to the formation of a Body for the Investigation of Indonesian Independence (Badan Penyelidik Kemerdekaan Indonesia, BPKI), which was inaugurated under the Indonesian and Japanese flags in May 1945 in the building where the Volksraad and the CSI had met. By July, the BPKI had drafted a constitution for independent Indonesia, and in August a successor body, the Committee for the Preparation of Indonesian Independence (Panitia Persiapan Kemerdekaan Indonesia, PPKI), converted that draft into Indonesia's first and current constitution.[43] Unlike their predecessors, these councils had the power not merely to suggest a future but to blueprint it.

In their composition the BPKI and PPKI did not build upon such gains as the Muslims had registered in the CSI but returned to the earlier tradition of the Volksraad, from whose seats the Islamic elite had been virtually shut out. In the political cockpit of Jakarta in 1945 the Muslim leaders were fewer than the national-

42. Sukarno's argument can be found in *Asia Raya,* March 9, 1943, Nov. 7, 1944; on events in 1944–1945, also see *Asia Raya,* May 10, 1944, Feb. 26 and 27, 1945.
43. On these events, see B. R. O'G. Anderson, *Some Aspects of Indonesian Politics under the Japanese Occupation: 1944–1945* (Ithaca: Cornell University Modern Indonesia Project, 1961), pp. 12–16 and 23ff., and "Japan," pp. 18–19; Benda, *Crescent,* pp. 182ff.; Dahm, *Sukarno,* pp. 285–287 and 294ff.; *Asia Raya,* May 28, Aug. 7 and 8, 1945.

ists and the administrators, less experienced, and had poorer access to the Japanese. Representatives of the Islamic elite made up 14 per cent of the CSI; they did about as well in the BPKI (15 per cent) but were cut in half (to 7 per cent) in the PPKI, the body that actually adopted the constitution. The nationalists, meanwhile, increased their strength from 31 per cent in the BPKI to an absolute majority (52 per cent) in the PPKI. The administrative elite provided about a third of the members in both the BPKI and the PPKI.[44]

Although the PPKI was the furthest removed in time from the Volksraad, proportionally more former Volksraad members served in it than in either the CSI or the BPKI. This continuity stemmed in part from a Japanese desire to install in an independent Indonesian government men of such long-standing experience that they could not be discounted internationally as mere creatures of the occupation. It also reflected, however, the greater affinity and overlap between nationalist and administrative elites than between either of these and the Islamic minority. Above all, the first two groups shared Western-style educational experiences, whereas Muslim leaders had been socialized in religious schools, notably pesantren. Although all three elites could communicate in the national language, Indonesian, the first two shared in addition an international language and culture-carrier, Dutch, which Arabic-oriented Islamic leaders had either not been exposed to or had consciously rejected as a colonialist medium.[45]

The power and, from the Islamic standpoint, the unrepresentative character of the BPKI and PPKI combined to pre-empt the dream of an Islamic state. The subcommittee of the BPKI in which Islam acquired its greatest representation did draw up a draft preamble to the constitution according to which the state

44. These figures were obtained—following B. R. O'G. Anderson, "The Pemuda Revolution: Indonesian Politics 1945–1946" (Ph.D. dissertation, Cornell University, 1967), p. 68, and *Some Aspects,* pp. 20–21—by classifying members according to their backgrounds as given in *Orang Indonesia Jang Terkemoeka di Djawa.* The procedure is explained in detail in my "Exploring Elite Political Culture in Indonesia: Community and Change" (Ph.D. dissertation, Yale University, 1972), pp. 193 and 214–215.

45. B. R. O'G. Anderson, *Java in a Time of Revolution: Occupation and Resistance 1944–1946* (Ithaca: Cornell University Press, 1972), pp. 64–65, and *Some Aspects,* p. 21; Emmerson, "Exploring Elite Political Culture," pp. 215–217.

would be based on belief in God, "with the obligation to carry out the laws of Islam for the adherents of Islam." This phrase could be interpreted in three different ways; in order of rising anathema to secular, abangan, and non-Muslim leaders, they were that Muslims should behave according to Islamic law, that the state should make sure they do, and that the state itself should execute Islamic law on their behalf. Seeing these ambiguities all too clearly, the nationalist-administrative alliance in the PPKI rolled back this effort, and the unadopted draft, termed the Jakarta Charter, became a painful reminder of the Muslims' defeat. Other Muslim initiatives were similarly rebuffed. According to the constitution passed by the PPKI, Indonesia's president would not have to be a Muslim, Islam would not be the state religion, and there would be no Ministry of Religion (which Muslims might have been expected to dominate).[46]

For all its anticolonial rhetoric, Indonesia's constitutional committee reinvigorated two colonial traditions: Islam was isolated as a political force, and the legislative branch was subordinated to a strong executive. By the afternoon of August 19, 1945, when the PPKI completed its work, Indonesia had a president (Sukarno), a vice-president (Hatta), and a constitution providing for an all-powerful but infrequently convening People's Consultative Assembly (Majelis Permusyawaratan Rakyat, MPR) and a Parliament (Dewan Perwakilan Rakyat, DPR). The DPR was to share responsibility for legislation with the president but could not unseat him or his cabinet of eleven ministers.[47] Before the month was out, the PPKI had enlarged and transformed itself into a National Central Committee (Komite Nasional Pusat, KNP) to discharge jointly with the president the functions that would devolve upon the MPR and DPR once those bodies could be formed. The KNP —its location, membership, and functions in flux throughout the ensuing revolution—and the 1945 constitution—its provisions

46. Emmerson, "Exploring Elite Political Culture," pp. 148–196 and references. Also see B. J. Boland, *The Struggle of Islam in Modern Indonesia* (The Hague: Martinus Nijhoff, 1971), passim, and Daniel S. Lev, *Islamic Courts in Indonesia: A Study in the Political Bases of Legal Institutions* (Berkeley: University of California Press, 1972), pp. 41–43. I am grateful to Daniel Lev for improving my translation of the key phrase in the Jakarta Charter.
47. Muhammad Yamin, comp. and ed., *Naskah-persiapan Undang-undang Dasar 1945,* I ([Jakarta]: Jajasan Prapantja, 1959), pp. 453–468.

effectively suspended by the combined force of emergency circumstance and executive will—survived into a 1949–1950 transition period that ended with the establishment on August 17, 1950, of a unitarian Indonesian republic under a new provisional constitution.[48]

In the years that followed, these two conditions of cultural politics in Indonesia—executive dominance and Muslim defensiveness —remained basically unchanged. Islamic fortunes appeared to rise in January 1946 when the PPKI's decision not to establish a Ministry of Religion was reversed by a government eager to attract all social forces to the republican cause. But in the long run the Ministry proved less a springboard than a cul-de-sac; in it the Nahdlatul Ulama, which gained control of it in the 1950's, was coopted into the secular bureaucracy and the community of Islam (*ummat Islam*) more or less ghettoized.[49]

Through the mid-1960's, Islamic political initiatives outside the establishment were basically of two kinds, insurrectionary and electoral. Neither approach worked. Central bureaucratic and military elites in Jakarta increased their prestige and extended their writ of authority as they outmaneuvered a succession of revolts, Islamic in tone if not always or purely in inspiration, in West Java, Sumatra, and Sulawesi. In the 1955 elections, Islamic parties won 48 per cent of the vote and 44 per cent of the seats in the DPR, but—repeating the pattern of a decade earlier, when Islam had achieved significant representation on the subcommittee that wrote the Jakarta Charter—this victory was short-lived. In the later 1950's the strongest Muslim party, Masyumi, was implicated in the regional revolts and struggled in vain for the old goal of an Islamic state against the opposition of a secular-abangan-Christian coalition in the Constituent Assembly charged with writing yet another constitution (Indonesia had by then already had three). In the Assembly the forces of Islam were only strong enough to ensure a stalemate, which Sukarno broke in 1959–1960 by dissolving Parliament, disbanding the Assembly, outlawing Masyumi, and reintroducing

48. On this period, see Kahin, *Nationalism and Revolution*.

49. *Peranan Departemen Agama dalam Revolusi dan Pembangunan Bangsa* (Bandung: Departemen Agama, 1965), p. 104; K. H. A. Wahid Hasjim, "Sekitar Pembentukan Kementerian Agama R.I.S.," *Mimbar Agama* (1951), reprinted in H. Aboebakar, comp., *Sedjarah Hidup K. H. A. Wahid Hasjim dan Karangan Tersiar* (Jakarta: Panitya Buku Peringatan, 1957), p. 856; and, especially, Lev, *Islamic Courts*, pp. 43–53.

the 1945 constitution with its strong executive. As a sop to the Muslims, Sukarno did, in his decree of July 5, 1959, declare that the 1945 document was "inspired" by the Jakarta Charter. The 1959 decree therefore joined the Charter as a symbolic legitimizer of Islamic demands. But an Islamic future for Indonesia had in fact again been cancelled.[50]

In the DPR that Sukarno appointed in 1960 to replace the elected model he had just dissolved, Islamic strength was roughly halved (to 20 per cent), as it had been in the shift from the BPKI to the PPKI in 1945; this time, however, it mattered less because Parliament had become a mere appendage of Sukarno's authoritarian-abangan regime. By 1966, just before Parliament was officially purged of its communist and presumed procommunist members, Islamic parties still occupied only 22 per cent of the seats; their subsequent gain to 28 per cent in 1968–1969 was a consequence not of their own doing but of the left's undoing.

In an anticommunist atmosphere ostensibly favorable to Islam, a caretaker organization, the Indonesian Muslims' Party (Partai Muslimin Indonesia, or Parmusi), tried to remobilize Masyumi's old base for the country's second legislative elections in 1971. But Suharto and the abangan generals around him could not forget the rebellions of the 1950's and did not relish the spectre of resurgent Islam. By reserving 100 of the 460 seats in the new DPR for its own appointees, by interfering in Parmusi's first congress to thwart the new party's plans to recapture Masyumi's votes, and by vigorously promoting its own electoral vehicle, the Joint Secretariat of Functional Groups (Sekretariat Bersama Golongan Karya, or Sekber Golkar; later simply Golongan Karya, or Golkar), the government succeeded in keeping Islamic representation in the 1971 Parliament down to 26 per cent. Whereas Masyumi alone

50. On this period, see Feith, *Decline,* and Daniel S. Lev, *The Transition to Guided Democracy: Indonesian Politics, 1957–1959* (Ithaca: Cornell University Modern Indonesia Project, 1966). The 1955 voting figures are in Herbert Feith, *The Indonesian Elections of 1955* (Ithaca: Cornell University Modern Indonesia Project, 1957); seat percentages in this and the following paragraphs have been calculated from data in Parlaungan, comp., *Hasil Rakjat Memilih Tokoh-tokoh Parlemen* (Jakarta: Gita, 1956), pp. 14–15 and 414–415, the files of the Documentation Section of the DPR in Jakarta, and *Sinar Harapan,* Aug. 7, 1971.

had held 22 per cent of the seats in the DPR in 1955, Parmusi obtained only 5 per cent in 1971.[51]

The Muslim parties at least had their religious community, the ummat, with its occupational roots in the private and rural sectors, to define themselves in contrast to the mainly urban, abangan, military governing elite. The PNI had no such distinctive self-definition. On the contrary, its essentially abangan-bureaucratic base of support on Java was easily penetrated and captured in 1971 by the similarly abangan-bureaucratic military leadership of Golkar. Public officials were expected to direct their subordinates' votes toward the banyan tree, the government's ballot symbol of paternalistic welfare and protection; and they did. Having held, like Masyumi, 22 per cent of the seats in 1955, the PNI's share shrank to 4 per cent in the 1971 Parliament.

Although Suharto's policies differed sharply from Sukarno's in economic matters and foreign affairs, in domestic politics the New Order intensified under mainly abangan military auspices a tradition of Islamic isolation and executive dominance over representative bodies that has continued almost uninterrupted since the colonial period. In the mid-1950's, Muslim parties did gain a significant share of the seats in the most representative and powerful Parliament Indonesia has had, a DPR whose membership was openly elected and broadly contested and that exercised important prerogatives in fields ranging from finance to foreign policy. But under Guided Democracy, Parliament was redomesticated, and Muslim organizations were either banned or bought off with bureaucratic positions in a patronage-swollen regime whose center of gravity, insofar as it had one, lay in Sukarno's latter-day kraton. In recognition of both its weakness and its Javanizing tendencies, Geertz called Guided Democracy a "cardboard Mataram."[52]

Suharto has made gestures toward rehabilitating the position of the DPR; whereas Sukarno delivered his independence-day addresses from the palace, for example, Suharto speaks in Parlia-

51. See K. E. Ward, *The Foundation of the Partai Muslimin Indonesia* (Ithaca: Cornell University Modern Indonesia Project, 1970); and two articles by Allan A. Samson, "Army and Islam in Indonesia," *Pacific Affairs*, 44 (Winter 1971–1972), 545–565, and "Islam in Indonesian Politics," *Asian Survey*, 8 (Dec. 1968), 1001–1017.

52. Clifford Geertz, *Islam Observed: Religious Development in Morocco and Indonesia* (New Haven: Yale University Press, 1968), p. 87.

ment. But Golkar's dramatically successful use of the official apparatus to overwhelm the parties in the 1971 elections, in which the government won an absolute majority of 71 per cent, leaves little doubt that the old tradition of bureaucratic dominance has been strengthened. The military-backed regime can and does penetrate more deeply into the society than its predecessor. To a degree, cardboard has been exchanged for steel.[53]

What has changed since the mid-1960's is not the basic power relationship between the bureaucratic and legislative institutions but their political coloration. Compared to its highly politicized predecessor, the New Order is avowedly depoliticizing, although the latter term in practice refers to party politics. The partial monopolization of particular ministries by the PNI and NU has been broken. The leftmost section of the political spectrum in Parliament has been lopped off. Stability and economic growth have replaced the rhetoric of revolution and cultural synthesis as hallmarks of the regime.

De Kat Angelino, the Dutch official who saw in the workings of the Indies government the gleaming rationality of a timepiece, also wrote of the administrative (essentially priyayi) class as if it were the representative body articulating popular will. Without this class, he warned, "the Government would lose its compass, its general sense of orientation, while the population would lose its best friend and mouthpiece. In truth, it would lose its very organ of speech." Decades later, on the floor of the DPR in independent Indonesia, Muhammad Yamin, a vocal nationalist from Sumatra, complained that Sukarno's palace favored the executive over the legislative branch even in matters of protocol. At a gathering to receive a visiting head of state, members of Parliament had been seated far back in the audience with ordinary civil servants. "But we are not civil servants!" Yamin thundered. "The Government considers us to be, and appoints us as, representatives of the peo-

53. On the elections, see Donald Hindley, "Indonesia 1971: Pantjasila Democracy and the Second Parliamentary Elections," *Asian Survey,* 12 (Jan. 1972), 56–68; R. William Liddle, "Evolution from Above: National Leadership and Local Development in Indonesia," *Journal of Asian Studies,* 32 (1973), 287–309; Oey Hong Lee, ed., *Indonesia after the 1971 Elections* (London: Oxford University Press for the University of Hull, 1974). On increased control, see my "Bureaucracy."

ple. Our status is very different" from that of mere government employees. Members shouted their agreement. But Yamin had admitted that he and his fellow legislators had been appointed to their posts, just as civil servants were. And a decade later Sukarno publicly renounced the idea that Indonesia's government should be separated into executive, legislative, and judicial branches.[54]

This picture of unclear and overlapping institutional boundaries, with a civil service presumed to articulate needs from the bottom up and a legislative body appointed or "elected" through indirect coercion from the top down, persists in Indonesia; this chapter has shown how it has developed and how executive dominance and Muslim defensiveness have reinforced each other since colonial times. These themes will be examined in microcosm in the next chapter, which is focused on the experiences and orientations of two individuals.

54. De Kat Angelino, *Colonial Policy*, II, p. 360; Dewan Perwakilan Rakyat Republik Indonesia, *Risalah Perundingan 1950/1951*, I (Jakarta: Pertjetakan Negara, n.d.), p. 113, citing Muhammad Yamin's speech of Aug. 22, 1950; Sukarno, "Trias Politica," speech to the plenary session of the National Planning Council (DEPERNAS), Aug. 13, 1960.

CHAPTER 2

INDIVIDUALS

One way of "mapping" the political culture of an elite, and the one used in chapters 4 and 5 of this book, is to relate context and content statistically across the full samples. Respondents are first divided successively along ethnic, religious, organizational, and institutional lines. A second series of maps is then drawn, each one showing the distribution of a politically relevant elite orientation. An attempt is then made to obtain the best fit between the two sets, that is, to find out which viewpoints are most and least consonant with which affiliations. This procedure permits identification of the orientations that are most deeply group-rooted, and thus sensitive and hard to change; it also reveals the degree to which similar groups have similar outlooks: whether, in elite political culture, opinion and origin are interdependent, densely meshed in distinct blocks of group identity and belief, or so unrelated that one cannot even be guessed from the other. A comparison of the power of different cultural and political identities to explain elite outlooks should then suggest appropriate strategies for change.

This approach is useful, but, like any mapping operation, it condenses and homogenizes reality. The uniqueness of the individual is lost in the effort to place him with others in one box of a matrix, and his wholeness is destroyed because that box classifies him along only a few of the myriad dimensions of his existence. The person is sacrificed to abstractions. To lessen this distortion and at the same time prepare for it, in this chapter the actual experiences of two people are portrayed in detail as they exemplify two important abstractions: the institutional and the religious. The two men's orientations are also explored in greater scope and depth than will be possible for the full samples.

The two men are "Purwoko," an abangan official in a ministry, and "Usman," a santri member of Parliament.[1] Of all the individuals in the samples, Purwoko grew up most familar with the kraton world of inland central Java on which abangan attitudes and priyayi status were for so long modeled, and Usman enjoyed the most prolonged, intimate contact with the pesantren world that fosters santri identity. If there are significant differences in experience and outlook between elite products of these two cultural milieux and between elite incumbents of the bureaucratic and legislative institutions, as chapter 1 suggests, the differences should appear in a comparison of these two men. And the qualitative differences thus revealed will point to possible lodes for quantitative analysis in the full samples.

Purwoko, an Abangan Administrator

I first met Purwoko a few weeks after Lebaran, the day of feasting and forgiveness that in Indonesia marks the end of the Muslim fasting month. Like many other Jakartans, he had left the city to be with his parents in their village home. He had not seen his aging father for a number of years, and the old man no longer recognized his son. Only when Purwoko identified himself did his father embrace him. Re-enacting the Lebaran ritual, as he had many times in the past, Purwoko asked his father's forgiveness for his faults and shortcomings and knelt before him in the classic Javanese posture of respect and homage: head bowed, palms and outstretched fingers together, fingertips level with his father's knee.

The gesture was not merely symbolic, for Purwoko owed to his father both his social status and his cultural identity. The first had opened doors to a Western education, which had smoothed his way into the administrative elite and the secular style of life he came to lead. The second had given him a sense of who he was: that, for all his intercourse with foreigners, his Western sense of time, and his use of foreign tongues, he would remain ineradicably Javanese. These debts suggest that the path to an understanding of Purwoko begins with his father.

1. Some of my informants would have wanted me to reveal their identities, but others trusted me not to. With apologies to the first group, I have given pseudonyms like these to about half the men in my samples and avoided giving names to the others. I interviewed Usman for six hours spread over three sessions, Purwoko for nearly nine hours over five sessions; additional time was spent getting to know them in social situations.

From age eighteen until senility finally forced him to retire, Purwoko's father was a village head in central Java. Although the post was (and remains) elective, the fact that Purwoko's father's father had been village head before him undoubtedly influenced the villagers in his favor. But there were other considerations as well.

The village lay part way up a life-giving mountain whose rich volcanic soil and plentiful water nourished the fields of rice the villagers tended on its flank. The peasants had prospered in this environment—their standard of living was higher than that of less endowed regions elsewhere—and they accepted their prosperity as a sign that the guardian gods of the mountain were beneficent.

But the gods had not been able to protect these peasants from the depredations of robbers and marauding bands, who, attracted by the wealth of the village, would come at night to make off with a water buffalo, a cow, or something else of value. The intruders were believed to use magic to accomplish their designs. Some, it was said, could make themselves invisible and steal with impunity; some were believed to whisper secret incantations that caused a victim to fall asleep in his fields while his water buffalo was stolen; others were said to be able to make themselves so small they could slip unnoticed through the woven bamboo walls of a house. When a victim discovered his loss he would ring the *kentongan* (a hanging piece of hollow wood, struck to signal danger), but in vain, for by then the thieves would have disappeared without trace. The only way to fight these supernaturally empowered persons, it seemed, was on their own terms.

It took Purwoko's father only a few years of residence in the village to establish his reputation for magical prowess. He was a mystic, a master of that ascetic self-control admired and emulated not only on this particular mountainside but throughout the cultural heartland of Java. It was said he could remain in trance, ingesting neither food nor water, for periods far exceeding the normal limits of human endurance. Often he would climb to the top of the mountain to meditate in search of the strength to overwhelm his opponents. His small size and slight build only confirmed the villagers' belief that he could defeat his enemies by spiritual means alone.

Purwoko's father also knew intimately the repertoire of wayang kulit plays, including the tale of Bima's search for the water of life. Local puppeteers often asked his advice on how to interpret a certain story. Although unlettered, he loved the Javanese language and could hold a village audience spellbound with his narrations, whether coarsely funny homilies or legends from the Javanese past.

Finally, he was an attractive man. At stag drinking parties, when a female dancer would circle the room, finally brushing with the tip of her scarf the man she had chosen to enjoy her company, Purwoko's father often felt her accolade. For all these reasons, and because of his experience in other villages west of the mountain, where, it was rumored, he had been spectacularly effective in rounding up thieves and brigands, the villagers agreed that Purwoko's father should become their head.

The village lay within the purview of one of four princely states created out of the colonial interventions and internal rebellions that had completed the disintegration of the Mataram empire. Upon becoming village head, therefore, Purwoko's father also became an official of the reigning king of the region and enjoyed the right to sow and harvest nearly six hectares (more than fourteen acres) of fertile wet-rice land as salary in kind. Considering that in the early 1930's three hectares was already a "large" holding, Purwoko's father was a wealthy man.[2]

Every year, Purwoko's father would don his finest clothes and go with the other village heads to assemble before the king. The king might offer them general advice on how to rule over the people, how to maintain the security and tranquillity of the state. Or he might hold up wayang heroes as models for their emulation: Bima for his steadfastness, or Rama for his eight statesman's virtues. In the latter event, one can imagine Purwoko's father being inwardly pleased at the recitation of the second and seventh virtues, the getting rid of thieves and evil-doers by natural or magic means, for he excelled at that.

---

2. The authors of a study conducted in 1932 in Kutowinangun, to the west of Purwoko's village, distinguished "large," "medium," and "small" landholders; persons in the "large" category owned an average of 2.95 hectares of arable land. D. H. Penny and M. Singarimbun cite the study—J. J. Ochse, et al., *Geld en producten-huishouding, volksvoeding en gezonshein in Koetowinangoen* (Buitenzorg [Bogor]: Department van Economische Zaken, 1934)—in their *Population and Poverty in Rural Java: Some Economic Arithmetic from Sriharjo* (Ithaca: Cornell University Department of Agricultural Economics, 1973), p. 88.

In the realm, Purwoko's father was a minor official; but in the village, he was king. The villagers would come to the *pendapa* of his home (a large roofed area in the front of the house, open on three sides), and there he would hold court, organizing compulsory labor, overseeing the collection of taxes, registering births and deaths, listening to a man ask for blessings on his daughter's approaching marriage or for advice on a matter of schooling for his son.

The men who held a share of village land and were therefore full members of the community took turns guarding the village after dark. Every night eight of them made the rounds to see that all was well. They carried a small kentongan with them, sounding it gently through the night to reassure the people that the watch was about and the village safe.

By religious belief and force of habit, Purwoko's father was a nocturnal man. Like many other Javanese he believed that an occasional white night did a man spiritual good; by curbing such wordly desires as the appetite for sleep a man could elevate himself to a higher, purer plane. Thus, as the safety of the village could be taken more and more for granted, and as the circumnavigations of the guards could become less frequent, Purwoko's father began to use the night hours and the undivided attention of the watch (for they feared and respected him too much to decline his invitation) to expound upon a range of matters philosophical and practical. Because sooner or later all the full citizens of the village took their turns in the watch, in this way he was able to reach the entire land-sharing community without losing the advantages of intimacy in a small group.

The eight men of the watch would sit cross-legged on the floor of the pendapa with Purwoko's father facing them from the elevation of a chair placed just inside the more hallowed *peringgitan* area of the house, so named because on nights of celebration plays from the classical shadow theater, or *ringgit purwa,* were performed there. To the night watch sometimes he told these wayang tales, or reinterpreted the virtues of Rama as he had heard them at his last audience with the king, but more often he spoke of mundane things. A frequent topic was the just allocation of water to irrigate the ricefields; in these quiet hours, disputes between individuals who happened to be on the watch together could sometimes be resolved. He would praise thrift and the prompt payment of debts, allude derisively to families who competed not in their efforts to be good citizens but in the lavishness of their daughters' weddings, remark that when a man heard his neighbor's kentongan ring out for help he should not feign sleep. Sometimes he outlined plans for a village project: where they might get stones for a dam, where the dam should be located, how the work details would be organized. Sometimes he might indirectly reprimand one of the eight men sitting before him; after a joke about a husband who cuckolded another with hilariously humiliating results, one of the watch might laugh more nervously than the rest. Another theme was the folly of Pak Tjikra and Pak Bedjo, whom Purwoko's father claimed to have known in his days fighting bandits west of the mountain. Pak Bedjo was a cunning thief and practical joker who enjoyed the discomforts of others. Pak Tjikra was the goodhearted, gullible sort who invariably did whatever his unprincipled friend told him to, and just as invariably suffered for it. Purwoko's father had a fund of funny stories about the evil of the one and the foolishness of the other.[3]

Purwoko's father divorced his first wife because she bore him no children. When his second wife also did not conceive, he took to immersing himself in the middle of the night in the river that ran down the mountain, squatting motionless for hours in water up to his neck, enlisting the assistance of the gods. When even this remedy failed, he divorced his second wife and married a third. She promptly bore him a son, Purwoko, who in time became the eldest of eight children.

Purwoko stayed with his parents until the age of four, when it was decided that he should go to live with relatives. Purwoko's maternal grandfather was approached. A relatively well-to-do man, he lived in a village not far away, and his five daughters had already married and left home, so there was more than enough room for Purwoko. Purwoko lived with this grandfather and his wife for

---

3. For example: Pak Tjikra and Pak Bedjo were neighbors. They lived near one end of a bamboo bridge slung across a stream. One day Pak Bedjo called Pak Tjikra over and, pointing to a submerged rock in the stream, said he had seen a big fish swimming there. "Why don't you go down and catch it?" suggested Pak Bedjo. Although he could see no fish, Pak Tjikra waded into the stream without further thought. By the time he had leaned over the rock to look for the fish, Pak Bedjo was on the bridge, his pants down, defecating onto Pak Tjikra's back.

two years while attending the local Volksschool, a simplified primary school for "natives" at which instruction was entirely in Javanese.

Purwoko's father, thinking that his son deserved much better than a "people's school," saw enrollment in the Volksschool as only a temporary step; he wanted to get the boy into the king's primary school. Located in the capital city of the region, the royal school was run by a Dutch headmaster along Dutch lines and in the Dutch language for the benefit of the king's family and their officials. Purwoko's father admired the Dutch and valued their education. But how was he to enroll the boy? As an official of the king, Purwoko's father was entitled to seek admission for his son, but as a lowly village head he would need the support of someone within the palace. He thought first of approaching a high official in the king's entourage whose father had been regent in the area west of the mountain where Purwoko's father had helped re-establish law and order years before. Surely this official would remember his own father's indebtedness to Purwoko's father; perhaps in return he would help get Purwoko into the king's school.

On a clear, bright day, Purwoko and his father, dressed in their best, went off to visit the official. Once in his presence, Purwoko's father adopted the highest speech level available in Javanese and an even higher respect vocabulary, reproducing in language the difference in rank between a village chief and a court personage. After many polite expressions of deference and praise, during which he carefully remembered to say how honored he had been to serve the regent in ending that unfortunate period of lawlessness some years earlier, Purwoko's father gently and obliquely raised his purpose in coming. The regent's son replied that of course he would be glad to do what he could to help the young boy and would let the father know in due course of any prospects. The conversation wound down through another set of formalities, ended, and the village head and his son took their leave. They never heard from the regent's son again.

Defeated but undaunted, Purwoko's father tried another route. The husband of one of Purwoko's maternal aunts was also serving in the king's palace, although in a lowlier position than the regent's son. Again there was a moral debt to be collected, for Purwoko's mother was the oldest of nine girls, and she had worked hard to help bring up her younger sisters. In the end, Purwoko's aunt and her husband agreed to accept the boy into their home, and Purwoko soon found himself, with the husband's help and to his father's great happiness and pride, enrolled in the king's school. Purwoko spent seven years there, including a year of introductory Dutch to enable him to follow the language of instruction.

In time and space, the king's school spanned two worlds: those of contemporary Holland and classical Java. The pupils were given an education comparable in its high quality and secular content to what they might have obtained in the Netherlands. The curriculum met the requirements of the colonial Department of Education and Worship in Batavia. Dutch inspectors from the Department regularly visited the school, with the king's permission, to see that academic standards were maintained. But outside the classroom lay the palace. There the pupils could observe the ritual and pageantry of Javanese kingship at first hand. They were given regular instruction in classical Javanese dance. The wayang puppeteers whose performances they were allowed to watch were among the best in Java. For Purwoko, the school opened the way to a secular, Westernizing future while simultaneously nourishing his roots in the Javanese past.

Most of Purwoko's classmates outranked him socially: they were the children of regents and district and subdistrict officers, not village heads. They brought bread and butter to school with them to eat during recess. Some wore fresh clothes every day, thanks to their families' washerwomen. Although a number wore the traditional Javanese sarong, by the 1920's Western dress, including leather shoes, had already become popular among the sons of the well-to-do. Purwoko could afford neither butter nor leather shoes, but his classmates did not mock his relative poverty or his lower social origin. The school stressed etiquette; its teachers trained their charges to behave toward one another in the refined manner of the Javanese aristocratic class. The fact of Purwoko's birth outside this class did not prevent his socialization into its ways. And he shared with most of his classmates an abangan religious upbringing and, now, the exposure to high Javanese culture.

Purwoko's adjustment was also made easier by his academic achievement, which more than made up for his social inferiority. He did especially well in the Dutch language. The highest possible grade in a subject was ten, but such a mark was almost never awarded; as the saying went, "Ten is reserved for God." When the headmaster, who also taught Dutch, awarded Purwoko a nine, Purwoko nearly burst with pride.

His ability in Dutch, and in languages generally, stood Purwoko in good stead throughout his life. Against a background of high marks in other subjects, it qualified him for further academic study in a four-year Dutch-language junior secondary school in the same city. The tuition was eight guilders a month, but Purwoko's good grades won him a monthly subsidy of ten guilders from a scholarship fund controlled by the king.

The city, in which Purwoko spent a total of eleven years, included, aside from the palace complex, markets, lower-status neighborhoods, and an area (the *kauman*) where practicing Muslims lived and congregated. Though he spent the bulk of his time in the king's school, in the palace, and at home at his aunt's, Purwoko became familiar with these other three milieux as well. The market was a place to make a killing, albeit on a small boy's scale. There Purwoko and his friends would buy candlenuts, say twenty for five Netherlands Indies cents (U.S. 2¢). They liked to play a kind of petanque, using the nuts instead of balls. A skilful player who emerged at the end of an afternoon of play with a much larger hoard of nuts than he had started with would run back happily to the market to convert his winnings into cash. The better-off children enjoyed matching movie-star cards—your Rudolph Valentino, say, against my Eddie Polo—obtained from packs of the expensive cigarettes their elders smoked.

Purwoko and his wellborn friends interacted with children from lower-status neighborhoods, the sons of commoners, on the soccer field. Each of the several schools in the city had a soccer club, and Purwoko played the game often. Children from other schools derided the pupils of the king's school as being soft and gentle and easily defeated; they probably also resented the latter's aristocratic advantages. Purwoko and his classmates wanted to prove that they were as tough as their opponents; interschool soccer therefore took on overtones of social class conflict, and violence was frequent. A favorite tactic of Purwoko and his teammates was to conceal pieces of wood or even metal between two pairs of knee socks to punish the barefoot enemy. Recalling these battles, Purwoko wondered if perhaps they had functioned as a kind of "catharsis" (he used the English word) to release the tensions and animosities of the players.

Although Purwoko did not reside in the kauman proper, next door to his aunt's house lived an Islamic teacher named Pak Hasan. Several times a week a dozen or so young girls came to Pak Hasan's house to memorize the Arabic alphabet and recite Koranic passages under his direction. Purwoko, who had no Islamic education to speak of, enjoyed pestering the girls. A favorite prank was to creep up to the house and poke the spine of a coconut leaf through a crack in the wall. At a particularly solemn moment, when the girls were in the middle of a prayer, Purwoko would jab the nearest with the sharp end of the spine. Startled, she would cry out. Pak Hasan would dash outside to catch the culprit, but Purwoko would be gone. As Purwoko and his friends continued to torment the old kiyai in this manner, Pak Hasan became more and more exasperated. Purwoko's eyes sparkled with amusement as he remembered how the old teacher looked, standing in the street in his baggy, thick-cuffed trousers, a cane raised in one hand to beat off the devils who kept interrupting the word of God.

During vacations Purwoko gladly left his aunt's house—where he was kept busy sweeping the yard, boiling water, and doing other chores—to return to his real home in the village. There he loved to join the children who tended his father's livestock. One villager had charge of twenty-five of Purwoko's father's goats. Purwoko enjoyed playing with this man's children; sometimes they would pass the time by picking two of the goats and matching them in combat. In the evenings Purwoko and his siblings would gather to listen while his mother's youngest sister, who had come to live with them, lulled them to sleep with folktales. And on nights when the watch had gathered at his father's feet Purwoko would sit on the pendapa or in the peringgitan or with his mother in the innermost room of the house, listening to his father's talk of wayang and the world.

It was a happy childhood. His father was firm but not harsh. Purwoko recalled being thrashed only once, when he talked back to his father. His mother was softer and more forgiving, but the two parents were on the whole consistent in disciplining their son. The village itself, perhaps two thousand souls in all, Purwoko remembered as his own family writ large. His father was the villagers' father, loved, feared, obeyed. And life was somehow "integrated" (again Purwoko used the English word), not like life in Jakarta in 1969. In the village, everyone and everything somehow fitted together. Since his childhood, the nation had traveled far, and so had he; but somewhere along the way, Purwoko felt, the peace and harmony of that village family had been irretrievably lost.

In junior high school, Purwoko decided he wanted to become a doctor. The house in which he lived with his aunt and her family was near a doctor's house. Purwoko could see that the doctor owned a car, had many servants, and enjoyed wide respect. The prestige of a doctor suddenly seemed to Purwoko higher even than that of a palace official. Purwoko wanted to be like his father; but if his father was a little king, Purwoko would be a big one, like the doctor down the street. To become a doctor, he would need further education. He wanted to go on to senior secondary school, but his father disagreed. The boy had had enough schooling; he should go to work to help finance the education of his younger brother and sisters, who had no scholarships and whose school fees might eventually weigh too heavily on the family budget. Besides, medical school would cost too much. In the end, a compromise was reached; Purwoko should enter a Dutch teacher training school, which would prepare him, in three years, to become a Dutch-language primary school teacher. Tuition in this kind of institution was much less than in a purely academic school, for the government needed teachers and was willing to subsidize their education. Not only did Purwoko continue to receive ten guilders a month from the king, for his school expenses, but his father gave him an allowance of five guilders a month to spend as he liked. In his new surroundings, among classmates less fortunate than he, Purwoko was a wealthy young man.

Purwoko's life at the normal school was far more regulated than it had been with his parents or his aunt. He lived in a dormitory and followed a strict regimen, with specific hours set aside for study, sports, meals, and other activities. The intellectual competition was tougher, so Purwoko studied harder, not to compensate for any social disadvantage—here he felt none—but simply to excel and to earn his teacher's praise. Once again he succeeded. Among the approximately sixty students in his class, Purwoko graduated second in overall academic average and first in Dutch.

Although he still visited his parents during vacations, his regimented dormitory life and his concentration on his studies meant that Purwoko was moving out of the family orbit toward a career. The horizons of his awareness were also expanding. In 1935, the Italians attacked Abyssinia. Between October, when the Italians invaded, and the following May, when Haile Selassie fled the country, Purwoko and his friends spent many hours listening to reports of the war on the radio, reading about it in Dutch-language newspapers, and debating the military strengths and strategies of the two sides. But, although they were not unaware of its racial aspect, the war seemed to these young men mainly a kind of international soccer match, exciting to follow between the bursts of short-wave static or the columns of sugar and rubber statistics but not more involving than that. Nor did their support of the underdog Ethiopian team conflict with the sympathies of the Dutchmen who ran the school.

Normally, a graduate of the teacher training school went straight into a teaching post at one of the Dutch-language primary schools in the colony, but Purwoko's academic standing won him an additional two years' study in the large city of Bandung to the west, where he and some thirty other promising Indonesian teacher trainees from around the colony were to be given further education to prepare them for positions as headmasters. Purwoko was proud to be thus honored, and his prestige soared, especially among the parents of certain eligible daughters.

Purwoko knew that in Bandung he would be subsidized by the Dutch East Indies government at the lordly level of forty-five guilders a month, including five guilders' pocket money. But what of his younger brother and sisters? Before going to Bandung, he sought an audience with the king. Duplicating the elaborate gestures and words of respect that he had seen his father use in the presence of royalty, Purwoko expressed his gratitude for the king's long support and asked whether the king might in future be willing to extend this support to Purwoko's younger siblings, who were also thirsting for an education. Was it not, he asked, important that they too be able to benefit from a modern education, as he had, and would not the Javanese people as a whole benefit through them? Would the king perhaps be willing to provide them with a stipend of twenty guilders a month? The king may at first have been taken aback by the straightforward mention of a specific sum —Purwoko's father would have been more circumspect—but in the end he agreed. Of the twenty guilders, Purwoko kept two and a half for himself; the rest went to his siblings, to be spent on tuition and other fees and to charter a horse-drawn carriage to take the girls to and from school each day. (Two of them later became university instructors.)

In Bandung, more than ever before, Purwoko lived in a European world. The city itself was an upland resort, business, and retirement community for Dutch colonial officials and plantation managers. The climate was cool, the streets tree-lined, the gardens around the European villas contoured and carefully tended. The European community frequented several first-class hotels and restaurants and two exclusive clubs, the Concordia and the Ons Genoegen (Our Pleasure), to which the tea and cinchona planters from nearby estates would repair for conversation and Dutch gin. Although Purwoko was accustomed to schools administered by Dutchmen, in his classes in Bandung even the teachers were Dutch. Purwoko and his classmates were told that they should be very proud, for they were the native elite, "the children of the [Dutch] queen."

Yet although he lived in a European world, Purwoko was not part of it. He could see that however much the school officials tried to instill in him a sense of having arrived at the apex of native society, that pinnacle was still dwarfed by the heights to which a white man could aspire. The gap could not have been more painfully visible than in the contrast between northern, upper, European Bandung and the southern, lower, indigenous section of the city. Purwoko was living at a standard far higher than the vast bulk of the local population; nevertheless, it was not the Dutch level. He knew that, despite identical educational qualifications, Dutchmen who were being trained as headmasters got bigger scholarships and would later enjoy higher wages than he or the other "natives" could expect. The queen had favorites among her children. Rather than endangering his position by objecting to these inequalities, however, Purwoko kept busy with his classes, assignments, and examinations. He also developed his interest in world affairs by reading widely and avidly in the Dutch-language press.

While in Europe Hitler carved out his Lebensraum, in Bandung Purwoko graduated and became, at last, a civil servant. His first assignment took him back to central Java, to the king's city. (A perquisite of the post was a five-bedroom house, where Purwoko promptly boarded his brother and sisters who were still in school.) Quickly Purwoko settled down to the routine of teaching and administration that would continue to organize the rest of his working life.

Many years and experiences separate Purwoko the colonial priyayi from Purwoko the Indonesian civil servant, but the discontinuities are few. The Japanese came in 1942; Purwoko's school was briefly closed, then reopened. The main change for Purwoko was that from then on he used Indonesian in the classroom instead of Dutch. He supported the revolution that broke out in the wake of the Japanese defeat and, in the patriotic spirit of the times, led a group of twenty of his pupils to Surabaya to help defend the city against a British attack in November 1945. Once there, however, the schoolmaster and his charges were more partisan spectators than participants in battle, and when it became clear that the republican forces would have to withdraw, Purwoko took his pupils home.

He stayed at his school until December 1948. By then nationalist sentiment among his students was in full blaze, and when the Dutch broke an uneasy truce and began to seize territory in central Java, he and his pupils withdrew to the rebels' stronghold in the mountains. There Purwoko tried to meet his classes in some semblance of an academic atmosphere, although the skirmishing and uncertainty sometimes made this impossible. Again his involvement in the physical struggle was more symbolic than real—he had had no military training and took no part in the fighting—but the excursion to Surabaya and this sojourn with the guerrilla forces did clearly identify Purwoko as a friend of the republic. For one who owed so much to the colonial aristocracy, this was no minor advantage. And when Sukarno and the other exiled nationalist leaders returned in triumph to Yogyakarta in July 1949 to establish their government there, Purwoko came down from the mountains to take up an administrative position with the republican regime. Having served the Dutch and the Japanese, he became, with the transfer of sovereignty later that year, a civil servant in the independent Indonesian state.

The revolution was not a democratizing experience for Purwoko; on the contrary, it reinforced his elite affinities. He identified strongly with the cosmopolitan idealism and diplomatic finesse of the Dutch-educated leaders of the revolution, while in Surabaya and in the mountains of central Java he saw the excesses and indiscipline of its ragged rank and file. Although it earned his sincere support for its goal of independence, the revolution did not turn Purwoko onto a political path; he remained a schoolmaster throughout.

The revolution also brought home forcefully to Purwoko the dangers of anarchy inherent in the violent assertion of popular will. His only brother, then an officer in the republican army, was killed by Indonesian communists in the Madiun area in 1948 during a short-lived revolt against the noncommunist (even anticommunist) leadership of the revolution. However, this event did not make Purwoko an anticommunist, for his essentially apolitical outlook was already uncongenial to appeals to proletarian or mass agrarian solidarity.

In independent Indonesia the need for expertise was great, and Purwoko advanced rapidly. By 1957 he was living in Jakarta, already a higher official employed by the ministry for which he still worked when I met him in 1969. After his initial appointment, however, his progress slowed; in those twelve years he moved only one grade higher on the wage scale. The channels of upward mobility flushed open by the upheavals of occupation and revolution had filled rapidly and become clogged with the continuing accretion in personnel.

In the 1950's, despite shifting political winds, Purwoko's job security was never in doubt. Turnover in the ministry was low; once in office, a man was likely to stay there. Purwoko's expertise made him more indispensable than many of his less talented colleagues and subordinates. And he remained scrupulously unaffiliated to any political group.

In the 1960's he was in more danger. His job entailed frequent contact with Westerners and the coordination of foreign, notably American, financial aid. He traveled widely abroad, mostly in Western Europe, the United States, and Australia. Acquaintance with Westerners was a mark of prestige in the 1950's, when Western aid was welcome, if not actually preferred, and when Western-style constitutional democracy was still at least a formal model for the fledgling state. But in the 1960's, with Guided Democracy in full swing, such contacts became suspect. Things came to a head when Purwoko declined to join a leftist political group within his ministry. The group promptly attacked him for being pro-Western and began a campaign to abolish his position. The leftists sought to arouse and represent the lowest strata, employees caught in the vise of pitifully low fixed wages and rampant inflation. Purwoko and his immediate subordinates, better educated, better paid, and enjoying working relations with various Western aid organizations, made ideal targets. In the end, however, Purwoko retained his position, in part because he had made himself sufficiently indispensable to the ministry, in part because the attempted coup and countercoup of October 1965 intervened.

Communists and leftist officials were implicated in the coup attempt, and within a matter of weeks a full-scale purge of suspected communists was on. The center of political gravity shifted drastically to the right; Purwoko's liabilities suddenly became assets; and he discarded his apolitical stance to join what he described as a "guerrilla" operation, coordinated by the army command, to weed out communists and leftists in the ministry. In 1966, Purwoko helped army officers arrest his own superior, whom Purwoko recalled as having been not only leftist but also—and more objectionable, to Purwoko—incompetent and corrupt.

Purwoko regretted that in the extreme anticommunism of the period many innocent people were imprisoned, people who had joined a leftist organization not because of its ideology but because their friends had or because it brought them certain welfare benefits. In contrast to the experience of these unfortunates, several leaders of leftist groups were able to evade arrest. One of the latter, a personal friend of Purwoko's, was fired from his job but, because one of his close relatives was a high-ranking military officer, never arrested; in 1969 he lived near Purwoko, having managed to obtain employment in the private sector. Purwoko saw him occasionally, and sometimes their children played together, although Purwoko knew their old friendship carried a political risk.

Purwoko survived not only politically but also economically. Much of his comparative prosperity he owed to his father and his wife. His father continued to send money to him even after he had grown up, married, and moved to Jakarta. The coffee, tea, and citrus fruit that grew in abundance in the large yard of his father's home were a welcome source of additional income to offset the inflationary erosion of Purwoko's fixed salary as a government employee. The older his parents grew, the more simply they seemed to live, and the greater became the excess income to be divided among Purwoko and his sisters. Purwoko's father denied himself new clothing and ate only the simplest fare. (As a mystic he sought thereby to keep his selfish desires in ever tighter check. As a father he would smile and explain his fasting by saying that the less he ate the more his grandchildren would be able to eat.) Partly because of his experience in the West, Purwoko felt that a grown man should not be so dependent on his father. Eventually he gently but successfully declined the old man's subsidy. One reason he could afford to do so was that his wife had meanwhile parlayed her cooking talent into a profitable business baking pastries for sale in stores that catered to the well-to-do.

Purwoko struck me as basically a contented man, but he was nostalgic about the past. He remembered that in Dutch times pupils were obedient, that even in the semianarchy of revolution the teacher retained their respect. "Nowadays," he lamented, "there is no discipline. The teacher pedals a bicycle to school while his pupil drives by in his parents' Mercedes Benz!" Above all, Purwoko remembered the village of his childhood, where everyone seemed to belong to a single family, living and working together. This retrospective view was idealized—after all, he had been the son of the village chief—but it was sincerely held.

When I met him, Purwoko's career was drawing to a close. More and more often he found himself returning in his mind's eye to the pleasures and meanings of Javanese culture and to his father's way of life for a remembered sense of permanence he could not find in the dissonant materialism of the city. He grew even less interested in politics than he had been before. To him, politics was all splitting and bickering; it disturbed. Wayang reunited him with his abangan origins; it reassured. Purwoko's life had reached a point where the present had begun to turn back upon the past and be validated by it in a slowly closing circle of unbroken meaning. Acts of divination—his father's prophetic dreaming or the accuracy of an old guru's predictions[4]—were recalled because they reconnected.

Purwoko was seeking a transgenerational continuity in life as well. He remembered how as a child he had wanted to be just like his father, like the "little king" his father was but on the grander scale of the doctor who lived down the street from his aunt's house. Although he had never fulfilled this dream, his eldest child was a medical student. "If a man's goals aren't achieved in his own life-time," mused Purwoko, "maybe they'll be realized by the children who come after."

The sun was rising in the sky; the ministry was filling up with people. Purwoko glanced at his watch and at the appointments calendar on the wall. It was time for me to go. He regretted that we would be unable to continue our conversations for a while be-cause he would be out of the country attending a conference. I thanked him for his hospitality and his time. We shook hands and said goodbye. As I walked past his window on my way out of the ministry he was already back at his desk, signing papers, asking for

4. Purwoko's father once dreamed he was walking down a road carrying two roosters, one under each arm. Suddenly someone came from out of no-where, grabbed one of the cocks, and slit its throat. According to Purwoko, the roosters were himself and his brother and the dream a true prophecy of the latter's death by violence in Madiun during the revolution.

Before he died, Purwoko's brother introduced Purwoko to a guru in cen-tral Java. On his first visit, Purwoko marveled at how much the old man knew about his life. On his second, Purwoko produced a photograph of his fiancée—an attractive girl he wanted very much to marry—and asked if she were destined to be his wife. The guru closed his eyes for a moment, opened them, and said, "No. You will only marry by way of a marriage. But the woman you marry will look like the woman in this photograph." Hurt and disappointed by this cryptic answer, Purwoko left the guru, thinking angrily to himself, "Who is he anyway? What can he know?"

Purwoko courted his fiancée on and off for three years, but in the end he had an argument with her father, who retaliated by forbidding him to see her. Later Purwoko married another girl, the daughter of a Javanese noble-man. When this first wife died, he married a second—in effect "by way of a [first] marriage"—and the second wife bore a remarkable resemblance to Purwoko's old sweetheart, the girl in the photograph. Impressed with the ac-curacy of the guru's prophecy, Purwoko went back to central Java to find him, but he had long since died. Retelling these stories in 1969, Purwoko seemed pleased that his father and an old Javanese guru, uneducated by Western standards, could foresee the future; their success seemed to validate abangan mysticism as a powerful tool.

files, and giving instructions—a busy administrator getting things done.

Usman, a Santri Politician

Some three hundred road miles northwest of the part of Java where Purwoko was born lies Usman's birthplace. The two regions are strikingly different. Purwoko was born on the slopes of an inland mountain. Usman's village lies on a flat littoral plain. Rice grows well in Purwoko's village, for the land is richly volcanic and fresh water is plentiful. The soil around Usman's coastal village is, by comparison, poor in nutrients, while the river water used for irrigation is more saline.

The two regions differ culturally as well. Usman's village lies not in the heartland of Javanese culture but on its periphery. Here is no palace complex, no royal nexus, no "magic center"[5] to serve as the source and standard of cultural norms. Here the great tradition of Hinduized central Java finds attenuated expression in coarser versions of its inland self. Respect vocabularies are less elaborate and less fastidiously used. Interpersonal encounters are less stylized, more direct. Even the wayang puppets are simpler, less finely incised.

To the west is Jakarta, with its ethnic mix and internationalism. To the south lie the upland springs of Sundanese culture. To the east, the royal house of Cirebon—the nearest interpreter of Javanese court tradition—lies decrepit and dying. The region where Usman was born is in every sense a fringe.

The area has its own culture, however: the Islamicized culture of Java's northern coast. Usman's and Purwoko's fathers were both Muslims. But as a frame of reference for personal and political identity, Islam meant very little to Purwoko's father, a great deal to Usman's. And at that time in childhood when Purwoko could be found in a far corner of the peringgitan listening as his father narrated to the night watch the myths of Java's pre-Islamic past, Usman sat at the feet of a village kiyai hearing parables from the life of the Prophet.

The village mosque was central in Usman's memories of child-

5. See Robert Heine-Geldern, *Conceptions of State and Kingship in Southeast Asia* (Ithaca: Cornell University Southeast Asia Program, 1956), p. 3.

hood. From roughly his fifth to his tenth year, he and the other boys of his age slept in the same corner of the mosque, went together to the kiyai's home for religious lessons, and, every year during Ramadan, circulated as a group under the direction of a mosque official distributing food among the villagers at dusk to help them break the fast. The boys shared a camaraderie that Usman remembered fondly long afterward.

At the feet of the kiyai, Usman and the other children memorized the sounds of the Arabic alphabet in order to recite, loudly and more or less in unison, from the Koran. They started with the first and shortest chapter and the easiest to memorize:

> Praise be to Allah, Lord of the Worlds,
> The Beneficent, the Merciful.
> Owner of the Day of Judgment,
> Thee alone we worship;
> Thee alone we ask for help.
> Show us the straight path,
> The path of those whom Thou has favored;
> Not the path of those who earn Thine anger
> Nor of those who go astray.[6]

These are the words every Muslim utters in the act of prayer; once he had committed them to memory, prayer also became possible for Usman. Yet he could not understand the meaning of the Arabic, nor was any effort made to explain it to him. It was the task of these fledgling santris, not to master the Koran, but to submit to its mastery of them. Recitation was an act of ritual, not comprehension, and it marked Usman's entry into the ummat, the community of Islam.

Once a week, on Friday, the kiyai would tell the children stories about the Prophet Muhammad and his times, about the lives of the prophets Abraham and Jesus, about Adam, the first man, or Noah and the ark. —Why, these are things you have to go to a university to learn nowadays!— said Usman suddenly in the midst of his

6. Surah I (Al Fatihah), *The Meaning of the Glorious Koran: An Explanatory Translation by Mohammad Marmaduke Pickthall* (New York: Mentor Book, New American Library, n.d.). Unless noted otherwise, all citations from the Koran are from this translation. For aesthetic reasons, Pickthall's practice of placing parentheses around contextually derived words and phrases has not been followed.

recollections. —I may not be an educated man, but I know the history of Islam.—[7]

In Usman's village, Islam did not replace pre-Islamic values but reinterpreted them. Shadow theater provides a good illustration. All-night wayang performances were held in the village from time to time.[8] After a session of Koranic recitation, the kiyai might ask Usman and his companions whether they had seen the performance held, say, the previous week at someone's circumcision celebration. He would then interpret at length the particular story performed that night, moralizing and dichotomizing the wayang in his commentary. The Pandawa were good, the Kurawa bad; the moral was that little boys should be good, not bad, for to be bad was to go against the way of Allah. Just as Muhammad fought and subdued the unbelievers who mocked him, so did the Pandawa fight and overcome the evil Kurawa. How could the forces of evil be defeated? By fasting. Just as Arjuna, the middle one of the five Pandawa brothers, went to the mountain to abstain from the world (*tapa*), so did Muhammad fast (*puasa*) to steel and cleanse himself that he might better execute the will of Allah. Did not Arjuna, after his ascesis, come down to the battlefield to defeat the Kurawa in the great war (Bratayuda), just as Muhammad defeated the unbelievers? So must men deny themselves food during the fasting month, to strengthen their resolve in the way of Allah. With what weapons could the forces of evil be put to rout? With the weapon of the eldest Pandawa, Yudistira, the Kalimasada. For that weapon was in truth the *kalima syahadat,* the Muslim confession of faith. At this point the kiyai would lead his charges in the careful, repeated enunciation of the kalima syahadat: "There is no God but Allah; Muhammad is His Prophet." In the kiyai's syncretic interpretation, Javanese tapa had become Arabic puasa and the Hindu Bratayuda the Islamic jihad.

7. Here and henceforth, dashes indicate paraphrased material; quote marks surround verbatim citations. Verbatim quotes were memorized in full or written down at the time they were spoken. Paraphrases were reconstructed from memory and/or summary notes as soon after the interview as practicable. On the method, see the appendix.

8. In Usman's mainly santri village, women were not allowed to watch these shows on grounds that the wives and daughters of good Muslims should not stay up all night in a public place lest they stray from the path of virtue. In Purwoko's abangan village no such restriction existed, although women and children in the audience were usually separated from the men.

Usman's father was too poor to send his son to a Dutch-language primary school, so the boy entered the village Volksschool. Instruction, in Javanese, was primitive. Usman remembered that the pupils used slates and writing stones in place of paper and pencils. They were taught the basic geography of the island of Java, to read and write simple Javanese, to count up to a thousand, and to solve elementary problems in mathematics.

Unlike the mosque, the Volksschool was strictly peripheral in Usman's childhood. He could attend only irregularly, for he had to work to supplement his parents' meager income. In an arrangement probably initiated by his mother, the boy sold snacks for a widow in the village. The widow prepared the food during the night so that it would be fresh when Usman picked it up at dawn. The snacks were piled on a bamboo platter, which Usman hoisted onto his head; and off he would go, crying his wares as he went. The important thing was to sell all the food during the morning hours, when demand was greatest.

So important was this enterprise that Usman remembered its smallest details. There were three types of cake: cassava, yam, and rice. He sold three cassava or yam cakes for half a Netherlands Indies cent; rice cakes were half a cent apiece. On an average day he took in about thirty cents, of which he got ten per cent and the widow the rest. Later, with the capital he had accumulated, he began raising chickens for sale.

Life in the village was not all work, however. There was soccer, which Usman loved and was good at, being fast and agile. According to him, he was the best soccer player among all the boys in the village. He recalled with particular pride one time after the harvest when his friends challenged a team from another village. The two teams gathered on the hard dry field, and Usman's friends implored him to join them. Usman agreed to play, provided they compensated him for the money he might have made selling the widow's cakes. Knowing he was poor, his friends took up a collection and paid him the three cents. And he played his heart out for them. Usman told the story with a relish that suggested embroidery of the facts but revealed how important it was to him in retrospect that he had excelled at something as a child. The vignette itself, whose essentials appeared to be true, showed the boy's precocity not only in soccer but in understanding that time could be turned into money by demanding reimbursement of an opportunity cost.

Usman's parents died when he was very young. By then he was already spending the bulk of his time away from home, so the event caused little disruption in his routine. Nor was he close to either parent. Nevertheless he retained through his adult life an acutely clear image of his father. In Usman's memory, his father was an angry man: angry at the Javanese officials who demanded his labor without, or with inadequate, compensation; angry at the Dutch who imposed so many taxes on the village and at the obsequious priyayis who collected them; angry at the Chinese moneylenders who ate forbidden meat (pork) and could claim a man's rice crop while it was still green in the fields. Usman's father could see only injustice in the prosperity of the priyayis who took the peasants' labor and boxed the people in with regulations until they could barely breathe. Why should they be able to dress their children immaculately and send them off to elite schools to learn foreign languages while landless peasants labored in the muck of someone else's fields for a few handfuls of rice?

The father's bitterness overflowed one day in an incident that became one of Usman's last memories of him. For a reason long since forgotten, father and son had gone on a journey to a trading center some distance away. The father's business done, they had walked through the streets of the town. When Usman grew tired, the father hoisted his son onto his shoulders, saying they must go a little further, for there was something Usman should see. Soon they were in the European section, walking past well-kept concrete houses and manicured lawns. Before almost every house was a wooden sign bearing a picture of a dog; Usman's father told him that the signs meant that no "natives" were allowed, that they would be attacked by dogs if they approached. —Or perhaps,— his father continued, —they think we *are* dogs! They certainly treat us that way.—

After his parents died, Usman was shuttled from one set of relatives to another, first in the village and later in a nearby town. These relatives gave the boy room and board but worked him like a servant. At the Volksschool in the town, the school authorities allowed him to sell snacks to the pupils during recess, which became his sole source of income. He was enrolled at the school for a while but rarely went to class.

In the town Usman could see for himself the inequalities that had so embittered his father. The sons of civil servants dressed in good quality sarongs or shorts, leather shoes, and clean shirts and attended the local Dutch-language primary school (Hollandsch Inlandsche School, HIS). There were other schools in the town, but Usman's attention was focused on the HIS. The pupils from the Volksschool and the HIS met frequently in interschool athletic competition on the field in the center of the town, where they played a local game reminiscent of baseball. The Volksschool children, deeply jealous, loved to ridicule the HIS pupils for being soft and weak. One way to retire a side was to hit a base runner with the ball. More than once a Volksschooler aimed for the head and threw as hard as he could. The ball was small and hard, and hurt. Yet the teacher-referees rarely intervened, discounting the violence as unintentional. Following the match, the two sides would return quietly with their teachers to their respective schools, but after classes were out in the afternoon the losers would waylay the victors, and the ensuing battle, often bloody, might rage on into the evening.

In the late 1930's a group of about thirty boys from the village, including many of Usman's friends from the mosque, the Volksschool, and the soccer field, were preparing to go off to a pesantren in south-central Java. For the villagers the departure was an event of the utmost importance; their sons were going off to study and to grow in wisdom and strength in the way of Allah. The kiyai glowed with pride at the thought of these boys, in whom he had tried to instill the word of God, becoming full-fledged santris in an Islamic school of some renown, just as he had himself years before. At the farewell celebration, old men spoke of the glory of Allah that would reflect on the village because of the dedication of its sons.

Usman longed to go with them, and the boys wanted him to. The parents, however, did not; they feared the poor orphan would sponge off their sons. If he could con them into paying him to play soccer with them here at home, what could he not do to them once they were far away? Usman set out to prove that he could make it on his own. He owned twenty-five chickens at the time, which he could sell for twenty-five Netherlands Indies cents apiece; after paying for his train fare, he would still have a little over five guilders to tide him over at the pesantren until he could find work. And why should he not work for his friends? He would cook for them and wash their clothes—if they would share their food with him and let him go along. The boys agreed, and finally the parents did too.

The train ride, Usman's first, was a humbling experience. At each stop along the way he could see how much more refined in manner and language the people were. On station platforms and in the railway carriage young Javanese bowed slightly and covered their genital regions with crossed hands in respect before an elder who had come to greet them or see them off. The fluency of their high Javanese so intimidated Usman that he resolved not to speak in their hearing. Even so he feared that his coarse clothing had already revealed him for the uncultured country bumpkin he suddenly felt himself to be.

His embarrassment did not lessen the thrill of the trip, however. Each stop was a fresh excitement. Usman would scoot onto the platform to explore and observe, climbing back on board again at the last possible moment before the train pulled out. The hawkers, the workers, the officials, the bustle and swirl of the crowd, the sight and sounds of the great engine all fascinated him. —And when I returned to my seat, my things were still there,— he noted. —There weren't any pickpockets or robbers then. Not like nowadays.—

Early that evening they reached Semarang. By prearrangement, they were to meet a kiyai in the city. He welcomed them, served them tea, and showed them the mosque where they would spend the night. The familiar atmosphere, the sounds of prayer, and the cool floor on which he spread his mat soothed Usman. That night before he went to sleep he comforted himself with the thought that, however backward he might be and however alone in the world, there would always be a mosque to sleep in and a kiyai to guide him.

The rest of the boys' journey was by bus. Along the way they stopped in a small town for lunch, and again Usman marveled at how refined the people seemed. In the more piously Islamic area from which he came, the men wore black overseas caps, simple tunics, and conservatively patterned sarongs made of relatively coarse cloth; but here in the Javanese heartland they wore caps of carefully tucked and creased batik, tunics with impressively large chest flaps buttoned across the front, and finely dyed batik cloth elegantly folded around their hips and legs.

Finally, the boys arrived at the pesantren, with its familiar, reassuring mosque and, clustered around that, the houses, dormitories, kitchens, and huts of the kiyais and their santris. The reputation of the teachers had attracted pupils not only from Usman's region but also from other areas of Java; there were several thousand at the pesantren when Usman arrived. Many stayed only a matter of months, or even weeks, being replaced by fresh arrivals in a continuing flux whose volume and direction depended on the fame of the resident kiyais.

Usman stayed for a decade. If the kraton enhanced Purwoko's status and identity as a member of the priyayi elite, only a few kilometers away, on the outskirts of the same city, Usman acquired his own status and identity as a santri. His pesantren experience was meaningful to him in several senses. The pesantren was the antithesis of the colonial bureaucratic world Usman's father had raged against before his death. It was entirely different from the progression of Dutch academic schools in which Purwoko studied. There were no application forms to complete in order to gain entry, no impersonal grading of a student's progress during his residence, no examinations to pass in order to exit honorably. Indeed there were no courses or classes, no matriculation or graduation in the Western sense at all. Typically, the santris sat around the kiyai and listened while he read aloud from a book of religious commentary, first in the original Arabic, then summarizing in Javanese. When he had finished, the kiyai would ask one of the santris to recite the same passage in Arabic and repeat the kiyai's summary in Javanese. To be thus singled out was an honor, and the pupils strove to repeat without errors what the kiyai had said. The process stretched out over the hours and days until, finally, the last page had been read and reread. If many santris were working on the same book, there might be a celebration of sorts to mark the completion of that particular volume, but generally the pupils merely went on to another book. Santris who joined the circle in mid-book were welcomed; nor did anyone mind if a pupil left the circle, and perhaps the pesantren as well, before the book was finished.

Dutch-language secondary schools were strictly hierarchial, not only in terms of the distinction between teacher and taught, but also in their practice of ranking students on an academic ladder. In the pesantren, the santris formed an undifferentiated community of believers who prayed jointly, fasted jointly, and jointly absorbed the wisdom of the kiyai. Each paid or worked his own way and was beholden to no one. Among Westernized priyayis and their sons Usman could only be conscious of his lack of social graces, his want of Dutch, and his poverty; in the pesantren he was part of a community of equals.

Pesantren life was loosely structured. There was communal work to be done—yards to be swept, floors to be cleaned—and there were group prayers in the central mosque. But within the limits of the behavior expected of a santri and the duties he was supposed to perform for the benefit of the school's community, pupils were largely left alone. How different, thought Usman at the time, from the colonial world of impositions, regulations, and obedience that his father had so despised; how different from the households of his demanding relatives. In the pesantren atmosphere a man could be independent and self-sufficient, prostrating himself before none save Allah.

In these congenial surroundings, Usman soon discovered a way to become financially independent and to stop having to cook and wash in return for food. Having noticed that many pupils wrote home regularly, Usman went to the local post office and bought postcards and stamps; affixing the stamps himself, he sold the cards to his fellow santris for three and a half Netherlands Indies cents apiece, clearing a half-cent profit on each card. With this money, he branched out. He began to buy soap in bulk to sell to the santris, needles and thread for them to patch their clothes, school supplies, even cheap underwear; his profit ranged between 5 and 15 per cent per item, depending on the turnover. Soon his cupboard was full of wares and his clientele had grown to the point that he began to lose customers because he could not always be there to serve them. To resolve this problem, he bought a noisemaker that his customers could use to summon him from wherever in the compound he happened to be. When he heard it, he came running to unlock his cupboard and make the sale.

Most of Usman's customers received an allowance from home

at the beginning of each month. By about the twentieth, many were asking for credit. Now the Koran enjoins against usury. If Usman extended credit at even a very low rate of interest he might open himself to charges of impiety, especially from his customers' parents, which, even if false, could endanger his good standing with the kiyais. Nor did Usman want the bother of having to calculate interest owed or dun debtors for payment. At the same time he did not want to see his capital drained off in unsettled accounts. In the end, he decided to give his customers interest-free credit to a limit of fifteen cents apiece, payable on arrival of the ensuing month's allowance, and nothing beyond that. Some months as many as a hundred customers had such a debt.

Usman's business prospered,[9] as did his relationship with the kiyais, who soon made him a kind of administrative assistant in the pesantren. Usman's monthly salary was two and a half guilders, half what Purwoko was then getting from the colonial government in pocket money alone. Usman's style of life was less costly than Purwoko's, however, and the santri managed to save something from each month's wages and profits. Usman had two brothers back in the village; although he had never been close to either, he paid for them to join him at the pesantren. —When I was in the village, before I knew the world,— he wrote them, —I was like a fish in a pond, ignorant of the outside because I could only look around in my little home. Now you, as I did, must leave the pond and see the world.—

For Usman, the pesantren experience was not monastic. He visited the city regularly to maintain his inventory; during Ramadan vacations he enjoyed traveling to other towns and other

9. Usman is typical of many santri traders, especially in such industries as clove cigarettes and batik, whose religion has proved to be no bar to commercial success. See Lance Castles, *Religion, Politics, and Economic Behavior in Java: The Kudus Cigarette Industry* (New Haven: Yale University Southeast Asia Studies, 1967). Nor does the Koran equate profit with impiety, despite its strictures against usury. Surah III (Ali 'Imran), v. 130, for example, says: "O ye who believe! Devour not usury, doubling and quadrupling the sum lent. Observe your duty to Allah, that ye may be successful." (Arthur J. Arberry, *The Koran Interpreted*, 2 vols. [London: George Allen and Unwin, 1955], translates the last phrase as "so you will prosper"; Zainuddin Hamidy and Fachruddin, *Tafsir Qüran* [3d print., Jakarta: Widjaya, 1963], as "so that you may profit.") The examples forbidden—"doubling and quadrupling"—are extreme and the verse concludes by endorsing economic success as a goal.

pesantrens. His store and his administrative duties diverted much of his time into strictly secular pursuits, while the academic specialty of the kiyai under whom he studied lay not in mysticism, nor even theology, but in the more prosaic field of Arabic grammar.

There was another reason why Usman's pesantren experience did not isolate him from the surrounding society. When he entered the pesantren, a variety of more or less political, more or less legal organizations on Java were already questioning the colonial relationship. This activity was not lost on Usman and his friends, who formed their own group, eventually affiliating with similar groups from other pesantrens to form an area-wide association. Informal and ad hoc in character, this organization served various purposes. Through it, the santris took part in parades (remembered by Usman as something less than impressive because he could never seem to keep the contingent from his pesantren in step), played supporting roles at mass religious observances, and were even able to send a delegation to a meeting of the moderate, priyayi-dominated Greater Indonesia Party (Partai Indonesia Raya, or Parindra).

Usman's participation in such activities neither stemmed from nor stimulated any consistent appraisal on his part of the colonial condition. What colored his outlook, whether toward Dutch or indigenous institutions, was his feeling of belonging to the ummat, in the sense not of an abstract kingdom of God but of the immediate community of kiyais and santris in the pesantren. Usman could accept easily the nationalist critique of colonial rule because the Dutch were so clearly outside his world. At the same time he could admire a Javanese king whom the Dutch had fully coopted into the colonial system (indeed whose very kingdom was a colonial creation) because, on a trip once, he had watched the king's retinue pass and had seen by the rank-determined patterns of the batik they wore that the status of the chief official of the central mosque equaled that of the high-priyayi regent.

Like many others in the pesantren, Usman was as pleased by the collapse of the Dutch colonial edifice in 1942 as he was astonished at its swiftness. The Japanese took steps almost immediately to indoctrinate and mobilize the Islamic community on behalf of their grand design in Asia; in the city, they orchestrated rallies, proclamations, and mass acts of militant allegiance. Meanwhile in the pesantren, Usman and his friends speculated endlessly on the meaning of the occupation for Indonesia. On the one hand, the alien colonial overlord had been defeated at a single stroke, a stunning achievement and one that opened a whole range of possible futures. On the other, the new rulers, for all their assiduous courting of Islam, were no more Muslims than the old had been and appeared to be in some ways no less repressive.

Before Usman's views had fully crystallized, he found that he had been mobilized. He was one of several in the pesantren chosen by the kiyais in late 1944 to undergo military training in Jakarta as part of an effort, sponsored by the Japanese with the cooperation of Muslim leaders, to establish an "Army of Allah" (*Hizbullah*). In three months he learned to shoot and to crawl under fire and acquired a rudimentary knowledge of battlefield tactics, training he was expected to pass on to his fellow santris.

Usman recalled his disappointment on discovering how quiet the former colonial capital seemed in contrast to the militant enthusiasms that were sweeping his pesantren and the area around it. For by the end of 1944 Indonesian independence, albeit within the Greater East Asia Co-prosperity Sphere, had become an officially sanctioned goal and rallying cry. In Usman's mind, the prospect of independence rendered academic the excited discussions that had gone on in the pesantren. Those talks had been among spectators; the point now was to act. He returned home flushed with enthusiasm. Although armed less with his training than with the prestige of having undergone it, Usman was determined to militarize the pesantren on behalf of the ummat. Soon the Koranic imperatives on waging holy war resounded among the santris, as Usman struggled to mobilize his assigned portion of the Army of Allah, in which by this time he held officer's rank:

Those who believe do battle for the cause of Allah; and those who disbelieve do battle for the cause of idols. So fight the minions of the devil.

Whoso fighteth in the way of Allah, be he slain or be he victorious, on him We shall bestow a vast reward.

Go forth, light-armed and heavy-armed, and strive with your wealth and your lives in the way of Allah!

Lo! Allah loveth those who battle for His cause in ranks, as if they were a solid structure.[10]

In August 1945, when the Japanese surrendered and the declaration of Indonesian independence ushered in the revolution, Usman's troops were hardly a "solid structure."[11] Above all they lacked arms with which to stop the expected return of the Dutch and prevent the hated status quo ante bellum being re-established. But, in the chaos of the moment, Usman and his santris-turned-soldiers were able, together with other republican youths, to seize and maneuver from the Japanese a limited stock of weapons. Then Usman and his "men"—Usman was still in his teens, and they were scarcely older than he—could fight.

Usman's story of battles lost and won need not be recounted here. What is important is his experience of revolution as compared to Purwoko's. Purwoko's participation was genuine but symbolic; he never took part in combat. By 1949, Usman, according to his own report, commanded four battalions, each two thousand strong. Whatever the accuracy of this claim,[12] there is no question that Usman did fight against the British (including Gurkha) forces and the Dutch troops that came in their wake. Aside from his trip

10. Respectively, surah IV (An Nisa), vv. 76 and 74; IX (At Taubah), v. 41; LXI (As Saff), v. 4. In repeating these verses, I do not mean to imply that Islam is a militaristic religion. I am quoting out of context, just as Usman and hundreds of other kiyais and santris did at the time. To illustrate, the injunction to "fight the minions of the devil" is significantly moderated later in the same surah (IV, v. 94): "O ye who believe! When ye go forth to fight in the way of Allah, be careful to discriminate, and say not unto one who offereth you peace: 'Thou art not a believer,' seeking the chance profits of this life so that ye may despoil him. With Allah [i.e., in the after-life] are plenteous spoils. . . . Allah hath . . . been gracious unto you. Therefore take care to discriminate. Allah is ever informed of what ye do."

11. Hizbullah itself was never a solid structure. Local units tended to be informally organized, poorly armed, self-financing, and largely free from central direction. Among the many revealing scenes of the revolution in the writings of Pramoedya Ananta Toer is a cameo of a Hizbullah fighter wearing shorts, a black shirt, and a helmet with the word "Allah" written on it in Arabic script, armed with three British-made grenades and a sharpened bamboo spear, and standing beside an empty kerosene can with its lid slit and the words FOND KEMERDEKAAN (Freedom Fund) written on its side (*Di-tepi Kali Bekasi* [3d print., Jakarta: Jajasan Kebudajaan Sadar, 1962], p. 185).

12. My own guess is that Usman's claim of 8,000 men may be accurate. He admitted, however, that only about 400 of these carried weapons.

to Surabaya, Purwoko did not actually join the revolution in a physical sense until December 1948, when he was forced by a Dutch general offensive to evacuate his school. Usman, by contrast, left the pesantren in September 1945, returning only during cease-fires and lulls in the fighting. Purwoko was thirty-three years old when he took his students to the mountains; the distance in age and status that separated the teacher from his pupils obviated any real revolutionary camaraderie between them. Usman and his santris, closer in age (fifteen to twenty-five years old), members of the same ummat, and sharing the same pesantren life style, were comrades-in-arms from the start.

In an important sense, however, the two men's experiences of revolution were identical. Despite the pan-Indonesian ethos and the common enemy, which stimulated a revolutionary spirit that could and sometimes did, at least temporarily, erase the birthmark of a man's social origins, the experience of revolution *confirmed* these two men's identities, Usman's as a santri and Purwoko's as a cosmopolitan priyayi. In the subjective experience of revolution, their social origins found not negation but validation and reinforcement.

The excesses of hot-tempered youths and the death of his brother in intrarevolutionary strife strengthened in Purwoko an appreciation of order and authority. His sympathies lay with the ministers in the republican government who were trying to impose coherence on the situation, not with the anarchically erupting masses. The first group he referred to as "idealists," in the sense not of dreamers but of individuals truly committed to a worthwhile goal (independence), while the latter he labeled, as charitably as he could, "a motley crew." He found greater heroism in the evacuated republican administrators' efforts to govern the revolution from the relative safety of the mountains of central Java than in the acts of the young who fought and fell in Surabaya. The latter were too viscerally fanatic for Purwoko; in the former he saw, I think, reflections of himself and his own predicament. In the mountains, deskless, at a time when the very system into which schools led and offices recruited was being violently contested, the schoolmaster and the officials must have found much in common: their priyayi background and Western education, the ideal of independence, and, not least, the felt impact of a revolutionary present in whose terms many of them had lived distinctly unrevolutionary pasts.

Usman found in the revolution status fulfillment and a reaffirmation of his religious identity. As a commander of men, the orphaned shopkeeper-cum-teacher's assistant enjoyed a prestige greater than he had ever known before, while the consecrated jihad furnished daily reminders of his identity as a member of the community of Islam. The typical Hizbullah fighter carried an Arabic-script quotation from the Koran as a talisman to protect him in battle and, should he die, enhance his glory as a *syahid,* a martyred soldier of Allah.[13] Many shouted the *takbir*—"Allahu akbar!" (Allah is incomparably greater!)—to tighten the lifeline between themselves and God at the moment of greatest fear of its sundering.[14] Usman recounted with unconcealed pride how, during inter-

13. Evidence that the syahid will enter paradise is to be found in one of the most martial surahs, IX (At Taubah), v. 111; also see surah XLVII, vv. 4–6. In Indonesia, the joys that await him were enticingly described in a popular epic of the anticolonial Acehnese War:
> To die as a syahid is nothing.
> It is like being tickled until we fall and roll over . . .
> Then comes a heavenly princess,
> Who cradles you in her lap and wipes away the blood,
> Her heart all yours.

A few lines later comes the (plaintive?) remark:
> If the heavenly princesses were visible,
> Everyone would go to fight the Dutch.

(James T. Siegel, *The Rope of God* [Berkeley: University of California Press, 1969], p. 76, citing H. T. Damste, ed. and trans., "Hikajat Prang Sabi," *Bijdragen tot de taal-, land-, en volkenkunde van Nederlandsch-Indië,* vol. 84.) Alone among men, the syahid is not washed before burial, for his glorious death has already cleansed him of all his sins.

14. The takbir is the defining cry of the ummat: the first words in the call to prayer, the opening statement in prayer itself, and the chant of the faithful in celebrations at the end of the fasting month and the beginning of the Muslim new year. "Allahu akbar!" may be the first words spoken into the ear of a baby born into a Muslim family or the last words a Muslim utters before he dies. See Hamka [Haji Abdul Malik Karim Amrullah], *Pandangan Hidup Muslim* (2d print., Jakarta: Bulan Bintang, 1966), pp. 149–150 and ch. 17, and compare the use of the takbir as life's closing slogan in two novels published nearly thirty years apart: *Sitti Nurbaja* (11th print., Jakarta: Balai Pustaka, 1965), p. 289, by Marah Rusli, which first appeared in 1922, and *Keluarga Gerilja* (3d print., Jakarta: Nusantara, 1962), pp. 213–214, by Pramoedya Ananta Toer, first published in 1950. In the second novel, unlike the first, the hero's takbir is a shouting down of the explicit doubts about his faith that assail him at the last moment before death, and he actually ends his life not with the takbir but its nationalist equivalent, the freedom cry: "Merdeka!" Pramoedya made clear his preference for the areligious slogan in the autobiographical story "Gado-Gado" in his *Pertjikan Revolusi* (2d print., Jakarta: Balai Pustaka, 1957), p. 78.

rogations of suspicious persons picked up along the roads, he had used his knowledge of the Islamic art of *ilmu firasah* (judging a man by his appearance) to distinguish friend from foe.[15] His pesantren education had found a practical and, to hear Usman tell it, unfailingly accurate application. —Even if we had evidence the man might be a spy,— Usman reminisced, —if he had an honest face, I let him go. I could always tell.—

But whatever the excitements of the jihad, however compelling the glories of martyrdom, Usman never became a fanatic. Although the excesses of war shocked him less than Purwoko, perhaps because Usman was closer to them, Usman too was critical of the youths of the "people's militias" who shot first and asked questions later. —Had they only possessed the santri's knowledge of ilmu firasah,— he reasoned, —many innocent people would not have died.— Nor did Usman's guerrilla experiences shift him politically to the left. His units clashed on more than one occasion with communist-led "red militias," but less for ideological reasons than to obtain more weapons.

Rather than leading Purwoko into partisan politics, the revolution, through the violent antagonisms it engendered or exposed, reinforced his preference for an administrative career. Purwoko's first job after the transfer of sovereignty in December 1949 involved processing demobilized youths back into their "proper" places in the classroom. But the revolution took Usman directly into party membership. Hizbullah had been created as a military extension of Masyumi, the wartime grouping of major Islamic organizations; after the occupation Masyumi became a political party and Hizbullah remained formally under its control.[16] By force of circumstance, Usman found himself with a party affiliation.

In 1949, Usman took his men and his weapons into the republi-

15. Imam Sjafii, founder of the school of legal interpretation favored by the overwhelming majority of Indonesian Muslim scholars, is said to have been particularly skilled in ilmu firasah. Originally a kind of phrenology of the face, ilmu firasah came to include appraisal of all aspects of a person's appearance. To use one of Usman's examples, if you meet a man with thin lips you should not be frank with him, for he may be a provocateur sent to incite you against your own men.
16. On the wartime Masyumi, see Benda, *Crescent*, esp. ch. 7; on Masyumi during the revolution, see Deliar Noer, "Masjumi: Its Organization, Ideology, and Political Role in Indonesia" (M.A. thesis, Cornell University, 1960), esp. part 2.

can army. Not long after the formal establishment of the independent Republic of Indonesia the following year, he took a government job under a well-known kiyai with whom he had studied once in another pesantren and whom he admired intensely. Usman stayed in the bureaucracy as long as his patron did—several years —and when the kiyai left to become a full-time party leader, Usman followed him.

In his subsequent career, Usman, like Purwoko, was neither laterally nor upwardly mobile. Between the mid-1950's and late 1960's, Usman did essentially the same kind of work, and for the same organization. If in the twelve years before I talked with him Purwoko had moved up only one rank in the civil service wage scale, it took Usman an almost equal length of time to rise one rung up his party's ladder. Purwoko never left his ministry; Usman never left the party.

For Purwoko, as has been noted, partisan politics normally held no attraction. Even his participation in the intradepartmental purge in the abnormal circumstances of 1965–1966 flowed at least as much from a felt necessity to survive as from a personal desire to act. Usman, on the other hand, was a partisan. His party's activities were at least vicariously his, and he identified strongly with its history. In our conversation on the postwar period, his party's life overshadowed his own.

The reasons for Usman's strong party identification and loyalty are in one sense obvious. He owed to the party his membership in Parliament, with its prestige and perquisites and a base salary even higher than Purwoko's. But at a deeper, less calculating (and, I think, more important) level, his party was for Usman an expression, just as Hizbullah had been, of the distinctive milieu and solidarity of the pesantren in which he first "became someone" (in the metamorphic meaning of the Indonesian, *jadi orang*). His sense of self-fulfillment rested securely in a larger sense of ongoing belonging in the ummat.

Purwoko's father and the king he served were lifelong models for Purwoko. Usman lost both parents early in life, and this fact had two consequences for him. First, he had no stake, no affiliation beyond the pesantren; it was not a boarding school, a phase in life, but home, life itself. The village boys with whom he had entered the pesantren enjoyed parental subsidies; the money orders that arrived each month reminded them of unbroken family ties. But Usman relied wholly on the school, as his retail market and the source of his assistant's salary; for him, life there was an unmitigated experience. Second, Usman could take part wholeheartedly in the veneration of the kiyai that characterized pesantren life.[17] There were no competing models.

Usman's patron, the kiyai whom he so admired and whom he had followed in and out of the bureaucracy, filled a void in the young man's life. "I was his closest pupil," said Usman (almost certainly exaggerating), in the proud yet personal tone of voice with which he might have said, "I was his favorite son." —He was warm and friendly. He always put his visitors at ease by remembering who they were, even though he barely knew them, and by giving them his full attention.— For an orphan, these were no minor kindnesses. —And he worked hard.— Just as Usman had done. Work, faith, and solidarity summarize Usman's life, as a pupil at the feet of his kiyal and as a figure in Islamic politics.

We had entered the full heat of the afternoon. Usman wanted to leave his office and go home. There, in an almost rural setting on the outskirts of Jakarta, he would work in his garden or perhaps check the accounts at his store. Purwoko lived in neat but impersonal surroundings in government housing for civil servants. That afternoon he would probably stay at his desk another hour or more, catching up on paperwork. Usman had a desk too, but he did not like to feel tied to it; he preferred the outdoors and the feel of soil. By this time, the indoor air felt warmer than our stale tea tasted, so it seemed natural to stroll outside. There Usman smiled goodbye and sauntered off to catch his bus.

Comparisons and Generalizations

In March 1968 the fifth general session of the Provisional People's Consultative Assembly (Majelis Permusyawaratan Rakyat

17. On kiyai-veneration in the pesantren and the role of the kiyai generally, see Clifford Geertz, "The Javanese Kijaji: The Changing Role of a Cultural Broker," *Comparative Studies in Society and History*, 2 (1960), 228–249; Samudja Asjari, "Kedudukan Kjai Dalam Pondok Pesantren" (M.A. thesis, Gadjah Mada University, 1967); and Abdurrahman Wahid, "Pesantren sebagai Subkultur," in M. Dawam Rahardjo, ed., *Pesantren dan Pembaharuan* (Jakarta: LP3ES, 1974), pp. 39–60. I am grateful to Benedict Anderson for bringing Asjari's thesis to my attention.

Sementara, MPRS), the nation's highest constitutional authority, ended with two of its committees stalemated.[18] The issues on which agreement could not be reached were familiar: Should the Jakarta Charter's controversial provision for the apparently official enforcement of Islamic piety be recognized as having constitutional status? What role should religion—and which religion—have in Indonesia's schools? And should freedom of religious choice include the freedom of Muslims to renounce their faith for another? The first and third questions had been debated hotly twenty-three years earlier, in the BPKI, and on many occasions since; they had never really been taken off the agenda. In 1968 delegates from the Islamic parties sought once again to protect the ummat from abangan laxity, from secular and Christian schooling, and from the blandishments of other faiths. Opposing them was a military and civilian, nonparty and PNI coalition around a core of delegates with priyayi-professional status and abangan-secular viewpoints; a Christian minority in this grouping felt especially threatened by the old bogey of an Islamic state.

Just over a year later, in April 1969, Indonesia's First Five-Year Plan was launched.[19] The plan had been worked out by civilian technocrats, mainly Western-trained economists, in collaboration with the World Bank and other foreign organizations for development aid, who hoped that five elements—political stability, fiscal stability, infrastructural rehabilitation, foreign aid and investment, and a stimulated agricultural sector—could be combined to achieve economic growth. But how could the various cultural communities participate wholeheartedly in a plan for economic development under a state whose cultural identity was, as the MPRS deadlock showed, still a live controversy among them? Would not the Muslim group feel left out of an essentially secular design for change?

Here a comparison between Usman and Purwoko can be instructive. How mutually alien were their self-identifications, and

18. Although its committees worked only in closed session, I was fortunate enough to be able to observe the Assembly's plenaries; this paragraph drastically compresses my impressions.

19. Articles on the plan include Rudy C. de Iongh, "Indonesia's New Five-Year Development Plan, 1969–1973," *Review of Indonesian and Malayan Affairs*, 2, 1 (Jan.-March 1968), 8–18, and K. D. Thomas and J. Panglaykim, "Indonesia's Development Cabinet, Background to Current Problems and the Five Year Plan," *Asian Survey*, 9 (April 1969), 223–238.

how did they orient themselves toward society and changes in it? Because they are polar types, a comparison of their religious and institutional experiences and their orientations toward secularizing change should yield some tentative propositions worth exploring in the full samples.

For Usman, the pesantren provided his most valued childhood experience. For many secular intellectuals, however, pesantren schooling is simply inferior. The derogatory view found perhaps its most forceful expression in the 1930's, in the rhetoric of a Western-educated intellectual from Sumatra, Takdir Alisjahbana. Takdir condemned the pesantren because, in his view, it stifled individual creativity and independence. The kiyai, he said, thought for the santris, who never dared contradict what he told them. Both kiyai and santri followed traditional custom as if that were "an unbreakable iron law." Because he never exerted himself or thought for himself, the santri's sense of self soon died and he slipped into a spirit of unity with his fellow santris and with the kiyai that was "nothing but the cozy idyll of a static society." It was certainly not by chance, Takdir said, that the greatest Indonesian leaders of recent years had been products of Western education. "For Western education taught them to think for themselves, taught them to criticize and contradict the kiyais, emboldened them to throw off all the customs and traditions that bind our people hands and feet." Takdir called for "the collapse of the traditions, an end to blind veneration of the kiyais, the smashing of static, passive unity, the disappearance of conservatism, and the bringing to life of the individual selfhood of each human being." The pesantren, he charged, trained "our people to become affable sheep, while the world is full of tigers." Years later, President Sukarno, another Western-educated intellectual, compared the pesantren to a barn, its doors and windows shut tight, where the santris read Islamic books and prayed five times a day as the air turned ever more stagnant; like Takdir, he urged the santris to break out of this stultifying world and exercise their long-fettered intellects.[20]

Usman would certainly reject this criticism, and his experience

<hr />

20. S. T. A. [Sutan Takdir Alisjahbana], "Didikan Barat dan Didikan Pesantren: Menoedjoe ke Masjarakat jang Dynamisch," *Poedjangga Baroe*, 3 (Dec. 1935), 182–184; Sukarno, *Negara Harus BerTuhan* (Jakarta: Departemen Agama, 1964), p. 40.

partly refutes it. As a santri, he was self-reliant. His veneration for the kiyai did not prevent him from taking the initiative in setting up an independent business that met the pupils' needs and made a profit for himself. Located on the fringe of a small city, his pesantren was hardly sealed off from society. In retrospect, Usman did not find the school confining at all; on the contrary, coming to it from the village he felt he had moved into a much larger world. (Takdir and Sukarno had spoken from an urban perspective.) Nevertheless, Usman was sensitive about the possibility of cosmopolitan intellectuals in the "metropolitan superculture"[21] of the capital city considering him uneducated, old-fashioned, or parochial; that was why, it later turned out, he discouraged my first attempts to talk with him. He was extremely proud to have been a santri, but he said he felt that label no longer fitted him—not, I think, just because he was no longer literally a pupil at the kiyai's feet but because he had moved into the even larger, secular, Western-influenced world of Jakarta in which one could be a Muslim (*orang Islam*) less defensively than one could be a santri. Usman's adaptation to Jakarta, far from weakening his religious identity, had assured its continued strength. In Usman's village, and even in the city near his pesantren, virtually the entire population was both Javanese and Muslim; labels of religious intensity that assumed the same ethnic and religious affiliation were appropriate. But Jakarta is the national capital, and there Usman mixed with Batak Protestants, Ambonese Catholics, Balinese Hindus, and Chinese Buddhist-Confucians. In relation to them, the distinguishing religious referent was his affiliation as an orang Islam, pious or not. (Similarly, in the full samples, which include a number of non-Javanese and several non-Muslims, the two dimensions, religious affiliation and religious intensity, will be kept analytically separate.)

Usman's shift in self-identification—from a specific, intracultural referent of intensity to a general, intercultural referent of affiliation —also involved a shift in the focus of his attention from a pious core within Islam to the defensive perimeter that marked the ummat off from worlds entirely outside it. In central Java, Usman was not so self-consciously Muslim because the religious milieu there was not so discontinuous. The village kiyai did not reject wayang

21. The phrase is Hildred Geertz'; see her "Indonesian Cultures," pp. 16–17.

as heretically abangan, even though its polytheism gave him reason to do so; rather, he reinterpreted it in an Islamic frame. The admired image of the chief official of the central mosque as he marched in the king's entourage linked the pesantren and the kraton complexes; holding priyayi status within the hierarchic center of abangan culture, he was yet a santri by piety if not education. The three labels—priyayi, abangan, santri—defined different aspects of the same culture.

Compared to these shadings, Usman's view of the contrast between Muslim and non-Muslim appears stark. Hizbullah's antagonism toward the Dutch was attenuated by neither religion nor ethnicity. In polyconfessional Jakarta, when it was said that Muslims should be "free" to commit apostasy by changing their religious affiliation, Usman could be expected to defend the entire, abstract ummat against proselytization by its presumed enemies—as in fact he did in the fifth general session of the MPRS when the issue arose.

What generalizations emerge from Usman's experience that are worth exploring with evidence from the full samples? Despite the tension often seen between these two labels, the cultural identities santri and abangan may be more coextensive than contradictory in the rural, prepolitical childhoods of Javanese members of the Indonesian elite. Despite the presumed seductiveness of the metropolitan superculture, members of the elite with strongly Islamic and rural backgrounds may not be markedly secularized by their experience in the supravillage sphere; their religious self-identification may, instead, become more abstract, more political, and more defensive. Only as an adult did Usman become aware of Islam's political disadvantage. In the course of village and pesantren life before the revolution there had been no need to activate the critical boundary around the ummat. But in Jakarta, Islam was a political minority, and he knew it. Usman's experience illustrates these tentative propositions: Politico-religious conflict at the elite level is not simply a translation of prior cleavages in the rural mass. What were once in rural settings subtle matters of cultural degree become polarized in the cities into matters of opposing political kind. The proximate cause of polarization is felt outgroup or minority political status. Because awareness of that status tends to occur in adulthood as a result of political contact between cultural groups, conflict in cultural politics may be politically avoidable and not culturally foreordained at all.

Purwoko's experience is similarly suggestive, though in a different direction. The label that he shunned was not abangan—a term he neither volunteered nor rejected as a description of his religious stance—but priyayi. For if Takdir and Sukarno had stereotyped and stigmatized the santri, so had other nationalist intellectuals disparaged the priyayi. Pramoedya Ananta Toer, for example, in an autobiographical short story, used the voice of a nationalist organizer who visited his village in the 1930's to denounce the priyayis in class terms:

Ever since there have been kings in this country the priyayis have been the sovereign class—and that sovereignty is misplaced. They feel they have the right to rule, but there are none who recognize or authorize that right or who are entitled to be addressed with high titles save the priyayis themselves. For the most part they're unmoved, insensitive to what's going on around them, too busy waiting for the coming of that rise in rank, prestige, salary. Sometimes their beautiful dream collides with a paranoid fear of getting fired, having their pay cut, being scalded by the boss' hot words. [But it doesn't matter now.] We've already begun to move [against dependence on the Dutch]. If the priyayis don't want to move with us, we'll leave them behind.[22]

Pramoedya's is no more a fair portrayal of Purwoko's life than Takdir's is of Usman's. Purwoko had, symbolically at least, supported the revolution, and he was not arrogant, craving, or insensitive. But the stigma was real, and though Purwoko recognized the term priyayi as a description of his social origins—much as Usman accepted having been a santri—he no longer wanted to associate himself with it. As Usman was self-conscious about religion, so was Purwoko about status. The term priyayi implied a natural right to rule, a sense of noblesse oblige that seemed to Purwoko out of date in postcolonial Indonesia. Moreover, his Western schooling and contacts had exposed him to the idea of democracy as a desirable form of government, and in that context

22. Pramoedya Ananta Toer, "Kemudian Lahirlah Dia," in his *Tjerita Dari Blora* (Jakarta: Balai Pustaka, 1952), p. 92; an edited English version is available as "Born Before the Dawn," trans. A. Brotherton, *The Atlantic Monthly*, 197 (June 1956), 114–116.

priyayi did have negatively elitist connotations. But neither post-colonial society nor Western democracy was without blemish in Purwoko's eyes. The first lacked the kind of moral integration he remembered from his childhood; as an experiment, the latter had somehow gone wrong, politicizing and undermining the old normative order and the sense of community on which it rested.

More objectionable to Purwoko than its elitist and undemocratic overtones were two other aspects of the priyayi label which explain why he preferred to be called a civil servant (*pegawai negeri*) or a government official (*pejabat pemerintah*). First, the priyayi category was not cosmopolitan. Pegawai negeri and pejabat pemerintah sounded modern and national; priyayi described a traditional status specific to Javanese culture. Second, the priyayi designation was not institutional. Pegawai and pejabat denoted government employment; priyayi only implied it. Usman, by comparison, felt no need for a label affirming his institutional role as a member of Parliament; to belong to the ummat was enough.

Purwoko was much more cosmopolitan than Usman. Usman could be unsentimentally critical about the narrowness of village life, but he still liked to work the soil in the fringe area of Jakarta where he lived and which reproduced the only partly urban setting of his beloved pesantren. Usman had never seen the West and had no Western friends. When he talked of retiring to become a farmer, he sounded practical, not nostalgic. I sensed that he could readapt to rural life. Purwoko, I felt, although he romanticized his childhood in the village, could never return there to live. Having traveled extensively in the West and being accustomed to conversing with foreigners and even writing for publication in foreign languages, Purwoko could probably not tolerate village life beyond visiting his parents on Lebaran every few years.

More propositions emerge from these comparisons: High civil service officials come from more cosmopolitan backgrounds than do most members of Parliament. Higher administrators are more likely to have had secular (Western) and advanced educations and to have traveled widely overseas. Members of Parliament are more likely to have parochial backgrounds, in the sense of more limited, and more religiously oriented, schooling and less international travel. The legislature contributes little to the sense of identity of its members. For most of them, Parliament is little more than a place created by the temporary juxtaposition of its participating organizations. Those organizations, including Usman's party, help shape the identities of their delegates in the DPR, but the DPR itself, as a body with an important and distinctive role to play in government, does not. In contrast, the civil service provides valued professional status and an institutional identity to its higher incumbents. These propositions can be combined with the historical evidence of bureaucratic dominance already presented to produce this tentative statement: The executive and legislative institutions in Indonesia are grossly imbalanced, in terms not merely of influence but also of identity and recruitment, with the bureaucratic elite being at once more dominant, more cohesive, and more advantaged in a secular society by its cosmopolitan background.

What do these generalizations imply for the content of elite political culture? Given their diverging religious and institutional experiences, do the two polar-typical men diverge in outlook as well? And if they do, in what directions? Is it accurate to see Purwoko, representing one extreme, as an agent of secular change opposing Usman, at the other, as the defender of embattled Islam? The answer is no, for complex and suggestive reasons to be seen in the following comparison of the two men's religious, social, and political opinions.

The basic difference in religious outlook between Purwoko and Usman lies in their conceptions of religious truth. For Purwoko, formal religions—Hinduism, Buddhism, Islam, and Christianity— were merely different. They were neither mutually exclusive nor collectively exhaustive versions of God. His relativistic understanding of religious truth led Purwoko to Disagree utterly with the statement, to which I asked him to respond during our final interview, that among all the religions of the world, there is only one true religion. Purwoko was prepared to accept God as single or multiple, perfect or imperfect, a concrete personality or an anonymous spiritual force. (Purwoko and Usman, like the others who completed my questionnaire, were asked to decide whether they agreed, tended to agree, were neutral, tended to disagree, or disagreed with each statement in it; for clarity and convenience in reporting their answers, I use "Agree" and "Disagree" to distinguish the extremes and "agree" and "disagree" for the less emphatic alternatives.)

Such indiscriminate eclecticism Usman could not accept. He Agreed completely with the idea that there is only one true religion. Religious truth and Islam were to him inseparably one and the same. Within the limits of the Islamic ummat, however, he was highly tolerant. On matters of Islamic practice, Usman characterized himself as lenient. Ascribing to a rival Muslim party the view that a Muslim who does not pray five times daily is a hypocrite, he demurred; that much could not always be expected of people. Nor did Usman object to the Javanization of Islamic ritual—the use of incense as a medium for carrying prayers to Allah, or of "Allah is God" as an endlessly chanted mantra at tombs and other spiritually charged places, or the equation of Islamic puasa or kiyai with Hindu-Javanese tapa or guru. (The pesantren itself may have evolved over the centuries out of communities of originally Indic learning and devotion.[23]) Usman's experience of rural Javanese Islam as a religion adapted to if not incorporating Hindu and animistic beliefs allowed him to tolerate, even to approximate, the abangan position according to which incense, mantra, wayang, and the ritual selamatan meal are all natural accompaniments of religious experience. But, unlike an abangan Javanese, Usman prayed with some regularity, had been to Mecca, and would have rejected out of hand the suggestion that he was anything but a good Muslim.

Purwoko's idea that all religions share a single truth and Usman's that one religion encompasses all truth are both similar and different. They are alike in that they permit a high degree of tolerance within each man's domain. Purwoko's tolerance was much more eclectic, of course; though formally a Muslim, he willingly accepted the Deity in almost any guise. But Usman's experience had carried him some distance toward an abangan version of Islam in which a good deal of laxity and syncretism were acceptable. As for the difference between their views, for Usman there was a *critical boundary* (around the ummat), whereas for Purwoko there was none. And in this difference lies the key to understanding the divergence between the two men's orientations toward society and social change.

---

23. Pigeaud, *Java,* IV, pp. 93–100 and 484–486; C. C. Berg, "Indonesia," in H. A. R. Gibb, ed., *Whither Islam? A Survey of Modern Movements in the Muslim World* (London: Gollancz, 1932), p. 257.

Usman considered each statement in the questionnaire from an Islamic perspective. He spoke from within the safety and brotherhood of the ummat. When we talked about the nature of human beings, Usman told me that man is born pure in the eyes of Allah and that his human environment then shapes him for better or worse. Usman acquired this belief in the pesantren; it was there that he learned the Muslim doctrine of pure birth.[24] Responding to the statement that poor people have fewer friends, Usman agreed that people in the cities tended to be materialistic. But what about the kiyais in the countryside? They were usually poor, and yet they were popular. In the pesantren, wealth was no precondition of friendship; there a man could develop in the right moral direction. Outside, things were different.

Purwoko made no such distinction. —Mankind,— he said, —is pretty materialistic, whether in the East or the West.— Having himself moved from rural to urban, abangan to secular, Indonesian to international settings, Purwoko had no closed community to which he could still relate and in which he could keep that kind of faith—nostalgia for his father's village notwithstanding.

When Usman Agreed that most people would rather be frank than hide their intentions and that there are no secrets between friends, he almost certainly had in mind the straightforwardness and camaraderie of his fellow santris in the pesantren, with some of whom he still kept in touch in 1969. But he excepted urbanites, intellectuals, and diplomats, whom he said were secretive and devious. About them he Agreed that, in general, the sweeter a man's words, the more evil his thoughts. But "ordinary" or good people were not this way. Besides, he could always penetrate a man's façade with ilmu firasah—and that skill too he learned from a kiyai in the pesantren. Purwoko, on the other hand, disagreed that frankness is the norm and that friends have no secrets; toward the notion that sweet words mean evil thoughts he chose neutrality. From his comments, I suspect that Purwoko had in mind the same urban environment that Usman so disparaged. Lacking one distinct community to which he could positively relate, and having lived in many more different settings than Usman, Purwoko had a much more ambiguous view of things.

24. See "Fitra" in H. A. R. Gibb and J. H. Kramers, eds., *Shorter Encyclopaedia of Islam* (Leiden: Brill, 1953).

The same contrast marks the two men's outlooks on conflict. Usman disagreed with the idea that friend and foe are hard to distinguish nowadays; using ilmu firasah, he could separate them. Purwoko pondered this statement at length before finally selecting the noncommittal response. —Personal friendships are one thing, political friendships another.— How should one treat a personal friend who, with a change in regime, became a political enemy? Purwoko had faced this dilemma in the post-1965 purges, and the memory was painfully fresh. For Usman, on the other hand, communists were the enemy and Muslims, especially those who shared his political affiliation, were friends. Conversely, since most of Usman's friends were members of his Islamic party he did not need to distinguish between personal and political relationships. He felt himself an integral part of a clearly bounded region of considerable affection, outside of which lay potential animosity.

More revealing still are the two men's responses to the idea that progress is worth its cost in conflict, that the dynamically advancing state is to be preferred over the tranquil one even if the latter is spared the upheavals of the former. By Takdir's logic, the Western-educated Purwoko should have welcomed bold, risk-taking progress, whereas Usman, his horizons stunted by pesantren life, should have rejected it in favor of pastoral, custom-bound calm. In fact, the reverse was true. Purwoko disagreed with the statement. Because there was no critical boundary across which he and his friends could be comfortably pitted against obvious enemies, because conflict literally knew no bounds, it was dangerous. Here Purwoko's childhood and his experience of revolutionary disorder influenced him deeply. His father's prime duty had been to guard the tranquillity of the village realm, discharging in microcosm the king's obligations. The idea of creative conflict is quite foreign to this view of the ideal Javanese kingdom as a place where officials attend to their respective duties in perfect harmony with one another, a land without robbers, disturbances, or fighting—to paraphrase the puppeteer's scene-setting prologue in the wayang kulit performances Purwoko loved to watch.[25] As he listened in the dark

25. Moertono, *State and Statecraft,* pp. 38, 83, and 89; Hardjowirogo, *Sedjarah Wajang Purwa* (5th print., Jakarta: Balai Pustaka, 1968), p. 7; A. Seno Sastroamidjojo, *Renungan tentang Pertundjukan Wajang Kulit* (Jakarta: Kinta, 1964), pp. 185–187.

on the edge of the pendapa while his father vulgarized the king's advice, as he observed and absorbed the models of priyayi etiquette in the king's school, Purwoko came to place a high value on order and serenity. His postwar experience of politics as essentially disruptive—popular revolution in the 1940's, governmental instability in the 1950's, mass violence in the 1960's—reinforced this orientation and gave it an even more "antipolitical" tone. He witnessed or gingerly participated in these events as a priyayi, uncomfortable in chaos, looking for the re-establishment of calm that would allow him to discharge his administrative duties once again.

Usman readily agreed that conflict was an acceptable cost of progress, although in answering the question he talked more about conflict than about progress. In his view, a clash across the critical boundary separating the Muslim ummat from the unbelievers who would insult or do injustice to it should never be avoided. Nor, in his own personal style, did Usman make any special effort to avoid disagreement. His manner was straightforward and direct, and he regarded the diplomatic finesse of certain Jakarta intellectuals as insincere, if not ill-intentioned. Tranquillity held no special attraction.

If for Purwoko the revolution was political and destabilizing, to Usman it was a politico-religious experience in which the gravity of his faith kept him securely on Allah's anticolonial path. The revolution was the most exciting period of Usman's life, a time when he was both leader of men and fighter for God. With no stake in the state, with the glory of the syahid in their minds' eyes, Usman and the ragged irregulars of the Army of Allah had everything to gain from revolutionary war.

When basic issues of religion and the survival of the ummat were not in question, Usman was entirely willing, even eager, to compromise, especially when not to do so might endanger his party's access to government jobs. —What is politics?— Usman asked himself at one point in our discussion. —Each group has an ideology, and politics is give and take between groups.— And if the honor or existence of the group were not at stake, why use confrontation tactics? Illustrating, he cited the controversy over Hwa Hwee, a Chinese game that had recently generated in Jakarta a gambling fever of epidemic proportions. The Koran expressly forbids gambling, and a number of Muslim politicians in Jakarta had publicly criticized the city government for permitting Hwa

Hwee and taxing its profits for revenue.[26] Instead of condemning the city officials, Usman and others in his party had quietly urged them to find another source of income, which ultimately they had done. —So now the government has its revenue and Hwa Hwee has been banned.— Despite the ideological divisions separating groups, politics did not have to be a crusade or a game with only winners and losers.

But Usman was ready to abandon this idea of cooperation based on mutual interest whenever he felt the ummat to be threatened. Once, in a committee of Parliament, a Christian leader charged that Muslims outside Java were dragooning Christians into the ummat by forcing them to utter the kalima syahadat against their will; Usman replied heatedly that if the matter were pursued further Muslims would have a lot to say about "aggressive Christianization." As has already been noted, in the committee debates on religious freedom and the Jakarta Charter in the fifth general session of the MPRS, Usman joined ranks with other Islamic delegates to defend the ummat. But on neither occasion did he take a public stand, outside the meeting room. Aware that the military government did not want a religious confrontation, and knowing how dependent his party was on official patronage, Usman refrained from rocking the boat too hard lest he fall overboard.

In taking this attitude, he shared with Purwoko an essentially statist bias. Both men saw the purpose of political activity as the acquisition of posts and influence in government. But whereas Purwoko, a career civil servant with needed skills, tended to regard politically appointed officials as incompetent hangers-on who violated criteria of disinterested service, for Usman, the number and importance of bureaucratic posts held by a party were criteria for judging its success. Party politics was seen by both men as a struggle for patronage—apprehensively by Purwoko, approvingly by Usman. For this reason, insofar as it insulated experts like himself from outside party pressures, Purwoko could accept the sharply increased penetration of the bureaucracy by the army since 1965; from Usman's point of view, the army's expanded role had

26. The injunction against gambling is in surah V, vv. 90–91. On the Hwa Hwee phenomenon, see my "Gambling and Development: The Case of Djakarta's 'Flower Organization,' " *Asia*, 27 (Autumn 1972), 19–36.

simply reduced the available spoils. Purwoko saw politics from the perspective of a professional in an institution, Usman from the standpoint of a Muslim in a party. Because Usman had a clearly circumscribed politico-religious base to orient him, he could handle the ambiguities of politics without Purwoko's anxiety—but only so long as the existence of that base was not threatened.

Usman had just such a possibility in mind when he Agreed that there are only two kinds of people, those who defend the truth and those who oppose it. Again he drew the critical line. His answer echoed his equation of Islam with truth, his memory of the revolutionary jihad as a defense of truth against its enemies, and his use of ilmu firasah to tell friend from foe. In religious conflict engaging the ummat against its opponents, there could be no middle ground. Purwoko disagreed with this statement, for if all religions shared the same truth conflict between them must be ambiguous. From Purwoko's experience of political struggle in the late 1940's and the 1960's, the victors' claims to a monopoly of virtue turned out on closer inspection to be exaggerated and to conceal excesses. In Purwoko's view of human affairs, there were no perfect moral dichotomies.

Does Usman's critical line circumscribe a majority or a minority? The last statement from the questionnaire worth citing is a rephrasing of John Stuart Mill's famous libertarian credo: "If all the members of society are of the same opinion save one person who has a different viewpoint, then to silence that one person would be as evil as silencing all the rest." Usman vigorously Agreed and poured into his answer all his feelings of defensiveness and frustration as a member of the beleaguered community of Islam. The minority should be given a fair deal; Islam had suffered enough, not only in Indonesia but throughout the world. —Why was Muhammad Ali's title taken away from him in America? Because he became a Muslim. Why is it that the northern Philippines is so advanced and the southern part so backward? Because the north is Christian while the south has a Muslim majority. And what of the ummat here in Indonesia? We [the members of his Islamic party] fought in the revolution. We served our country well. But after independence, who got the ministerial posts? The educated people. Not the masses. We were the masses, and we got nothing. Intellectuals filled even the middle levels of administration. We wanted to move up, at least taking over the middle posts. But we were blocked.—

Usman's bitterness is doubly revealing. It echoed the grievances of Muslim leaders over a string of defeats dating all the way back to the isolation of Islam under the colonial regime; Islam had been shortchanged, cheated, deprived of the fruits of its victories. But it was also a tacit admission that political Islam was a minority, that silencing it was tantamount to silencing a *single* voice. Most of the Western-educated people who became ministers after the revolution were Muslims, but in a statistical sense only. By affiliation they were inside the community of Islam, but in actual behavior they were not. Although he emphasized the border around the entire majoritarian ummat, Usman knew that there was a second, much shorter circumference that marked off a small minority of practicing Muslims and Muslim leaders like himself within the Islamic community. To recognize that latter boundary explicitly would have meant acknowledging Islam as a political minority in Indonesia and therefore accepting the meagerness of its gains in the revolution and ever since. Preoccupation with the larger boundary, around the more abstract community, spared Usman that sobering recognition.

Purwoko Disagreed with the paraphrase of Mill. He identified with the effective majority, Muslim in name but seldom in practice or party preference, and with the Western-oriented intellectual bureaucrats who carried on their forefathers' roles as guardians of the state. Extreme civil libertarianism had no place, in his view, in a country where only a minority had been properly (that is, Western-) educated. Like Usman, he used the majority to defend his minority. He rejected the idea that the right of a single man to speak out was morally equal to the right of the rest of the population to voice its views, but his solicitude for majority opinion was colored by the presumption that civil servants like himself should articulate it. The elite bureaucratic minority of which Purwoko was a part purported to speak for the voiceless majority, just as the Dutch had said it did; respect for the rights of one individual should not allow the upsetting of the clockwork and its keepers, who were working, after all, in the popular interest.

These differences in outlook suggest consequences for the way

the two men conceived of and related to modernization. For Purwoko modernization meant, above all, improved education, which
would permit people to acquire necessary technical skills and to
make a better life for themselves, their families, and their society.
Purwoko's professional identity and daily work were geared to just
this objective. Modernization was learning. For Usman, it was a
more alien concept, something external to his own experience. He
had acquired useful secular skills in the pesantren, including
knowledge of commerce and agriculture, but those talents were
rooted in a religious community that now found itself on the
defensive in relation to the machines and achievements of modern,
non-Islamic countries. To Usman, modernization was technology.

Ironically, by defining modernity as something foreign, by
thinking of it as an apparatus rather than, as Purwoko did, the
acquisition of skills needed to run the apparatus, Usman could
simply incorporate it into Islam. He mentioned space flight and
interpreted it as a sign of the greatness of Allah, who created the
universe that it should be explored. The fact that the explorers
were not Muslims did not bother Usman because he had not defined modernization in behavioral terms.[27] He mentioned tape
recorders as another sign of modernity, and treated them the same
way: —We can tape the conversation of two people and then play
it back years later when they're already dead, right? Well, [the
Islamic] religion tells us that as long as we live an angel notes
down our evil deeds, while another one keeps track of the good
things we do. When we die we face a judgment based on their
notes, on the diaries they've kept of our lives.[28] If we've done more
bad than good, we go to hell, if the other way round, to heaven.
As the angels record, so does the tape recorder. Therefore the tape
recorder doesn't lessen our faith in Allah. On the contrary!— By
finding correspondences between technology and Islam, Usman

27. It did bother Sjamsu Anwar. In "Apollo, Islam & Ummat Islam," *Indonesia Raya,* Aug. 12 and 19, 1969, he listed the names of the astronauts
and others responsible for man's travel in space and then noted that "not a
single one of these names is Muslim or Arab. Where lies the reason? Within
Islam as the religion of the Muslims? Or is it merely because of the inade-
quacies, mistakes, or stupidity of the human beings who call themselves
Muslims?"

28. Cf. Koran, surah LXXXII, vv. 10–16. Or Usman may have had in
mind the extra-Koranic tradition of the interrogating angels, Munkar and
Nazir; he had almost certainly heard about them in the pesantren.

could claim that modernization had already been foreseen by Allah and that it could only renew one's faith in Him. Had he defined modernization as a change in behavior, and especially as secularization, he could not have embraced the term; on the contrary, he would have had to throw up the critical barricade across which Muslims must defend their faith.

For the student of cultural politics, the question is: Over what issues will the barrier go up, and how can those issues be resolved so that, rather than feeling threatened by the secularizing aspects of social change, committed Muslims will take part in it to make it more responsive to the needs of their community?

Contrary to Takdir's image, Usman was no affable sheep; contrary to Pramoedya's, Purwoko was not an arrogant patrician. Purwoko derived satisfaction and identity from his profession and his institution, Usman from his religion and his party. Each lacked something the other had. Purwoko had the skills and the position to be able to contribute to the general welfare. His role was validated by its output: decisions made, manuals published, buildings erected. His actions brought change, and in material terms the change was generally salutary. But Purwoko also felt the lack of spiritual meaning in his performance and was therefore driven back to his abangan past for a renewed sense of linkage with supernatural forces and meanings. Usman already had that sense of linkage and belonging. But he belonged to a community whose leaders largely lacked the professional skills and institutional position of a cosmopolitan high official such as Purwoko. Usman was not an agent of religious reaction; his feeling for politics as "give and take" made him flexible within the broad limits of his critical boundary. Purwoko was less political, and in some ways less flexible too; as an educated, skilled individual he honestly felt that he knew what was best for the people. Nor was Purwoko a ruthless agent of secular change; not only was he too tolerant for that, but, in addition, as he thought of retiring, he saw the need to moor his own life more securely to its spiritual origins. I am sure that the two men have never met; if they did, they would probably not be comfortable in each other's presence, so different are their positions and personalities. That is a pity, for they have much to offer one another.

Beyond challenging Takdir's and Pramoedya's caricatures of the santri and priyayi types, the attention paid here to Usman and Purwoko has yielded a number of propositions for further exploration. Baldly stated, the argument looks like this: The socialization and recruitment of members of the Indonesian bureaucratic elite have made them culturally more homogeneous and more cosmopolitan than members of Parliament are; they are also more powerful. As a result of this institutional advantage, members of the bureaucratic elite relate to their changing environment more positively than do their counterparts in Parliament; the latter are more negative, partly because they are politically less powerful and partly because they are culturally more representative. Overlapping and reinforcing this institutional hypothesis is a second proposition: Compared to cultural majorities, cultural minorities (for example, minorities defined by religious affiliation or, as in the case of Usman, religious intensity) feel more disaffected from their environment and are more likely to see the changes occurring in it as potentially threatening; and they feel and see this way as a result of their own distinctively minoritarian experiences. In chapters 4 and 5, these hypotheses are explored using evidence from the full samples. First, however, the samples themselves, and how they were drawn, must be briefly described.

CHAPTER 3

SAMPLES

"The elite" in this study has been defined as the members of the higher central bureaucracy and the national legislature. Specifically, it includes persons who in 1969 occupied positions of higher, but not highest, central authority. Excluded from the populations from which the samples were drawn were nineteen men at the very top: ministers heading the eighteen departments in the Development Cabinet and the chairman of Parliament. These men would have been difficult to meet, might not have had time to talk with me, and, given the constraints of high office, might have been less than frank. At the bottom I excluded all administrators who were two or more layers of authority removed from the ministers. I did not try to sample the politically most powerful individuals. Of the forty men selected, some were widely known and considered influential. Quite a few others were at least occasionally reported in the Jakarta press as having said or done this or that. But only one had a consistent influence on decisions on a wide range of vital matters at the highest level of government; and none of the politicians was an organizational leader of the first rank.

Tapping the center meant ignoring the periphery. Provincial parliaments were not sampled, only the national body in Jakarta. Among administrators, all nondepartmental bodies were excluded, a decision that reinforced the vertical exclusion of insignificant clerks and supersignificant ministers, for some of these organs were utterly incidental—those on archival librarianship and space flight, for example—while others were too highly placed and sensitive to sample—those dealing with security and intelligence, for example, and the president's personal advisory staff. In the legislature, the numerically smallest and politically least significant organizations were also excluded in order to ensure adequate coverage of the major party, military, and civilian groups. In sum, individuals were included for sampling purposes in each institutional population through a working compromise between my access and their influence.

Higher Central Administrators

The twenty men in the bureaucratic sample were drawn from a list of 651 officials.[1] Eight departments were selected to contribute two randomly chosen members apiece. The remaining four members were randomly chosen from all the other departments combined, with the proviso that none of these latter departments could contribute more than a single member of the sample. The eight favored departments were chosen because they were relatively large, important, covered a broad range of governmental activity, and might be expected to have some impact on cultural politics; two were in the political sphere (Defense and Security, Home Affairs), three in the economic sphere (Finance, Trade, Agriculture), and three in the cultural-social-communications sphere (Education and Culture, Religion, Information). The remaining members of the sample happened to be in Foreign Affairs, Manpower, Industry, and Transmigration and Cooperatives. Not represented were the Departments of Justice, Health, Social Affairs, Communications, Mining, and Public Works and Electric Power.

Among departments that were represented, several bore responsibility for large numbers of people. Defense and Security coordi-

1. The document used was "Daftar Nama-nama Pedjabat Alamat & Telepon" (List of Officials' Names, Addresses, and Telephone Numbers), prepared by the secretariat of the (revised) Ampera Cabinet and dated Dec. 1, 1967. (The name Ampera, an abbreviation of Amanat Penderitaan Rakyat [Message of the People's Suffering], was given to the cabinet of 1966–1967 and to its reshuffled version in 1967–1968.) The full list was broken down as follows: 651 departmental officials, excluding ministers; 5 second listings of departmental officials (individuals holding two posts); 21 departmental ministers; 13 vacant departmental posts; 69 posts in the state secretariat; 88 posts in the highest state organizations; 128 posts in nondepartmental organizations; and 9 posts in the state ministers' offices, including the state ministers. There were 984 entries in all. The sample was drawn from the first category only, after the names in it had been regrouped under the eighteen departments of the Development Cabinet announced in June 1968. The absence of women in this and the legislative sample reflects their rarity in the elite.

nated a military establishment of over three quarters of a million men, while two other departments (Education and Culture, Religion) together accounted for a majority of the nearly half a million civil servants in the civilian core bureaucracy.[2] Still other departments—Manpower, for example—were quite small. Within each of the nine sampling categories—the eight major departments and the ninth residual category—the names chosen averaged 5.0 per cent of the names listed. The twenty men selected made up 3.1 per cent of all the names on the list.

In a typical department, the first layer of titular authority below the minister was made up of a secretary general and one or more director generals or inspector generals. In a second layer were a larger number of directors, inspectors, and bureau chiefs. In the universe—that is, the full list of 651 individuals—for every person in the higher layer there were four in the lower; in the sample, the ratio was one to three. In other words, the higher layer was slightly overrepresented in the sample.

The personal ranks of these men indicated their seniority. The civilians were all in the highest basic category (F) in the civil service pay scale; their base pay was higher than that of 99 per cent of all civilian government employees.[3] Of the military men in the sample, three were brigadier generals, one was a colonel, and one was a lieutenant colonel (or equivalents of these). On a scale of bureaucratic prestige based on perquisites of office, these twenty men also ranked high: a few had airconditioned offices; nearly half worked in spacious rooms, alone or with one or two unobtrusively

2. Of an estimated 450,000 civil servants, Education and Culture accounted for about 150,000, Religion for around 100,000. The next largest department (Home Affairs) had less than 40,000. "Djumlah Pegawai Negeri/ABRI/Sipil ABRI/Pensiunan dan Pegawai Daerah Otonom Pada Achir Th. 1967 KBN/DSPP," dated April 24, 1968. Such figures vary widely because of redefinition and misreporting. The "Djumlah" figures exclude military personnel, regional employees, nondepartmental employees, pensioners, and occasional workers. President Suharto has estimated the total number of state employees in all categories at about 2,500,000 (Antara, *Warta Berita*, Aug. 18, 1968, AB).

3. In 1967, salary ranks ran upward from A to F in accordance with the Regulation on Civil Servants' Pay (Peraturan Gaji Pegawai Negeri, PGPN) of 1961; military personnel were paid according to the regulations of their own service. The Institute of Public Administration estimated that of all the civilian (PGPN-salaried) civil servants in Indonesia, one per cent were in category F (*Angkatan Bersendjata*, Oct. 30, 1967).

placed aides; most had official cars; and all but one had a telephone. The distribution of these status attributes in the sample appeared roughly to reflect their distribution in the universe.

By type of bureaucratic purview, the sample also closely matched the universe: 23 per cent of the universe worked in the political sphere (Defense and Security, Home Affairs, Foreign Affairs, Justice) compared to 25 per cent of the sample; employees in the economic sphere (Finance, Trade, Agriculture, Manpower, Industry, Public Works and Electric Power, Mining) accounted for 45 per cent of the universe and 40 per cent of the sample; for the residual cultural-social-communications sphere (Education and Culture, Religion, Information, Transmigration and Cooperatives, Health, Social Affairs, Communications) the percentages were 32 and 35.

To ensure adequate representation of the military, the sample was also divided according to officer versus civilian status. By ensuring that 25 per cent of the sample (five of its twenty members) were officers, I could closely approximate their 23 per cent share of the universe. I did not sample the military elite as such, for that would have taken me from the mainly civilian bureaucracy into the command structures of the armed services themselves. At the end of 1967, the closer a government body was to President (General) Suharto, the greater was the military's participation in it: compared to the 23 per cent of higher central bureaucrats who were officers, 43 per cent of the cabinet, 64 per cent of the (then still acting) president's personal advisory staff, and 100 per cent of the State Intelligence Coordinating Body (Badan Koordinasi Intelijens Negara, BAKIN) were military men.[4] I limited my military subsample to the first of these four groups; although proportionally the smallest it was in absolute size by far the largest of the four and thus reflected well the officers' ubiquity and influence in administration, if not in the inner ring around the president.

4. The total numbers of people in each of these categories were 651, 21, 28, and 7, respectively. The makeup of Suharto's personal advisory staff illustrates the character of the New Order as a tandem of high-ranking officers and highly educated technocrats. More than a third of the officers were brigadier generals or above, while over two-thirds of the civilians held Ph.D.'s (and the rest M.A.'s), obtained mainly in economics from American universities. "Daftar Nama-nama" is my source for these and most of the following figures.

Some changes have taken place since 1967. In the Development Cabinet announced in June 1968 the proportion of officer-ministers was down to 33 per cent; and criticism of Suharto's advisory staff eventually led to its dissolution in 1974. When I did my interviewing in 1969, however, the armed forces' participation in government remained decisive and widespread.[5] Subsequently the military's presence in the central government has been made less noticeable by the civilianization of successive cabinets; at the same time, however, the military appears to have increased the number of positions it holds in the publicly less visible layer of authority just under the ministers.[6]

Most influential and ubiquitous of all the armed services in government was the army, whose share of posts among the officer-bureaucrats also rose roughly with the posts' rising importance. In the higher central bureaucracy, 70 per cent of all officer-officials were army men; in the sample, 80 per cent were. Although in the cabinets of 1967–1968 the figure was only 67 per cent—the greater national visibility of ministerial positions may have encouraged more generous allocations to the air force and navy—the army contributed all members of the president's advisory staff and BAKIN.

The administrative sample, then, was made up of senior military and civilian officials in relatively high posts in major ministries in Jakarta. Compared to the half million members of the core bureauc-

5. The military's share of personnel was of course highest in the Department of Defense and Security. In the universe sampled, three-quarters of the men in this department held military rank. Officer strength in the Departments of Industry and Trade (37 per cent and 23 per cent, respectively) reflected the military's stake in the economy. The armed forces had been a trustee of industry at least since the takeover of Dutch enterprises in the mid-late 1950's and were also profitably engaged in importing and exporting and related activities. Military strength in Communications (31 per cent) reflected the prominence of the armed forces in land, sea, and air communications. Home Affairs' involvement in the political aspects of internal security also attracted the military (24 per cent). These were the five most penetrated departments in the universe as restructured to conform to the organization of the Development Cabinet. Of the seven ministers in the revised Ampera Cabinet responsible for these fields, only one was a civilian; in the Development Cabinet, two. The five least penetrated departments in the restructured universe were Manpower (11 per cent), Information (8 per cent), Religion (7 per cent), Social Affairs (3 per cent), and Justice, which had no military officers at all. In both cabinets, four out of five of these ministers were civilians.

6. On this point, see my "Bureaucracy."

racy, and the two and a half million public employees, the twenty men were a tiny, stratospheric elite. From the perspective of the ministers, let alone the man who named the ministers, they were subordinate figures. However, all of them influenced policy, if not always its inception certainly its interpretation and application; located as they were just under the apex of government, the relative tension or overlap in the patterns of political culture embodied in the backgrounds and opinions of these high officials would be a crucial enabling, or limiting, condition in any official action affecting cultural politics.

Members of Parliament

The twenty men in the legislative sample were drawn from a list of 369 members of the "Mutual Help" People's Representative Council (Dewan Perwakilan Rakyat Gotong Royong, also DPR for short).[7] Eight major parliamentary groups were selected to contribute one or more randomly chosen members apiece. The most important groups in Parliament, numerically and politically, were the Armed Forces (Angkatan Bersenjata Republik Indonesia, ABRI), the Development Group (Pembangunan), the PNI, and the NU. Four members were drawn from each of these delegations such that together these groups' share of the sample (80 per cent) matched their strength in the universe (81 per cent). The ABRI contingent was subdivided by selecting two army members and one each from the navy and air force to reflect the 2:1:1 ratio of representation of these services in Parliament. Finally, one member of the sample was drawn from each of four delegations that had few

7. The document used was "Daftar Nama dan Alamat Anggota-anggota DPR-GR" (List of Names and Addresses of Members of the "Mutual Help" People's Representative Council), prepared by the documentation section of the DPR and dated March 1, 1968. The full list was broken down as follows: 369 members of PNI, NU (excluding the NU member who chaired the DPR), Pembangunan, ABRI (Army, Navy, Air Force), PSII, Parmusi, Parkindo, and Partai Katholik; one chairman of the DPR; 14 members of ABRI (Police); 4 members of ABRI (Civil Defense, People's Defense, and Veterans); 11 members of IPKI; 4 members of Partai Murba. Nine seats reserved for Perti but not filled and two otherwise vacant seats raised the total to the 414 seats then in the DPR. The sample was drawn from the first category only. Abbreviations are explained in the text, except for IPKI (Ikatan Pendukung Kemerdekaan Indonesia, the League of Supporters of Indonesian Independence) and Perti (Persatuan Tarbiyah Islamiyah, the Islamic Educational Association).

seats but represented significant groups or communities: the Party of the Indonesian Islamic Union (Partai Sarekat Islam Indonesia, PSII), Parmusi, the Indonesian Christian [Protestant] Party (Partai Keristen Indonesia, Parkindo), and the Catholic Party (Partai Katholik). Of these various contingents in Parliament, the Development Group and the PNI, with 90 and 78 seats, were the largest, and the Protestant and Catholic Parties, with 17 and 15, the smallest. But all of them could be expected to play some role in cultural politics. On the average, 5.9 per cent of each of the eight sampling categories appeared in the sample. Of the total universe, the twenty men chosen constituted 5.4 per cent.

In an elected, voting, uncoerced house of representatives, numerical and political strengths are the same. The groups' margins of electoral victory and the size of their constituencies usually determine the number of seats (legislative votes) they control. In 1969, however, the Indonesian Parliament was not elected and did not vote. All members were appointed or approved by the government. Given the political power of the military generally and the fact that the legislature could not vote it down, it is not surprising that ABRI carried more than its numerical weight in Parliament.

As for the mainly civilian Development Group, which included mostly nonparty professional people—lawyers, students, intellectuals, and the like—it had less influence than its large size would suggest. A new and heterogeneous grouping, it was not united by religion or a common past as the other groups were; nor was it so able, beyond being vaguely "progovernment," to impose discipline on its members or to articulate a shared outlook. Nor, of course, did it have the authoritative position or coercive potential of ABRI.

I took these imbalances into account by slightly overrepresenting the three armed forces and slightly underrepresenting the Development Group, so that ABRI members made up 20 per cent of the sample, compared to 15 per cent of the universe, and the Development Group only 20 per cent, compared to 24 per cent of the universe. In no other case did a group's share in the sample deviate by more than one percentage point from its share of seats in the universe. Among officer-legislators were two brigadier generals, one colonel, and one lieutenant colonel (or equivalents), a distribution almost identical to that among the five officer-bureaucrats.

Although exact comparisons are difficult, the salaries of members of Parliament in 1969, including various allowances and increments, were certainly less than the salaries of the category F civil servants in the bureaucratic sample. This did not mean, however, that the DPR members had less total income than the administrators; some clearly did, but others were obviously much wealthier. Although almost all the members in both samples supplemented their incomes from other sources, there was much less variation in these outside amounts among bureaucrats.[8] The administrators held only two outside professional roles: soldier and teacher. They augmented their civil service pay through other means: for example, commercial cooking, sewing, and petty trading by their wives, or the sale at home of something bought abroad. Aside from the five officers and the two men who held teaching positions in addition to their civil service assignments, they were unambiguously bureaucrats.

Not so the members of Parliament. Between legislative sessions, if they were not traveling with a delegation or detained in Jakarta to work on a standing committee, they returned to their homes in the regions, taking up again whatever their "normal" job happened to be. Among my sample were officers in the armed forces, civilian government employees, businessmen, landowners, religious leaders, a newspaperman, and student, youth, and labor organizers. Some were full-time party politicians, and several fitted more than one of these descriptions. Legislators differed in socioeconomic status not only among but also within these categories. Beneath the "businessman" label, for example, could be found both Usman, a shopowner of modest means, and the wealthy manager of a nationwide business whose sphere of operations extended to Singapore and Hong Kong. Among the landowners were some whose effective holdings, including land registered in the names of friends and

8. As an army officer or an instructor in a public university, for example, a member of Parliament would already receive a salary from the state. In theory, the DPR would pay such a person only the difference between his legislator's salary and his other government wage, assuming the latter was lower; in practice, however, both incomes could sometimes be enjoyed. If the member's extralegislative income was from private sources and/or not in the form of a recorded fixed wage, he was still luckier, for adjustments in such cases were not even attempted.

relatives, were substantial and some who had plots just large enough to sustain the families who worked them.

The parliamentary sample was also geographically dispersed. Less than half were permanent residents of Jakarta, and among these all but two had relatives in the provinces and were in the habit of returning there during legislative recesses. Most of the bureaucrats also had close kin in the regions whom they visited periodically, but these men were obliged by the year-round nature of their jobs to reside in Jakarta. Several of the legislators, in contrast, lived in Bandung with their families and managed to return home almost every weekend.

In Jakarta the legislators lived in a variety of neighborhoods, many on an ad hoc basis with friends or relatives or in government hostels; one even slept on a couch in the office of the organization he represented. Those who had their own homes in the capital lived for the most part not in the posh Menteng area but in more crowded, noisier surroundings toward the port or on the less urbanized outskirts of town. A few of these homes were well furnished, with a telephone, an icebox, and the large nature-scene paintings and stuffed Sumatran tiger typical of the houses of prominent people in Jakarta. But many had no refrigerator, and one had neither phone nor electricity. Most of the legislators did not own cars. Again, however, the generalization conceals the variety; several civilian members relied entirely on buses, while the generals had chauffeurs and at least one official-business vehicle apiece.

The age of the two samples followed the same pattern of legislative diversity and bureaucratic homogeneity. At the time I interviewed them, the administrators' mean age was 48, the legislators' 45. A more striking difference lay in the shapes of the two distributions. Although the bureaucrats' years of birth ranged across two decades (1912–1931), the mean, median, and mode (respectively, the average, middle, and most common year) all coincided in 1920. The politicians' range was over three decades (1908–1938), and their mean, median, and mode were all different: 1923, 1921, and 1938, respectively.

To summarize, by age, residence, and socioeconomic status, the legislators were a dispersed and differentiated group compared to the administrators. And in this contrast can be seen the old difference between the more representative Volksraad-CSI-BPKI-PPKI and the more monolithic precolonial-postcolonial administrative elite. Both the contemporary contrast and the historical difference can be seen in the first of the two main generalizations, restated below, to be explored in chapters 4 and 5.

According to the institutional hypothesis, the socialization, recruitment, and historic dominance of the bureaucratic elite have made it more homogeneous, more cosmopolitan, and more powerful than Parliament. In turn, these advantages—the homogeneity and historical weight of the bureaucracy that facilitate identification with it by its senior officials, those officials' preferred social and educational position, and their overall power superiority compared to members of Parliament—should engender in members of the bureaucratic elite a more positive, less distrustful outlook on their changing environment. According to the cultural minority hypothesis, members of religious or ethnic minorities, whether by affiliation or the intensity with which it is kept, have felt disadvantaged in life compared to cultural majorities and have developed a strong in-group identity. These minorities should therefore be more defensively negative in their orientations toward majoritarian society and toward social change under majority auspices. Insofar as cultural minorities are more widely represented in Parliament than in central administration, the two propositions should be reinforcing.

Chapter 4 on the experiences of the elite will emphasize the first parts of the propositions; chapter 5 on orientations will explore the second parts. Along the way other dimensions of elite political culture and its contexts will be identified and related to these core generalizations.

CHAPTER 4

EXPERIENCES

Distortions in the recollected past are conscious or unconscious. From the interviewer's standpoint, while the second kind cannot be avoided, the first can. In Indonesia in 1969, the elite was more inclined consciously to alter or hide the recent than the further past (Surjowidjojo's account, given below, was an exception). Left-wing political positions legitimate under the Old Order had become dangerous under the New; the afterimages of that violent transition were still vivid, its repercussions still being felt. "Communist subversion" still preoccupied the military and, through them, the media. Letters certifying noninvolvement in the attempted coup of October 1, 1965, were still widely required for entrance into schools and jobs. Jails and camps around the country were still receiving persons suspected of leftist connections. Sukarno was neutralized, but alive; Suharto's full presidency had only just begun—in March 1968. One of the twenty administrators in my sample was, in fact, arrested—and later released—during the interview phase in 1969; he had apparently allowed a relative with some indirect connection to the outlawed Indonesian Communist Party (Partai Komunis Indonesia, PKI) to stay in his home.

Morally, if not operationally as well, interviewing in depth requires scrupulous respect for the individual; in addition, I was interested in enduring patterns of affiliation and experience likely to bear on general attitudes toward society, not in the painful self-justifications of people whose previous associations might, in the light of some current orthodoxy, make them want to "set the record straight." Many informants talked about recent events, but I only asked an individual about them if I was sure that the confidence established between us would not be jeopardized.

In relation to the further past, say before the late 1950's, when Sukarno's Guided Democracy began to take shape, distortions were not absent, but they tended to be of the unconscious kind. Some administrators, for example, romanticized the tranquillity of the colonial order; some politicians exaggerated their roles in the revolution. Purwoko and Usman are cases in point. But these were not deliberate embellishments, and they did reveal how a characteristic orientation toward peaceful stability or violent change had grown out of experiences and how the memory of those experiences had been enhanced to fit more perfectly the orientation.

This chapter takes up first the parental status and social origins of the members of my samples and the nature and intensity of their ethnic and religious ties; moves on through the socializing impact of their fathers and siblings, of the schools they went to and the associations they joined; and then considers the terms of their encounters with the Japanese occupation, the Indonesian revolution, and, lastly, the bureaucratic and legislative institutions they were affiliated with in 1969. After being presented, this evidence is summarized and related to my guiding propositions: that the bureaucratic elite is more homogeneous and cosmopolitan than the legislative elite, and that members of cultural minorities feel themselves disadvantaged compared to cultural majorities.

Family Status: Bureaucratic Continuity

One way of situating someone by social status is to locate him in a genealogy. Almost all members of both samples could recall the names of their great-grandparents, but some could trace their ancestries from memory in astonishing detail. Several of these latter genealogies were regarded by their beneficiaries as important sources of personal status. The dazzling bloodline of Drs. Harun, an urbane and world-traveled Sumatran whose title signified possession of a master's degree, wended its way back across twenty-three generations of kings and saints, picking up ancestral glitter at almost every bend. One cascade of names descended from a royal source in Kalimantan, another from a former kingdom in western Sumatra, yet another from Dang Hyang Dwijendra, the great sage of Majapahit and the father-founder of the Balinese priestly caste.

Apart from the lustre they offered, these ancestral chains were malleable. Through selective recollection they could be reinterpreted in the light of changing criteria of contemporary status. The ancestry of an individual is one history he can reannotate with little fear of contradiction. An illustration is provided by Surjowidjojo (Surjo for short), a Javanese member of Parliament who traced his descent, down a route he admitted was rather indirect, from a deified lord of Majapahit. Surjo had been a nationalist in the revolution and was vocally antifeudal. He took pains to show how a fork in his originally high-royal genealogy had led to his current position as a man of the people. (He was the only member of the legislative sample who had ever been elected to the DPR—in 1955.) Among his great-great-grandfather's sons, he said, was one who grew up to be a patih and another who was "just a peasant." The patih fathered a succession of Dutch-appointed civil servants, but the peasant's descendants were village officials, elected by the people, and it was this latter line that had produced Surjowidjojo. With a supernatural lord for a distant relative and one helpful corrective bifurcation, Surjo could relate himself simultaneously to the sacral, hierarchical past and to the modern preference for a democratic, defeudalized future. In fact, Surjo's father and grandfather had been, not village heads like Purwoko's father, but officials responsible for several villages; and Surjo's great-grandfather, the patih's younger brother, was probably not "just a peasant" but a man of some wealth or position.[1]

Administrators and legislators were about equally inclined to claim noble relations; but along a less manipulable and far more important dimension of childhood status—father's occupation—a different picture emerged. First, noble persons and high priyayis were scarcely represented among the fathers of the elite; second,

1. In 1974, a popular magazine published an article claiming that President Suharto was descended from royalty. Although the president made a dramatic public show of rejecting the story and raffirming his peasant origin, his denial appeared to open a small loophole for those familiar with kraton customs in the Yogyakarta region, where he was born, to believe that he might have some royal blood in his veins after all. If that loophole was intentional, Suharto, like Surjo, may have been accommodating the preferences of democrats and aristocrats together. Whatever the truth of the matter, the affair underscores the political importance of elite genealogy in Indonesia. As for the offending journal, it was shut down and its editor tried and sentenced to a prison term. On the affair, see the Jakarta press in late 1974 and early 1975; the interpretation cited above was only one of several circulating privately in Yogyakarta at the time.

the bureaucratic elite showed markedly greater status continuity than the legislative. Table 1 makes both points.

Table 1.   Father's primary occupational status and sector

Primary occupational status	Administrators		Legislators		Totals	
Public sector						
Royalty	–		1		1	
Subdistrict head (assisten wedana)	2		1		3	
Railroad official	1		2		3	
Village head	2		1		3	
Schoolteacher	4		1		5	
Other official	6		2		8	
Totals	15	[78.9]	8	[42.1]	23	[60.5]
Private sector						
Businessman	1		4		5	
Landowning peasant	1		3		4	
Craftsman	2		2		4	
Petty retailer	–		1		1	
Landless peasant	–		1		1	
Totals	4	[21.1]	11	[57.9]	15	[39.5]
Grand totals	19	[100.0]	19	[100.0]	38	[100.0]

Note: Aside from the primary occupations shown, a number of fathers had secondary jobs and sources of income. One was a shadow play puppeteer, several were engaged in trade, and almost all either owned or had access to agricultural or commercial land. For two individuals, no information on father's occupation was obtained. Here and henceforth, brackets enclose percentages.

The father of only one individual could qualify by blood and position as royalty. By the time my informants were born, well into the twentieth century, the Dutch had either destroyed or, more often, bureaucratized the indigenous nobility. The great majority of the Javanese had priyayi backgrounds, but this was evidence of administrative status, not royal parents.[2] The office and

2. Observers have not always made this distinction between the bureaucratic elite and the blood nobility. For example, in his *Social Status and Power in Java* (London: Athlone Press, 1960), pp. 81–83, Leslie Palmier equated nobility with priyayis, although he did distinguish a higher (hereditary) from a lower (occupational) nobility. I prefer to recognize an overlapping but by no means identical Javanese hereditary nobility (*ndara*) and

the book of accounts had already replaced the palace and the golden umbrella. The one son of royalty was not even Javanese. Most of the fathers of the elite were officials of the colonial government.

The occupational status of only two fathers, Usman's and Sumarno's, can be considered economically depressed. Neither father either owned land or could afford to send his son to a Dutch-language primary school. But the important point about these two fathers is that they both died when their sons were very young. Usman's story has already been told. After the death of Sumarno's father, the boy's mother packed him off to be raised by relatives on his father's side who were better off than she. They accepted him, but, for reasons Sumarno did not relate, forbade him any further contact with his mother; he never saw her again. The early deaths of these fathers meant that low parental status could not harden in a mold of visibly inherited social inferiority to constrain the children's sense of what they could become. In each case, the child was ejected from the nuclear family altogether and left to make his way on his own or with the help of relatives. Had these parents lived, and the sons stayed at home, Usman and Sumarno might not have risen as high as they did. With the exception of these two fathers and the ambiguous case of a third—whose social status was similarly low but whose carefully accumulated income from the stall where he sold fruits, cigarettes, and other small items had at least bought an education for his son—the fathers of the sample members were all in the middle and upper strata of colonial society.

Between a fourth and a third of the thirty-eight fathers whose primary occupations were identified could be said to have been unusually wealthy. Among the five businessmen, for example, one owned a factory, another a plantation, and two others big stores, while the fifth was a large-scale trader. Two of the three subdistrict heads were also very wealthy, as were at least one of the craftsmen (a goldsmith) and two of the "other officials" (a slaughterhouse head and an irrigation expert). Those who lived and worked in villages tended to form a rural elite, the village chiefs and school-

bureaucratic elite (priyayi). On the ndara-priyayi distinction, see Koent-jaraningrat, "Javanese of South Central Java"; Sartono, *Peasants' Revolt*, p. 50, n. 84.

teachers among them; although seldom as rich as their counterparts in the cities, they lived in comfort and enjoyed great respect.

Among the sample members who came from wealthy families
were Hadiwidjaja and Wiradiwarsa (Hadi and Wira for short).
Their childhoods and Usman's or Sumarno's were poles apart.
Hadi, a high-ranking military officer and bureaucrat, had not been
burdened with household chores as a child; there were servants for
that. His father's career as a colonial official won the old man a
medal, but it was the land he owned and rented out—some 200
hectares—that guaranteed the family a materially good life. Each
tenant, who might in turn have several people beneath him actually
tilling the land, paid Hadi's father in cash an amount equal to the
sale price of 50 per cent of the crop after taxes. Hadi's father, who
liked to keep his relationships businesslike and had a talent for
accounting, wrote down all these transactions in his credit book,
keeping an eye on the crop market to make sure that his tenants
were not understating the sale price. —Although in those days,—
Hadi added, a little wistfully, —the price of rice was generally
stable, so that everyone knew what it should be.— Wiradiwarsa, a
member of Parliament, remembered how, in the palmy times before
the depression of the 1930's, he could order the coolies on his
father's tea plantation to collect crickets for him and his friends to
match in combat; how he rode the train to school in the city on
weekdays and filled his holidays with swimming and table tennis.
Both Hadi and Wira grew up in the rich agricultural heartland of
western Java.

The bulk of the sample fathers fell between the extremes of
wealth and poverty, but closer to the former. About three-fifths of
of them were in public service (see Table 1), an indication of that
sector's ongoing importance as a source of the politico-administra-
tive elite. Within that sector, however, an important change had
occurred. The prewar elite had been recruited mainly from the
nobility and the territorial administration. Table 1 shows the results of the functional differentiation of government service in the
Indies in the first decades of this century. The technical services—
railroading and "other" government jobs such as irrigation, forestry, and land surveying—account for a significant portion of elite
fathers. There are no regents, or even district heads, and, as already
noted, only one member of royalty, but instead, to stretch an old

category, "new priyayis" (in the technical services) and "lesser priyayis" (public primary school teachers, village heads, and territorial administrators beneath the district head).

Table 1 also shows two marked differences in recruitment to elite status between the bureaucracy and the legislature. Whereas a large majority (four-fifths) of the administrators were sons of public officials, a majority (three-fifths) of the legislators' fathers were in the private sector. Parliament, if these samples are an accurate representation, had nearly three times as many private-sector sons as the bureaucracy. In addition, the range and variety of occupational origins among members of Parliament—from wealth and royalty down to the landless peasantry—were substantially wider than among bureaucrats, who tended to carry on a tradition of government service.

The military component in the samples bears special mention. One of the rationales sometimes offered by Indonesian generals to justify their dual (politico-military) role in national life is that the armed forces sprang from the people as a revolutionary guerrilla movement and are consequently more representative of the nation as a whole, and less a product of the colonial past, than the narrowly recruited civilian political elite. The military has indeed provided channels of upward mobility for low status individuals, but a broadly recruited soldiery need not imply a socially representative officer corps. Proportionally most overrepresented among the eight officers' compared to the thirty civilians' fathers represented in Table 1 were businessmen, economically the single most advantaged group. As for service in the colonial regime, the proportions of officers and civilians whose fathers had worked for it in one capacity or another were almost identical (about three-fifths in each group). However, *within* the two institutions of administration and Parliament, the social origins of the officers did have a diversifying effect. Among the civilians the ratio of public to private sector sons in the bureaucracy was an overwhelming 7:1; among officers it was 1:1. In the legislative sample, the ratio among civilians was 1:2, among officers 3:1. Although military and civilian components were about equally narrowly recruited in the elite as a whole, the effect of officer participation in the two institutions was to diversify them.

Before leaving the subject of bureaucratic continuity, the question should be asked: through what mechanisms did it operate? One possibility is that the bureaucrats' fathers—nearly four-fifths of whom worked in the public sector—had a greater formative impact on their sons' lives than the fathers of the legislators. The more important the father in his son's eyes, according to this logic, the more likely the son would be to follow in his footsteps.

Table 2 supports this possibility. Bureaucrats' fathers were remembered as having a stronger impact on their sons than legislators' fathers on their sons. The contrast between Purwoko the

Table 2. Father's impact as remembered by son

	Absent	Weak	Moderate	Strong	Totals
Administrators	3 [16.7]	4 [22.2]	3 [16.7]	8 [44.4]	18 [100.0]
Legislators	4 [21.1]	7 [36.8]	7 [36.8]	1 [5.3]	19 [100.0]
Totals	7 [18.9]	11 [29.7]	10 [27.0]	9 [24.3]	37 [99.9]

Note: "Absent" means that father and son were separated by death or departure when the son was very young. "Weak" means that the memories of his father expressed by the son were few and insignificant, either because of infrequent contact or early separation or because the father made little impression on the son. "Moderate" means that in the son's recollection the father exerted some influence over the son in a family situation involving fairly frequent and significant son-father contact. A "strong" father loomed very large in his son's memory as a decisive referent in the boy's life. Three respondents could not be classified because of inadequate information. In a dichotomous version of this variable, moderate-intensity informants were reallocated to the extremes.

administrator, with a strongly influential father, and Usman the politician, with an absent one, held for the full samples. Whereas eight, or 44 per cent, of the bureaucratic fathers made strong impressions on their sons, only one (5 per cent) of the legislative fathers did. Whereas nearly three-fifths of the politicians remembered their fathers as either weakly influential or absent, less than two-fifths of the bureaucrats did. Seven of the eight strong fathers of administrators worked in the public sector—as village heads, teachers, and officials of the colonial state and its appurtenances—while of the fifteen bureaucrats whose fathers were in public service seven, or nearly half, remembered their fathers as having a strong impact on them.

From those memories emerged a portrait of the typical strong father as an energetic, oak-willed man who was strict with his son in the interest of the boy's advancement. Whereas mother-son relationships in these families were remembered as comparatively warm and loving, toward their fathers the sons recalled feelings of respect, deference, and, occasionally, fear. This distance from the strong father stemmed in part from customary parental role differences; mothers spent more time with their children than did fathers who worked and traveled outside the home. But influential fathers also often encouraged distance as a condition of manly self-reliance. For example, one administrator, Lieutenant Colonel Suhardi, grew up an eldest male child with a strong-willed influential father. As recounted in our conversations, two of Suhardi's most vivid memories were of going to new schools, first the Dutch-language elementary HIS several miles from his home and later the Western-style junior secondary school (Meer Uitgebreid Lager Onderwijs, MULO) in a city where he lived away from his parents. Young Suhardi had been sent off for the first time to each of these institutions unaccompanied by relatives or even a household servant— despite the boy's anxiety and reluctance to make the trips alone— because his father wanted to teach him to be independent. Tousling his own young son's hair as he recalled these experiences, Suhardi swore that he would never be so cruel to his children. But he admired his father for trying to instill in him feelings of self-confidence. His father used to stress to Suhardi that the Dutch were ordinary people, no better than anyone else, and that Suhardi should not fear them. Whenever Dutchmen came to the house, Suhardi remembered, his father made a point of treating them neither better nor worse than he would a Javanese colleague or acquaintance.

Most of these sons remembered their fathers as strict disciplinarians when it came to schooling. Ibrahim Lubis, an administrator and an eldest son like Suhardi, had a father who could neither speak nor read Dutch, but in the evenings when the son was doing homework, the father would come and stand behind him. Suddenly the old man would point to a page of the Dutch textbook open on the table and ask for a translation, just to make sure that Ibrahim was keeping up with his studies. Ibrahim would hastily summarize the page and his father, satisfied, would go away.

His father also encouraged Ibrahim's self-confidence and allayed his fears even while sharing them. The father, for example, believed that malevolent spirits inhabited certain trees. Yet he would joke about such "superstitions" to build up the boy's courage. As they were walking past a cemetery one night, Ibrahim worried aloud that the spirits of the dead might come alive to bother them. The father replied jovially that since most of the cemetery's inhabitants were from the Lubis clan, the boy should instead welcome the chance to meet some of his relatives.

Ibrahim's schooling was a controversial matter. The Lubises had been village heads in north-central Sumatra for generations. Ibrahim's grandfather, fearing that a Western education would turn the boy away from this ancestral calling, objected vehemently when the time came for Ibrahim to be sent to a Dutch-language primary school. But Ibrahim's father, who had only spent five years in a vernacular-tongue village primary school learning a few basic skills, wanted his son to get more of an education than he had had, to be able to converse with Dutchmen on their own terms. His father prevailed, and Ibrahim went off, first to an HIS not far away and later to a MULO in Medan, Sumatra's largest city, repeating the pattern of progress through Western schools followed by Suhardi and many other administrators. Another of these was Abdul Rasjid. For the sake of his education, his father refused to follow a local custom whereby young boys, once circumcised, slept in the Muslim prayerhouse; the boy was made to spend the nights at home instead. The prayerhouse, Abdul remembered his father saying, did not have lights to read by, so how could the son prepare himself there for the modern (Western) education he should have?

Finally, these strong-impact fathers had occupational ambitions for their sons. Ibrahim's father wanted him to become an administrator or a teacher: the former because it involved giving orders instead of taking them, the latter because it meant working only half a day. Other strong fathers were similarly decisive. Virtually all preferred administrative work for their sons or, failing that, a teaching career; a few almost physically propelled their sons along these lines.

Moderately and weakly influential fathers were less strict, but many of them also cared less. Their expectations were few and lighter, for they had invested less emotional energy in their sons' futures. They attached less importance to whether their sons became public officials or did something else, and this attitude, at least as it was later recalled by their sons, showed less a sense of respect for a boy's freedom than simple indifference. Insofar as the authoritarian firmness of the strong fathers followed from genuine concern, their sons felt on the whole more advantaged than not.

If administrators tended to be the sons of strong fathers, did they also tend to be earlier born sons, and therefore more likely to have been moved into bureaucratic careers by the greater weight of their fathers' expectations? Comparing sons of the same father and mother, subtracting sisters, and excluding siblings who died in infancy, in order to focus on a limited set of most likely competitors for fatherly career expectations, the administrators were indeed slightly more likely to fall above the median birthrank than were the legislators. Yet even a measure refined in this manner is imperfect. One administrator who had thirteen siblings, most of whom survived infancy, grew up virtually as an only child because he was the only one to live past the age of seven. In another case, an elder half-brother appears to have received greater attention and guidance from the father than the individual who by the above measure would qualify as the eldest male. Overall, the evidence merely suggests that sibling rank could be an intervening variable between a strong-willed, public sector father and his son's future membership in the bureaucratic elite.

The data do show a high proportion of older sons in the two samples taken as a whole. More than two-thirds of the thirty-seven individuals for whom information was obtained were older or oldest children (including sisters). The relationship between elder sibling rank and elite status appears especially strong for socioeconomically more advantaged families in which the older son did not have to suspend his own training to provide for his younger siblings. Finally, half of the Javanese members of the elite were eldest children, compared to less than a fifth of the non-Javanese, and, as the next section will show, the Javanese are also overrepresented in the bureaucratic sample. But the evidence that sibling rank affects bureaucratic elite continuity is weaker than the case for father's impact doing so.

To recapitulate the findings of this section, the samples showed marked intergenerational continuity in elite status. The members' fathers were typically men who enjoyed fairly high social status or substantial wealth, or both, under the colonial state. Continuity was especially pronounced in the bureaucratic elite. This evidence is consistent with the picture of administrative continuity drawn in chapter 1 and, for Purwoko, chapter 2. The samples also support the earlier impression from historical evidence of greater diversity in the legislature. Compared to fathers of the bureaucratic elite, the legislators' fathers not only were much more likely to have worked in the private sector, but also spanned a greater range of occupations. By this measure, the administrative elite was more homogeneous. Like the civilians in the samples, the officers were mainly recruited from among the sons of advantaged social strata. They did, however, diversify the samples in that they tended to reverse the public or private character of the recruitment base typical of each institution. Finally, the continuity of the bureaucratic elite appeared to be at least partly the result of the greater and more career-shaping impact of the administrators' fathers on their sons, and perhaps especially on their elder sons.

Ethnicity, Religion: Overlapping Majorities

Since the Javanese priyayis were the mainstay of the colonial administration and kept this position, shaken but essentially intact, through the occupation and beyond independence, it might be expected that the bureaucratic sample would include a high proportion of Javanese. This expectation is borne out. Two-thirds of the administrators were Javanese (Table 3). Of the remaining seven, four were Sundanese from West Java who had been raised in upper class families that were somewhat more purely Islamic in atmosphere than their Javanese priyayi counterparts but had also been influenced by Javanese abangan culture. A Balinese, a Batak, and a Minangkabau completed the sample.

Once again, by comparison, the legislators were diverse. Javanese were most numerous among them but made up less than half of the parliamentary sample and were accompanied by three Sundanese, two Minangkabaus from West Sumatra, a Banjarese from Kalimantan, an indigenous Jakartan, an Indonesian of Chinese descent, and one man apiece from three small groups on three different islands in the eastern reaches of the archipelago.

Table 3 suggests that the ethnic intensity of the elite is not strikingly high. Ethnicity was a very important part of the self-

Table 3. Ethnic affiliations and their strength

	Ethnic affiliation	Strength of ethnic affiliation			Totals	
		Weak	Medium	Strong		
Administrators						
	Javanese	7	3	3	13	[65.0]
	Non-Javanese	2	3	2	7	[35.0]
Totals		9	6	5	20	[100.0]
Legislators						
	Javanese	4	3	2	9	[45.0]
	Non-Javanese	3	6	2	11	[55.0]
Totals		7	9	4	20	[100.0]
Grand totals		16	15	9	40	

Note: Strength of ethnic affiliation is the importance of his ethnicity to an individual's self-image as revealed in his behavior, verbal and nonverbal. A person who was married to a Javanese, who had an intense interest in Javanese history or culture, who used Javanese expressions with some frequency, and who tended to contrast the Javanese favorably with other ethnic groups in Indonesia, for example, was considered a "strong" Javanese. "Weakly" ethnic informants were those for whom very few of these indicators were present. "Medium" is an intermediate category. In a dichotomous version of this variable, medium-intensity informants were reallocated to the extremes.

definition of less than a fourth of the men interviewed. However, the table conceals some subtleties. All of these men considered themselves Indonesians, including the one person of Chinese descent who had taken an Indonesian name. But they were well aware of their ethnic origins and of ethnic distinctions in Indonesia generally. They were not indifferent to ethnicity; it cropped up in reference to others if not always to themselves. But they had more or less subsumed ethnic we-feeling under a broader sense of being Indonesian. The acquisition of a national identity had been for most of these informants, especially the older ones, a highly successful but highly self-conscious process.[3]

The process can be seen to have operated in two phases of the socialization of these elites. First, in the Indies, many of these men obtained Dutch-language secondary and higher educations in com-

3. In his *Ethnicity, Party, and National Integration: An Indonesian Case Study* (New Haven: Yale University Press, 1970), esp. ch. 7, R. William Liddle argued similarly that ethnic identity has been incorporated into national identity, not replaced by it.

pany with students from all over the archipelago. By bringing them together and giving them a shared sense of class status that cut across their disparate ethnic and regional origins, the colonial school system played an integrative role. Second, the still rather abstract Indonesian identities of most of the elite took concrete shape in the vivid experience of a national revolution. But the struggle to realize the Indonesian idea did not, through some unifying imperative, simply override ethnic and regional differences. The politicization of these differences in fact made them more explosive than before. The elite consciously reinterpreted them, in the revolutionary context, as divisive givens to be transcended. Bound as it was to a unique historical experience, that view became less and less realistic the more the nation-making achievement of the revolution could be taken for granted.

Table 3 shows that the bureaucrats were more Javanese than the legislators in a quantitative sense. Were they qualitatively more Javanese too, in terms of the intensity of their sense of ethnic belonging? At the extreme, such a combination could mean that the most intensely committed members of the Javanese majority in one institution are pitted against ethnic minority group members and more weakly identifying Javanese in the other. In fact, however, strength of ethnic affiliation cuts across the institutional line; Javanese administrators were actually less intensely ethnic than Javanese members of Parliament. These data do not support the picture of an aggressively Javanizing bureaucratic elite using its institutional position to promote ethnic ends. On the other hand, the overrepresentation of Javanese in the bureaucracy could encourage such a view among persons who already feel themselves disadvantaged on ethnic grounds. From this circumstantial evidence, an institutional version of ethnic grievances as an issue in cultural politics appears more latent than actual.

What of the cultural group hypothesis? If members of ethnic minorities were more strongly ethnic than the Javanese majority they might be more likely to perceive ethnic aggrandizement by the Javanese bureaucratic elite because of an already heightened sense of identification with their own ethnic groups. For such individuals, ethnic defensiveness could be as natural a stance as religious defensiveness for a similarly "doubled" (quantitative and qualitative) religious minority. Table 3 gives some support to this possibility. Ignoring institutional affiliation, proportionally as many Javanese had strong ethnic identities as did non-Javanese. But whereas half of all the Javanese were weakly ethnic, only a little over a fourth of the non-Javanese were; and whereas half of the non-Javanese were medium-strength ethnics, only slightly over a fourth of the Javanese were. These are not dramatic differences, but they do suggest a picture of the elite in which more strongly committed ethnic minority groups on the one hand face a more weakly ethnic but numerically predominant Javanese majority on the other.

Table 4. Religious affiliations and their strength

	Religious affiliation	Strength of religious affiliation			
		Weak	Medium	Strong	Totals
Administrators					
	Muslim	13	4	1	18
	Catholic	1	–	–	1
	Hindu	–	–	1	1
Totals		14 [70.0]	4 [20.0]	2 [10.0]	20 [100.0]
Legislators					
	Muslim	8	2	7	17
	Catholic	–	1	–	1
	Protestant	–	1	1	2
Totals		8 [40.0]	4 [20.0]	8 [40.0]	20 [100.0]
Grand totals		22 [55.0]	8 [20.0]	10 [25.0]	40 [100.0]

Note: Strength of religious affiliation is the importance of his religion to an individual's self-image as revealed in his behavior, verbal and nonverbal. Someone in whose conversation references to Islam were frequent, who was observed to pray, and on whose walls hung Koranic invocations, for example, was considered a "strong" Muslim. (In several cases, independent assessments were unobtrusively elicited from friends and family to ensure that an image of piety projected in an interview situation was in fact genuine; in every case, it was.) "Medium"-strength Muslims were individuals who normally kept the fast, for whom the Islamic religion was not insignificant as a personal referent, but who neither prayed regularly nor referred frequently to their religion. The "weakly" religious were those whose formal affiliation affected their self-image and behavior minimally or not at all. Religiosity here refers to one of the world religions; a "weak" Muslim might be a private mystic. In a dichotomous version of this variable, "medium" and "strong" were combined as one category. There were no atheists or antireligious persons in the samples, and only one informant had actually married someone of a different religion (compared to five who married across ethnic lines).

Table 4 presents comparable evidence on religious affiliations and their strength. A first clear impression is that, as with ethnic affiliations and their strength, the numerical majority is qualitatively weak. Nearly 90 per cent of the men interviewed were Muslims, but among them "weak" religious identities were proportionally three times more common than among non-Muslims. If a score is assigned to each individual according to his religious intensity (0 = weak; 1 = medium; 2 = strong), if Muslim and non-Muslim scores are averaged separately, and if it is assumed that one average score can be legitimately expressed as a fraction or multiple of another, non-Muslim religious identities (0.6) can be said to be only half as strong as Muslim identities (1.2).

The prevalence of "weak" Muslims—sometimes called "statistical" in Indonesia because they are counted as Muslims in official statistics even though they rarely practice Islam—has an institutional and an ethnic aspect. Nearly two-thirds of the nominal Muslims in the two samples were bureaucrats; in contrast, the legislative sample was almost equally balanced between weak and strong Muslims. The more finely the samples are divided, the less representative are the resulting subsamples, but it is nevertheless noteworthy that among bureaucrats more than four-fifths of the weak Muslims had fathers in the public sector, whereas only half of the medium-strength Muslims did.[4] In other words, the greater part of the weakly Muslim majority among these forty men was made up of persons who were at least second-generation public officials. Again the survey and the historical evidence are consistent, for in this continuity—and, at its core, the linkage of abangan outlook with priyayi status—can be seen perpetuated the old Dutch-fostered distance between the native administration and "fanatic Islam." The picture of a culturally homogeneous bureaucracy compared to a more heterogeneous Parliament is further supported.

Roughly speaking, the smaller the ethnic group the stronger its Islamic identity. Among Javanese Muslims in the samples, 71 per cent adhered only nominally to their religion; among Sundanese

4. One of the thirteen weak Muslim administrators could not be included in this calculation because his father's occupation was not known. Since there was only a single strong Muslim in the administrative sample, he was not included either; his father, however, was a public official.

Muslims the figure was 57 per cent, among Minangkabau Muslims 33 per cent, and among Muslims of all other ethnic origins 25 per cent (see Table 5). Heirs to an important Hindu-Buddhist tradition predating the coming of Islam, the Javanese, of all the predominantly Muslim ethnic groups, had one of the most prolonged and embracing acquaintances with the secularizing colonial state. The other group that experienced similarly long and pervasive colonial contact was the Sundanese, but their cultural milieu and governing elite, although close to the Javanese and not lacking in pre-Islamic models, were on the whole more thoroughly and devoutly Muslim. Among the Minangkabaus and other groups Islam shows its strength. But the proportionally stronger ties to Islam of these ethnic minorities do not begin to counterbalance the single dominant (upper leftmost) cell in Table 5: the abangan Javanese.

As for the non-Muslims, their distribution in Table 5 conforms in still more extreme fashion to this pattern. The one Javanese non-Muslim had a weak religious identity; none of the four non-Javanese non-Muslims did. Again roughly speaking, size of ethnic group and strength of affiliation to any religion were inversely related.

The cultural minority hypothesis is supported: more strongly religious ethnic minorities appear to face a more weakly religious but numerically predominant Javanese majority. Again the phenomenon of the doubled minority emerges. The fact of being both outnumbered by and more religious than the nominally Muslim Javanese could make strongly Islamic outer islanders more likely to see themselves as discriminated against by a militantly abangan Javanese majority.

How accurate would that negative perception be? How naturally anti-Islamic is the mainly abangan viewpoint of the Javanese majority? Generalizing from the Purwoko-Usman comparison, I suggested that the abangan and santri categories in early elite socialization were more extensions than negations of each other, that what really drove apart the groups defined by these labels were political considerations, that abangan antipathy toward rigorous Islam and vice versa may be more a matter of adult political socialization than a reflection of sharp mass cleavages learned early in life. Is this true for the full samples?

Basically, yes. From the santri side, Usman did not pick up a hostile view of abangan Islam as a child, and his sense of being a

Table 5. Religious affiliations and their strength, by major ethnic group

	Javanese			Sundanese			Minangkabaus			Others			Totals		
	\multicolumn{15}{c}{Strength of religious affiliation}
	W	M	S	W	M	S	W	M	S	W	M	S	W	M	S
Muslim	15	3	3	4	1	2	1	1	1	1	1	2	21	6	8
Catholic	1	–	–	–	–	–	–	–	–	–	1	–	1	1	–
Protestant	–	–	–	–	–	–	–	–	–	–	1	1	–	1	1
Hindu	–	–	–	–	–	–	–	–	–	–	–	1	–	–	1
Totals	16	3	3	4	1	2	1	1	1	1	3	4	22	8	10

Note: W = weak, M = medium, S = strong, as defined for Table 4.

committed Muslim, which took a highly political form, was acquired as a young adult in the revolutionary Hizbullah and later in his Islamic party. In Purwoko's childhood, the kraton and the Western school played a religiously more pre-emptive role, but his case is balanced by those of several other abangan members of the samples whose experiences ran more nearly parallel to Usman's.

One of the latter is Ahmad Sutikno, like Purwoko a weakly Muslim high official in one of the larger ministries. Compared to Purwoko's father, Ahmad's was much more interested in Islam, but he too remained a culturally mainstream Javanese. Ahmad remembered his father as a self-made "priyayi Muslim" who had worked his way up to a position of some responsibility in the colonial forestry service. In the father's mind, Islam and abangan values had been partly blended, partly compartmentalized; he had discovered his political identity in being a Muslim, his cultural identity in being an abangan Javanese. In the 1920's, in the area in which the family lived, feelings of resentment against the Chinese merchants, whose economic power and political contacts in Dutch colonial circles gave them unassailable strength in the marketplace, were running high. Sharing these feelings, Ahmad's father decided to join the Sarekat Islam. Once in the party he helped set up retail cooperatives among (Islamic) Javanese that could withstand the competition of the (non-Islamic) Chinese. Ahmad's father never became either a "fanatic Muslim" or an antagonist of the colonial government—he preferred to remain with the cooperative Tjokro-aminoto wing of the party—so he was never in danger of losing his job. Islam was simply a counterdefinition to the non-Muslim Chinese and a political means of cutting into the latter's monopoly. At home the obligations of Islam were undertaken irregularly or not at all. Ahmad's father was more interested in the wayang, which he loved to watch and even write about. As a grown man, Ahmad treasured an heirloom common among deeply Javanese families: a picture of an upside-down banyan tree whose branches were covered with notes on Javanese genealogy and philosophy; his father had drawn it in a spidery hand years before.

For Ahmad, growing up in his father's house, abangan and santri outlooks were not opposed. Shorn of its behavioral demands upon the believer, Islam blended naturally into the world of wayang. Ahmad remembered in particular an evening when his father told him the story of how Yudistira, eldest and purest in heart of the five Pandawa brothers, met his end. All of Yudistira's brothers had long since died, but he could not; he felt he still lacked something, he knew not what, something that would enable him to end his life a completely fulfilled man. One day he met Sunan Kalijaga, one of the nine great Muslim missionaries who, according to tradition, spread Islam through Java. All my brothers have died, he told Sunan Kalijaga; but I still seek fulfillment. Where is it to be found? In response, Sunan Kalijaga looked at Yudistira's magic weapon, a piece of paper that had been written on, folded, and tucked into Yudistira's headpiece, and asked what it was. That is the Kalimasada [the weapon's name], answered Yudistira. No, replied Kalijaga, that is the kalima syahadat [the Islamic confession of faith]. Whereupon Yudistira took the paper, opened it, and read, in Arabic, "There is no God but Allah; Muhammad is His Prophet." The instant he completed this first obligatory act of all Muslims, Yudistira entered the ummat, gained life's perfection, and died a completed man, a Muslim. This story echoes the village kiyai's interpretation of wayang to Usman from the other side of the abangan-santri line.

Names and words were important to Ahmad's father. In keeping with Yudistira's example, which showed that for a man of pure intentions it was sufficient to recite the words of witness to "become a Muslim," he gave his sons Arabic names, as if their names alone would make them Muslims. As for their behavior, the father brought them up not as devout santris, let alone future kiyais, but as abangan priyayis, eclectic enough in religious outlook to enjoy the partly Islamicized meanings of the wayang and looking to careers in government service for social prestige and material welfare.

Abangan and santri can also describe different phases in a man's life. Another Javanese informant, Djokosutrisno (Djoko for short), a member of the PNI's legislative delegation, recalled how as a young child his parents had introduced him to the arts of Javanese music and dancing and how, later, he learned to recite passages from the Koran. Later still, thus familiarized with abangan and santri values, he gained elite priyayi status as a civil servant.

Djoko's abangan orientation both diluted and incorporated elements of the santri outlook. He found no contradiction between the two viewpoints. Was not the highest god of the wayang, Sang Hyang Wenang, the same as the Allah of Islam? But although he had made the pilgrimage to Mecca and kept the fast in public during Ramadan, Djoko was not a fully practicing Muslim. A member of an essentially abangan political party, in matters of politics his referents were un-Islamic, even anti-Islamic. In this, Djoko illustrated another way of compartmentalizing political and cultural identities. Whereas Ahmad's father had a Muslim political and an abangan cultural identity, Djoko had found his political expression in an abangan party while keeping a place for Islam in his cultural self.

Generalizing for all fifteen abangan Javanese in the samples, a childhood experience of rural religion that was more or less syncretic gave way to an adult urban experience of religion-linked politics as more or less divisive. Abangan viewpoints are not naturally anti-santri; they become so in the context of political competition between elites. Problems of cultural politics may, therefore, be more manageable than they would be if they merely translated mass cleavages; by the same token, however, elites may have too great a political stake in cultural divisions to be able to overcome them.

Since military men have the greatest effective say in cultural politics, and politics generally, in Indonesia, the position of the officers interviewed is of special interest. The officers' ethnic makeup differed little from the civilians, but the evidence suggests that military men may be more inclined to come down on the secular-abangan side of religious issues. Whereas nearly a fifth of the civilians belonged to minority religions, all of the officers were Muslims. More important, among the nine officers, the distribution according to strength of affiliation was 7-2-0 (weak-medium-strong); 78 per cent wore their affiliations very lightly and none was devout. Among civilians, the distribution was 15-6-10; only 48 per cent were nominal and fully 32 per cent devout. All four of the Javanese officers were thoroughly abangan; one of these was the single most influential man in the samples, and his outlook on life was the least Islamic and most Hindu-Javanistic of all. Other officers were extremely secular in outlook. Religiously committed minorities in general, and the strongly Islamic minority in particular, would appear to have few voices in the key military segment of the elite. When their experiences with Islamic militancy since independence are considered later in this chapter, the secular-abangan bias of these officers will become even clearer.

Both the institutional and the cultural group hypotheses have been strengthened. Ethnically and religiously, the bureaucratic elite is more homogeneous than the parliamentary group. In quantity, it is more Javanese and more Muslim; in quality, it is less strongly Javanese, less strongly Muslim. In the basically abangan bureaucratic elite, cultural majorities overlap. Parliament, in contrast, tends to include the intensely identifying members of cultural minorities, ethnic or religious. The cultural group hypothesis is also supported in that, regardless of institutional affiliation, the smaller the cultural group the more strongly its members identify with it. Elite conflict between the santri minority and the abangan majority among the Javanese appears less the reflection of a general cultural cleavage experienced in childhood than an adult political response to questions involving the cultural policy of the state (for example, the Jakarta Charter). As for the military component of the elite, its secular-abangan stance suggests the likely bias in its approach to cultural politics.

Schools, Associations: Differentiated Minorities

Everyone in the samples had at least a secondary school education, but whereas a majority (three-fourths) of the bureaucrats had continued through institutions of higher learning, a majority (three-fifths) of the politicians had not; among the administrators there were proportionally almost twice as many higher-educated persons as among the legislators. In addition, proportionally more of the administrators had postgraduate degrees; six of the fifteen highly educated bureaucrats held a master's degree or its equivalent, compared to only two of the eight highly educated politicians. Overall, twenty-three of the forty men had had Western-style higher schooling of some kind, while only three had been essentially pesantren-educated.[5]

5. Educational levels were defined in Western (secular) curricular terms. Although the pesantrens attended by three individuals clearly imparted a "higher" knowledge of Islam, the training received in secular subjects was comparable only to the Western secondary level; these three men were therefore classified as having attained, by Western secular standards, a sec-

In 1944, on the eve of the revolution, two institutions of higher education were cited far more frequently than others in the biographies of leading administrators and politicians: the Higher Law School in Batavia and the University of Leiden.[6] Twenty-five years later there were no dominant institutions. The higher educational experience of the elite as sampled in 1969 was more varied; among institutions attended were the University of Indonesia (four individuals), Gajah Mada University (three), Pajajaran University (two), and five other universities (one man apiece) in Indonesia alone. No one had studied at the University of Leiden or at any other university in the Netherlands. In contrast to the 1944 figures, which show Holland as by far the most popular site for overseas higher education, by 1969 the ex-metropole had been displaced by the United States. Of the nine individuals in the samples with higher overseas training, four obtained it in the United States (including two cases of advanced military training), only three in Holland (in higher vocational schools, not universities). And whereas eight of the fifteen highly educated administrators had pursued higher studies or training abroad, only one of the eight highly educated members of Parliament had.

These figures reinforce the historical evidence presented earlier in support of the institutional hypothesis that the bureaucratic elite in Indonesia is more cosmopolitan than its counterpart in Parliament. In fact, a comparison of the social backgrounds of the elite in 1969 and 1944—as revealed by the sample interviews and the biographies, respectively—suggests that the gap between administrators and politicians has widened. A process of indigenization and diversification of the channels of recruitment to elite status has occurred among the highly educated politicians, who now come from a wide variety of Indonesian universities whereas before they tended to come from a few institutions in the Netherlands and the Indies. Among the highly educated administrators, the location of

---

ondary education. The decision to use secular rather than religious criteria was dictated by the majority experience of the samples and implies no value judgment about either type of education. Finally, no distinction was made between academic and vocational schooling. The secondary category includes graduates of postprimary teacher training schools, for example, while among those classified as having had a higher education are several alumni of the armed forces' postsecondary staff and command schools.

6. Calculated from *Orang Indonesia*.

favored training sites seems not so much to have shifted to Indonesia as to have moved from the former metropole, Holland, to
what is intellectually already a neometropole, America.

Table 6. Secular versus religious education

	Secular	Islamic	Christian	Hindu	Totals
Administrators	14 [70.0]	1 [5.0]	4 [20.0]	1 [5.0]	20 [100.0]
			6 [30.0]		
Legislators	10 [50.0]	7 [35.0]	3 [15.0]	– [–]	20 [100.0]
			10 [50.0]		
Totals	24 [60.0]	8 [20.0]	7 [17.5]	1 [2.5]	40 [100.0]
			16 [40.0]		

Note: "Secular" means that the individual received no formal religious education.
(Three of the twenty-four persons thus classified, however, remembered having memorized Koranic passages, either at home or in a group, before entering secular primary
school.) All other individuals received some formal religious education, defined both in
terms of content and auspices. An Islamic religious education for example, might include
an experience in a pesantren or *madrasah,* the latter also a Muslim school but more
formally organized; Christian schooling took place typically in a primary or secondary
institution run by missionairies or under Christian auspices; the one Hindu instance oc-
cured in a school very roughly equivalent to a higher pesantren or theological seminary
in the Muslim or Christian system. Individuals who had studied in more than one religious system were classified under the one in whose schools they spent the greater amount
of time.

The differences by secularity of curricular content and school
auspices shown in Table 6 further strengthen the image of a cosmopolitan bureaucratic elite. Whereas 70 per cent of the administrators received entirely secular educations, only 50 per cent of the
legislators did so. Furthermore, comparing the two groups of six
bureaucrats and ten politicians with at least some formal religious
education, for 70 per cent of the politicians that schooling was
Islamic while for 67 per cent of the bureaucrats it was Christian
(Catholic or Protestant). The samples diverged both in relative
secularity of schooling received and, strikingly, in its major confessional aegis.

Once again these findings relate to earlier differences. The bureaucrats tended to have more imposing fathers. The strong-impact father commonly placed his son in the best available Western-style school and then, through a mixture of encouragement and coercion, pushed the boy to study hard. The importance of a quality education that would equip their sons for high, especially administrative, positions overcame in the fathers' minds any qualms about crossing religious boundaries. Christian schools not only kept high academic standards but were also, because of the evangelizing rationale on which (at least historically) they rested, more accessible to non-Europeans than the costly elite European primary ELS (Europeesche Lagere School) and secondary HBS (Hogere Burgerschool).

All degrees of father significance were equally represented among informants with some Islamic education; of the seven with some Christian education, however, four remembered their fathers as having had a strong impact on them. And these four were themselves all Muslims, as were their fathers, whereas the other three Christian-schooled informants and their less imposing fathers were all Christians or, in one case, animist.[7] It took a strong-willed father, with great ambitions for his son's success in colonial society, to send his son to a school operated by representatives of an alien minority religion he had not adopted.

None of these Muslim sons was converted to Christianity by his school experience. But the risks of apostasy were real. Zainal, for example, the only politician with a strong father, was a devout Muslim, as was his father. But the father wanted Zainal to have a good Western education that would lead to a job, as Zainal recalled his words, "where you can use your brains and not just your hands." So the father sent Zainal to what he thought was a good Dutch-language primary school, even if it was run by Protestants, and after three years there Zainal went on to a Protestant-run junior high school in the regional capital. Although the pupils were required to pray to God before and after classes and to say grace, the curricula at these two schools were essentially secular and, Zainal remembered, of extremely high quality.

7. The animist was a father on one of the least developed outer islands; he never succumbed to the appeals of the Protestant missionaries active there, although his son did. This is the only instance in the samples of an informant adopting a religion that was not his father's.

So happy was Zainal with his Protestant schooling that he wanted to take the further step of entering a Protestant teacher training school in order one day to teach in such a fine system himself. But at this suggestion the father recoiled, realizing that he was unintentionally moving his son toward a Christian career and perhaps later even a Christian identity. His objections overruled, Zainal found himself at his father's insistence in a school training Muslim teachers. Subsequently he became a regional leader of the same Islamic party that his father belonged to. His early Christian education augmented Zainal's experience without cutting his ties to Islam.

This incident illustrates a conflict between two socializing sites, a Muslim family and a Christian school. The disagreement between father and son is atypical; most informants did not oppose their father's choice of schools or vice versa. But it highlights a discontinuity that, in varying degree, was common to the experiences of all. The worlds of the family and the colonial school were far apart. The content of Dutch-language curricula—several men recalled with as much pride as hyperbole that they had mastered the map of Holland down to the tiniest creek—had little in common with the traditional wisdom of the informants' generally less well educated fathers. Western schools meant expanded cognitive horizons for the boys who entered them. At the same time, outside school, these boys experienced something of the social reality of the Indies. In this extracurricular socialization, the peer group was an important third socializing site.

In various extracurricular milieux, the colonial pupil acquired, simultaneously, a sense of the differentiated character of colonial society and a sense of solidarity with certain of his peers. Growing up in a plural society of reinforcing racial and class cleavages meant associating with one group against other groups. Sugijono, an administrator, remembered the society in the town in eastern Java where he went through HIS as sharply stratified; the priyayis were on top, the workers on the bottom. Sugijono's father's job, in railway administration, carried middle-rank priyayi status; Sugijono's mother's claim of descent from a lesser noble of Mataram added to the family's prestige; and the HIS where Sugijono studied was a distinct social cut above the local Volksschools. But the town also boasted an ELS, to which some of the sons of still higher priyayis had been granted access. Sports contests pitting Sugijono and his classmates against these even more advantaged boys often degenerated into street fights, one stretching into another like running battles in a miniature class war. Sugijono and his comrades were well aware that the ELS was mainly a place for white Europeans, and they resented the fact.

Racial and class differences were similarly reinforcing in the experience of Margono, who grew up in the 1920's in a central Javanese town where streetfighting was so common that, as he put it, the boys went to school by day and practiced *pencak* (roughly, a Javanese equivalent of karate) by night. Regular targets were the black Ambonese and the Eurasians, whose proximity to the racially and socially elite Dutch exposed them to the derision of Margono and his friends. The boys would gather in front of the building in which the Ambonese and mixed-blood soldiers in the Dutch colonial army were billeted and taunt them, shouting "Black Dutchmen!" At the same time, the local kraton served, just as the palace in Purwoko's childhood had, as a nucleus of identity and cultural pride in relation to which Margono came in time to see himself as distinctly Javanese.

At their Dutch-language schools, the boys sat in ethnically mixed classrooms and learned about such incorporative abstractions as the "Netherlands Indies." In interaction with peers they differentiated themselves and learned the specifics of racial and class inequality. While school made them intellectually aware, social awareness they picked up in the streets.

As for political awareness, the fathers of a few informants had nationalist leanings; in these homes, politics formed part of the child's earliest environs. But for the great majority in the samples, political knowledge and activity were not associated with the family. The fathers, especially the strong-impact ones, wanted their sons, and particularly the eldest, to study hard, to excel, to rise high in a colonial hierarchy that many of the fathers expected to continue indefinitely, and not to risk the future playing politics. The fathers were not disappointed. By and large, the sons did study hard, achieving grades that ranged from satisfactory through outstanding, and did not risk their careers; none was ever arrested by the Dutch. In fact none committed an act of protest much more serious than singing "Diponegoro" instead of "William of Orange" in the Dutch national anthem. (As already noted, Prince Diponegoro led a revolt against the Dutch in the nineteenth century.) Political socialization occurred essentially outside the family— whether the nuclear family or the kin with whom many students boarded while attending secondary school.

Political experience was discontinuous in another sense as well. At the verbal, symbolic level, anticolonial identification with the idea of an Indonesian nation was strong. But, with some important exceptions, the organizations these pupils joined did not encourage the articulation of that idea in petitions and protests. Furthermore, again with some exceptions, these associations were not often transethnic in membership; and even when they were, they were not particularly integrative. The unitary nationalism to which the famous youth oath of 1928—"one nation, one people, one language"—had given such dramatic expression was endorsed no less sincerely for being an abstraction without any serious behavioral implications in the years before the coming of the Japanese. As students, these men were neither timid nor hypocritical. But they felt the weight of the academic expectations placed upon them by strong fathers, demanding uncles, or solicitous teachers eager to develop the intellectual promise of their charges. And parents and teachers alike discouraged political activity of an overtly antiregime kind. Nor was the atmosphere of the Netherlands Indies in the 1930's Manichean. School pupils did not feel pressured by events or opinion to take a stand politically one way or another. The Pax Neerlandica was fully in effect; the uprisings of the late 1920's were history. Volksraad nationalism and the Sutardjo Petition had not yet been discredited as ineffective or rendered irrelevant by the Japanese invasion.

Political consciousness was fired in the minds of several informants by the platform personality of Sukarno, whom they saw as a kind of forensic Diponegoro. One of these informants, then a youth, was mesmerized when he heard Sukarno, just released from prison, speak in Bandung in 1932. Another wore full Javanese dress in order to pass as an adult and enter, with an indulgent smile from the doorkeeper, a mass meeting in Blitar addressed by Sukarno. A third, having sneaked out of his school dormitory to occupy a front-row seat long before the appointed hour, heard Sukarno in Kediri. All three were enthralled; all three marked the experience in retrospect as a crossing of the threshold of political awareness.

But although they became politically conscious, they did not take political action. Sukarno inspired these three men, and a number of others who heard him during this period, but incited none of them. Asked to recall the content of his speeches, these informants said Sukarno had not been seditious but had stressed instead the positive and ostensibly peaceful theme of national unity embodied in the youth oath of 1928. (Having previously been jailed for his political activities, he operated under certain constraints.) For those who heard him, Sukarno gave compelling appeal to the idea of one Indonesia; by the same token, he represented less a path of action than a grand ideal, one that enthusiastic high school students could applaud in principle without having to attempt to achieve in practice.

A similar disparity between principle and practice can be seen in the apolitical, subnational character of most of the extracurricular associations these pupils joined. The prewar youth groups they favored—scouting and outing clubs, for example—tended to be regionally, ethnically, or religiously based, or more recreational than political, or both. When it came to moving beyond symbolic commitments into radical action, most informants were neither organizationally equipped nor personally willing to risk the consequences. This pattern held as well for the legislators as the bureaucrats.

Martinus Wande, for example, a Protestant politician from eastern Indonesia, felt inspired by Sukarno's vision of the greater unity of Indonesia even though he had never heard the man speak. But the vision was one thing, reality another. Sukarno's solidarizing rhetoric about one nation, one people, and one language did not alleviate Martinus' loneliness in the bustling anonymity of a large city on Java where he felt himself a foreigner, someone from a different people and a different culture, speaking a different language that the Javanese could not understand. Even when he found a job in an institution where he could work and go to school at the same time, he was constantly reminded of his "otherness." In music class, for example, Wande played the Javanese instruments clumsily and with great embarrassment, to the concealed amusement of his Javanese classmates, who found in his halting performances confirmation of their view of him and his culture as primitive. In the face of this quiet ridicule, he and his friends from the islands east of Bali lashed out at other targets, using with relish the contemporary epithet for Eurasians: *orang tiga suku* (two-bit half-breeds). Although at the abstract level Martinus took pride in national symbols, at the practical level he joined a defensive-identity youth group strictly limited in membership to those from the eastern islands, and informally limited as well to those of non-Muslim faiths (Christians were a majority in Martinus' home region). This group had its own athletic team, and Martinus spent much of his free time in intensely fought sports competition with other ethnically, regionally, or religiously exclusive youth clubs.

This young man's initial entrance into politics was similar to Usman's in that it occurred far away from his family in an educational establishment on Java where he was able both to study and to earn his keep. Wande's teacher, a highly educated man, was quite active at the time (the 1930's) in the reformist-cooperative stream of Indonesian nationalism and would occasionally deviate from the subject of his lectures to discuss the idea of Indonesia and the country's future. One day he said to the class, as Martinus recalled his words, "When I die, we will not be free. When my children die, we will still not be free. But my grandchildren's generation will see freedom come to Indonesia." What struck Martinus about this statement was not its political content but the fact that, taken literally, it contradicted what was well known: that the teacher did not have any children, let alone grandchildren. So Wande stood up and asked how freedom could come to the teacher's grandchildren when the teacher did not even have children. The teacher smiled, not knowing the boy except as a name on an enrollment list, and replied, "He who asks the question . . . is my child." Although the other pupils laughed at him and whispered "Konjol!" (Nuthead!), Martinus was deeply pleased that this great man, a Javanese with a high degree, could even think of Martinus as his son. A relationship developed between them not unlike that between Usman and his kiyai.

If in the pesantren before the war Usman had looked to the moderate-reformist Parindra, to the urban mosque official marching with the priyayis in the kraton parades, not to any sort of drastic action against the colonial regime, as a student Wande too was not attracted to radical politics. Aside from belonging to the regional youth group previously mentioned, Wande did join a more militant, national organization, Young Indonesia (Indonesia Muda, IM); but an incident in the early 1930's shows the young man's unwillingness to risk his situation to make a political point. When rumors of a clash with colonial authorities swept the building where Martinus worked and studied, his friends in IM ran out to join the fray. He told me he was "ordered"—by whom, it was unclear—to remain inside with the women and girls and to help them care for the wounded who came limping in off the streets as the fight progressed; in fact he was probably already sufficiently reluctant to go outside that an order to stay inside would have been superfluous. The police soon triumphed, and some 250 boys from his institution, including Martinus, were identified as IM members and taken for questioning. The boys were lined up and told that any who promised to resign from and renounce IM and to abstain from rioting in the future would be freed; of the 250, only about 25 accepted this offer, but one of them was Martinus. Years later he justified his decision to cooperate as enabling him to continue his education and prepare himself, as he put it, to "fight again" another day. Besides, had not his teacher said that freedom would be a long time coming?

Very few in the samples even joined IM. Those who were adolescents or older in the 1930's were politically aware, and many were sympathetic toward and impressed by Sukarno and the kind of integral nationalism he stood for; but the interests and activities of these future members of the elite were on the whole apolitical, and their networks of friends tended to develop around shared regional, religious, or ethnic origins. Most popular were scouting and outing groups. Six informants joined the PNI's scouting movement and wore its nationalist symbol, a red and white neckerchief. Two joined the scout wing of the Islamic Muhammadiyah movement and donned its green and white scarf. Others joined the Dutch-sponsored scouts, kraton scouts, regional and moderate party-affiliated youth groups, and, at the most purely recreational level, vacation clubs.

If the type of association characteristically joined by bureaucrats versus legislators is considered, earlier findings are extended. Although in both samples moderate organizations were preferred over radical ones by large margins, the administrators were more likely to have joined interethnic or nonconfessional, as opposed to ethnically or religiously particularistic, organizations than were the legislators. Three-fourths of the politicians who joined extracurricular societies belonged to the latter type, compared to only a little over half of the bureaucratic joiners. Along this dimension, once again, the administrators were more cosmopolitan, the politicians more parochial.

Overall, affiliative activity involved political awareness but not political action. For most in the samples, the prewar era was doubly a "normal time," as Purwoko called it. The stability, predictability, and apparent permanence of the colonial order were not only reassuring; in addition, they permitted the beneficiaries of that order to separate themselves from it intellectually and symbolically without having to translate an abstract commitment into action. Because Indonesia did not yet exist, it could be supported without the Indies having to be rejected.

In sum, the institutional hypothesis that the bureaucratic elite is more cosmopolitian is confirmed by the more advanced, more secular, less Islamic, and more international character of their education and their tendency to join interethnic or nonconfessional organizations, compared to the schools and associations of the legislators. As for cultural groups, extracurricular socialization in the streets and on playgrounds made virtually all the members of the samples aware of the partly reinforcing racial, ethnic, and class differentiation of a plural colonial society. Religious distinctions were also visible to these youths, but to a lesser degree than ethnicity, which was the more identifiable by looks, dress, and language. Generally, whereas religious conflicts became important later in life but were more expressly political, ethnic conflicts occurred earlier but were more broadly social. The implication is that the more ethnic identity discriminates between elite orientations, the more the political culture of the elite can be said to reflect nonpolitical divisions internalized early in life; the more religious identity discriminates, the more clearly can the sources of conflict in elite political culture be located in the adult political world.

Occupation, Revolution: Opportune Discontinuity

War shattered the luxury of endorsing the national idea without opposing the colonial status quo. The Japanese destroyed the

Netherlands Indies and in three and a half years made Indonesia possible. Indonesia and the Indies became contradictions in terms, and eventually in blood as the self-proclaimed Republic of Indonesia fought the returning colonial power. Which side are you on? became a question of paramount importance. In the reminiscences of my informants, 1942–1949 was above all a time of action and alignment.

Compared to the colonial era, these were years of social anarchy and material deprivation, but administrators and politicians evaluated that fact differently. Bureaucrats saw the period basically as a deviation from colonial norms. Some of them recalled being implicated in its abnormality. One, a student at the time, stole books from his school library to buy food; another made money by selling for profit materials the Dutch had left behind; a third was involved in a smuggling operation between Sumatra and Singapore. Some cited the corruption of others. Yet by emphasizing, even exaggerating, these lapses from the civil servant's ideal of disciplined conformity with the law, these men buttressed that ideal. A great majority remembered the violence of the times, whether a public execution by the Japanese secret police or the excesses of republican hotheads of the sort from whom Purwoko had recoiled; and the vividness of these recollections, too, suggests a retrospective oversharpening of the contrast between an agreeably stable colonial order and postcolonial chaos.

The politicians recalled this period no less vividly, but to most of them its chaos was creative. The few instances of larceny they cited were recalled less with disapproval than with admiration for the ingenuity with which people had improvised survival. As for violence, about four times as many politicians as bureaucrats had actually fought battles and fired weapons during the revolution, and the legislators were prouder of it. On this score, the Usman-Purwoko contrast held for the samples as a whole. Among members of Parliament the revolution was also a deviation from colonial norms, but one more welcome than regrettable.

These years also offered opportunities. For the legislators, the opportunities were political; hardly a man among them did not become in some way politically affiliated during this period, and some belonged to three or four different groups, including pseudomilitary units set up by the Japanese and a variety of more or less irregular organizations that sprang up during the revolution. For the bureaucrats, the opportunities were less activist than administrative. The demolition of the colonial state meant, for many of them, promotion in its wartime successor. Nearly three-fourths of the bureaucrats held administrative posts directly under the Japanese, compared to only one-fourth of the legislators. Nor were politicians in Japanese-sponsored organizations part of a supervised hierarchy in the same direct way that translators, district heads, intelligence agents, and forestry officials (to cite just a few of the administrators' wartime occupations) were. Three of the administrators worked from the demise of the colony right through the occupation at virtually the same jobs, their daily routines barely disturbed by the change in regimes.

The occupation meant mobility, upward for many individuals in the samples, lateral for others, downward for a few; overall, in career terms, the elite benefited more from the occupation and the revolution than they were hurt. An extreme exception was Surono, a bureaucrat. Nostalgic for the colonial past, he resented the subsequent decline of his fortunes. His monthly wage before the war, when he worked as a bookkeeper for a Dutch-language newspaper, bought nearly three times as much rice as his civil servant's salary did in 1969. He blamed the Japanese for shattering his "normal" life. When they came, in 1942, they closed down his newspaper and threw him out of work. When they later announced an opening for a telephone repair and maintenance man, Surono applied and was hired. He hoped to learn the job properly from the Dutchman he was to replace, but the Japanese grew impatient and hustled the man off to a camp before Surono really knew the work. Although he had laborers underneath him who actually dug up the cables, Surono hated his job; the Japanese were impatient and often abused him, physically and verbally, for his slowness and his mistakes. Ever since, Surono felt, he had been abused—by acquaintances, superiors, fate. He saw the occupation as the beginning of the end of his life.

For most in the samples, however, the beginning represented by the occupation was auspicious. The officers especially remembered this period as a springboard; of the nine, the military careers of six began then. One man rose rapidly through the Japanese-sponsored Defenders of the Homeland (Pembela Tanah Air, Peta) to become a garrison commander. Another received naval training. A third merely exercised with a wooden rifle. But all six first tasted military life under the Japanese.

The revolution also opened opportunities for these men; the three remaining officers began their military careers during these years. Even men with little training could, almost literally, walk into ranking positions in the expanding republican forces. Surono would have joined the regular People's Security Army (Tentara Keamanan Rakyat, TKR) if he could have been made a first lieutenant; but he had not even a semblance of military training behind him, and the TKR refused. That his hopes could have been so high shows how upwardly mobile during this period were many of his acquaintances who did manage to get in on the TKR's first or even second floor.[8]

Recalling the revolution, civilian administrators stressed the need for order in chaos and how they had tried to meet it. Drs. Harun had been assigned to guard the stores of Chinese merchants who had fled from the fighting. Most of the stores were empty, having already been looted by anti-Chinese militants, but Harun had been proud even at a purely symbolic level to protect the revolution from vandalism and greed done in its name. Another administrator, Sumarno, had been similarly appalled by acts of looting and violence aimed at Chinese and well-to-do Indonesians. One of Sumarno's jobs for the republican government was to investigate rumors of profiteering by its officials, one of whom was fired from his job on the evidence Sumarno was able to gather against him. In an irregular time, Sumarno felt, norms of proper conduct had to be guarded all the more zealously. In his efforts to protect certain assets of the republic, R. A. Wiroto had to avoid equally the attacking Dutch and rampaging young republican irregulars. The fact that only a few days after he reported the successful completion of his mission to Vice-President Hatta in

---

8. Abdul Rasjid, a high-ranking officer, once set up a regional branch of the TKR simply by picking out someone he thought looked tough and competent and making him a colonel. About 2 o'clock the following morning, this newly commissioned and not a little disoriented commander knocked on Rasjid's door and said, in effect, "Me a colonel? I didn't even finish primary school!" Rasjid could recount the incident with relish because the man's heroism had later confirmed Rasjid's judgment.

Yogyakarta most of Wiroto's clothes were stolen from his hotel room epitomized, in Wiroto's mind, the lawlessness of the times.

Another civilian bureaucrat, Sutikno, recalled with admiration verging on awe the republican leader Sutan Sjahrir's skill as a negotiator with the Dutch and his attempts to calm the stormier petrels on the Indonesian side: "He was like ice on a hot forehead." Ibrahim Lubis was the only administrator who said flatly that he had opposed a negotiated end to the revolution. The rest either expressed no view or said they had strongly preferred the diplomatic path. Even Lubis had spent long weeks during the transition to Indonesian sovereignty trying to apply ice to the foreheads of a "wild battalion" that was refusing to give up its arms and integrate itself into a peaceful postrevolutionary order. All these men—Harun, Sumarno, Wiroto, Sutikno, and Lubis—responded to a felt need for a firmly holding center lest, in Yeats' phrase, "things fall apart."

If colonial nostalgia marked the civilian bureaucrats, their counterparts in Parliament—and especially members of the PNI, NU, and PSII—tended to romanticize the revolution. Between these two groups fell the officers; like many politicians, they had engaged in violence, but like many administrators, they had tried to protect the nascent republican order. The military men remembered facing a symmetry of internal oppositions: communists on the left, Muslims on the right. Several officers had taken part in the quelling of the revolt-within-a-revolution in the Madiun area of east-central Java in 1948 in which the Communist Party was involved. The ostracizing of the PKI since 1965 encouraged the officers to remember even tangential brushes with communists as examples of leftist treachery. Similarly, on the right, the Darul Islam uprising that had broken out in western Java just after the revolution loomed more prominently in the officers' recollections because of the persistence of the vision of an Islamic state through succeeding years. A large majority of the officers had been involved, directly or indirectly, in countering one or the other type of threat to the integrity of a secular, national state.

The officers tended to trace these disloyalties back to the revolution. A brigadier general in the Department of Defense and Security cited an attempted minicoup in the Cirebon area in 1946 that had involved several PKI leaders, while the roots of the Darul Islam movement, he believed, could be found in the refusal of some members of Hizbullah to integrate themselves and their weapons into the regular republican army in 1947. —I am part of the generation of 1945,— this man said. —We fought for something the younger generation takes for granted: the unity of this republic. We fought for it against the Dutch, against the PKI, against the Darul Islam. We fought for it in the 1940's, the 1950's, and the 1960's. We remember the revolution. But will our children?—

An interesting difference between informants' recollections of colonial childhood and postcolonial adulthood is that, with a few exceptions, in more recent memories reference was made less frequently to ethnic than to religious differences. Excepting racial hatred of the Chinese, instances of ethnic animosity were extremely rare in reminiscences about the revolution. Outer island ethnic minorities, for example, generally did not feel themselves discriminated against during the revolution. The issue of an Islamic future for Indonesia, on the other hand, had been visible and controversial from the constitutional debates of 1945 onward. The revolution appears to have been more successful in creating in the elite a sense of transethnic nationhood than a sense of agreed-upon religious freedom or interreligious trust.[9]

The occupation and the revolution, then, appear to have been differently experienced by civilian administrative and political elites. Along a spectrum of roles between the preservation of order at one extreme and the promotion of disorder at the other, between the guardian and the guerrilla, most sample members fell toward the order-preserving end. But the civilian bureaucrats were closest to and the civilian politicians farthest from the pure guardian type, with the officers clustered in between. In essence, the politicians tried to gain as much as they could, the bureaucrats to avoid losing more than they had to, and the officers simultaneously to protect the revolution from internal subversion and win it against external assault. On the whole, the struggle intensified ethnic identities and activated political competition between them less than it intensified and politicized religious identities and antagonisms.

9. On the subjective meaning of the revolution, also see my "Thoughts on 'Remembered History' as a Subject of Study, with Reference to Indonesia's Revolution," *Review of Indonesian and Malayan Affairs*, 8, 1 (January-June 1974), 3–6.

Institutional Status: Legislative Weakness

On the basis of the comparison between institutions and individuals made in chapters 1 and 2, it might be expected that the institutional identities of legislators would be much weaker than those of bureaucrats; such is indeed the case. In addition, both groups of individuals generally recognized the subordinate position of the representative body.

Table 7 compares administrators, members of Parliament, and officers according to the strength of their institutional affiliations. The armed forces were the greatest source of personal identity; the bureaucracy followed, and the DPR was the weakest of all. The strengths of the officers' military and civilian affiliations were inversely related: the stronger a man's military identity, the weaker his legislative or administrative affiliation. A majority of the officers (five out of nine) identified only weakly with the civilian institution to which they belonged; none identified strongly.

Table 7. Institutional affiliations and their strength

	Weak	Medium	Strong	Totals
Administrators	6 [30.0]	7 [35.0]	7 [35.0]	20 [100.0]
Legislators	9 [45.0]	10 [50.0]	1 [5.0]	20 [100.0]
Military	1 [11.0]	2 [22.0]	6 [67.0]	9 [100.0]

Note: Strength of institutional affiliation is the importance of his institution—the bureaucracy, Parliament, or the military—to an individual's self-image as revealed in his behavior, verbal and nonverbal. The more time he was observed to spend on activities relating to the institution, the more voluble he was about it and his involvement with it, and the more he used it in conversation as a self-locating frame of reference, the stronger his institutional identification was judged to be. Each officer was classified twice, once for the military and once for the bureaucracy or Parliament; in the first instance he was compared to all other officers, in the second to all other administrators or legislators. Affiliations were treated as independent, so that in theory, for example, the same person could be held to identify strongly with both the military and a civilian institution.

The primary nature of military loyalties among the officers is not merely a consequence of the armed forces' premier position in the regime; other reasons, structural and stylistic, also affect military pride. In the first place, all the officers owed their extramilitary jobs to ABRI. Lieutenant Colonel Suhardi, for example, joined the TKR during the revolution and stayed on. By the early 1960's he felt he was not being promoted fast enough, so he approached a general to see what could be done. The general offered him a job helping manage a network of rubber plantations that had been nationalized and placed under army management in the 1950's. The plantations were turned back to their original foreign owner in 1968, but Suhardi's army superiors decided he should remain in a civilian job, so he was transferred to an economic ministry; he had been working there for about six months when I first met him. Despite their civilian employment, all the officers continued to be paid by the armed forces according to military regulations.

The military structure of vertical authority and unambiguous command also influenced the officers' identities and working styles, and many had trouble adjusting to the relatively amorphous structure of the bureaucracy or to the formal horizontal equality of Parliament. Suhardi had not only been socialized in the armed forces to adopt a command style of decision-making; that style had attracted him to a military career in the first place. While still a student, during the Japanese occupation, the no-nonsense manner of the man in whose house he lived impressed him deeply. The errands Suhardi ran for this man, to help earn board and room, always had a clear beginning, middle, and end, and his host made him report back on the success of every one of these little "missions," as Suhardi called them. When the revolution broke out, Suhardi made plans to leave the city on a particular date, in the evening. At the last minute, however, he found that his school friends had decided to leave the morning after, so he agreed to postpone his departure by one night and go with them. But when he told his host of this change of plan, the man scolded young Suhardi for being inconsistent: once you had decided to do something, that was that; decisions were made to be carried out, not reconsidered. Suhardi took the advice and left in the evening, without his friends. By his own admission, Suhardi's growing preference for clarity, order, and consistency in work situations predisposed him toward the military life.

Compared to army life, Suhardi had not relished his assignment overseeing rubber plantations in the early 1960's; there, he felt, politics had made a shambles of command. One of his superiors, a PKI member, had tried to flatter Suhardi by acting as if Suhardi were equal to or even above him in rank; in narrating the experience, Suhardi appeared less upset over the man's communist affiliation than with his attempt deliberately to blur a clear line of authority. For the same reason, Suhardi admitted, he found it hard in his current position to accept the tendency of some of his civilian subordinates to mix social and professional relationships. He had tried to be sociable and to joke with them outside working hours. But when these civilians had tried to treat him in the same informal, egalitarian way in the office, Suhardi had felt obliged to stop them, despite the cost to him in popularity. —In the army you give an order and it will be carried out,— Suhardi protested further. —But with civilians an order may just sink down one or two levels and then stop, with nothing done.— Suhardi also complained that in the bureaucracy orders had to be explained, in great detail, whereas in the military that was not necessary.

From one of the generals killed in the coup attempt of 1965, a man Suhardi admired greatly and who had been at various times his commanding officer and mentor, Suhardi learned two managerial imperatives. First, if you do not know what to do, do not share your indecision with your subordinates. Upon taking up a mission in the 1950's, Suhardi's commander had immediately ordered all junior officers (including Suhardi) to prepare detailed reports on the geography, military strength, and political sympathies of an area then being contested with rebel forces, even though the commander did not know whether the reports would ever be used. In the end, the work proved to have been unnecessary—the reports were never read—but Suhardi thought it had been justified because it gave the men a positive, immediate (and false) impression that their leader knew just what to do. It also kept them occupied, and that was the second lesson: whatever happens, make sure your subordinates stay busy; they will have no time to get in trouble and, in Suhardi's admiring phrase, "the machinery will keep working." A critical observer might object to this advice as being a recipe for ignorance through makework, but to Suhardi it was a model of good leadership that he was trying hard to apply in a civilian department whose job definitions were vague and whose large staff was underemployed.

Some of the same difficulties of adjustment were revealed in my conversations with Kusumabrata (Brata for short), an officer in Parliament. One of his assignments was to help socialize incoming ABRI members into legislative ways, to explain to them that they could not adopt in the DPR the same command style they were accustomed to in the armed forces. Brata took pains to try to show that ABRI was not the preponderant group in Parliament—"our only weapons are those the other members use: thoughts and opinions"—but in his language he showed clearly the special status of military men. In Parliament, he noted, sometimes a general will find himself in a committee meeting chaired by an "ordinary person" (by which Brata meant a civilian), yet the armed forces must stand above all political groups, and an officer's first loyalty must always be to the doctrines of ABRI. Suhardi made the same point when he said he would never execute an order that violated his soldier's oath, not even if it came from his own (civilian) minister.

A final reason for the greater identification of officers with the military than with a civilian institution lies in what the revolution meant to them. Asked to name the happiest time in their lives, about half of them referred to the revolution, and the revolution was intimately bound up in their self-assigned purposes as military men: to secure, integrate, and maintain the nation. Most of these men had been involved in the work of building a regular military organization out of the congeries of units that fought the revolution, and the idea of the military as an integrative force was common among them. The revolution was also used in conversation by a number of officers to validate in retrospect the "dual function" of ABRI in military and nonmilitary realms—in popular struggle against a common enemy the boundary had naturally been ignored —and thus stress ABRI's popular support. One or two others, sensitive to contemporary criticism of generals who interfered in politics and the economy, looked back to those years as a time when they could be especially proud of their military status; but even they said they would never choose civilian careers.

Table 7 shows Parliament to be distinctly weaker as a source of personal identity than the bureaucracy. The legislative role did not imply a career; administration did. Parliament had not been elected and was not in that sense a "real" legislature at all. Administrators went daily to their offices; but legislators, by contrast, came to the

DPR buildings only irregularly, depending upon the legislative calendar and the press of other affairs, and only one of them had even a desk there. The army officer who was the most powerful man in both samples apparently never bothered to attend legislative sessions at all—either because he disdained Parliament's impotence or because he was unwilling to put himself in the anomalous position, pointed to by Brata, of sitting under the chairmanship of an "ordinary person," and probably for both reasons.

In the terms of one enumeration of possible functions of legislatures[10]—elite recruitment, elite socialization, regime legitimation, system transformation, constituency representation, law-making, investigation of the bureaucracy, and acting as a safety valve for the expression of grievances—the DPR in Indonesia in 1969 was basically a legitimizing safety valve. But its ineffectiveness in comparison with the Western model of an active legislature (itself, as noted earlier, more theoretical than real) was not the result of some abstract executive will to power; there were concrete reasons for its weakness, and they showed up in the experience of both politicians and bureaucrats.

First, the administrators had an average of fourteen years' continuous service in the same or an equivalent ministry behind them, compared to an average among legislators of only four years in Parliament. (When officers are excluded, the first figure increases to seventeen while the second stays the same.) Three-fourths of the legislators in the sample were appointed in the period 1966–1968 as part of the revamping of Parliament undertaken to strengthen support for Suharto's government in the MPRS sessions of 1967 and 1968 that named him first acting and then full president. Among both samples, length of service correlated strongly with strength of institutional identification.

Second, Parliament was a penetrated body. If not always agreeable to the politicians, that condition at least had familiar precedents, which several politicians had even helped to establish. A PNI legislator with a long record of service in the pamong praja recalled how in 1945, as a district head in west-central Java, he had, on instructions from above, set up a district legislature, with himself as chairman, by selecting the names of prospective members

10. Malcolm Shaw, "Introduction: Legislatures in Comparative Perspective," *International Journal of Politics*, 1 (1971–1972), 291–298.

and submitting them to the regent for final choice—a procedure that roughly duplicated that by which many of his fellow members of the national Parliament had been appointed. A member of NU in the DPR remembered how, as chairman of another local parliament, in the province of East Java, he had obtained guidance in advance from the regent on every issue that arose, in order, as he put it, to "facilitate" the process of legislative decision-making, a procedure he considered altogether appropriate for a national legislature as well. A young civilian administrator had received a telephone call from a minister telling him that his name was among the list of new appointees to Parliament to be announced the following day and explaining that "Pak Harto" (General Suharto) needed his support. This individual saw his role in the DPR as being to represent the interests of the department in which he had been working and through which he was still salaried; he said he accepted membership in the DPR because it would allow him to continue doing what he had been doing all his professional life: serving the government. The partial election of a new DPR in 1971 did not reduce its penetration by the bureaucracy or alleviate the resulting problem of accountability. In December 1973, a well-known Jakarta lawyer spoke out against the presence in Parliament of so many civil servants and officers, asking rhetorically how a civil servant-legislator could be expected to evaluate the work of his own minister, or a colonel-legislator the work of a lieutenant general-minister.[11]

A third factor inhibiting legislative review of the executive's plans and acts, as one businessman-legislator noted, was the lack of information and expertise among DPR members. Having had to balance expenditures and revenues in his own firm, he could understand the government's budgets; but most members, he felt, lacked the necessary training and knowledge. He found it easier to talk with a minister or with the secretery general of a department than with his colleagues in Parliament. In fact, by working closely with the Department of Finance, he told me, he hoped to be able to protect its policies in Parliament from criticism by other ministries. (Departments often feel that in Finance's allocations they have been given less than their due; as the secretary general of one

11. Statement by Yap Thiam Hien as reported in *Sinar Harapan*, Dec. 3, 1973.

ministry put it, "Negotiating with Finance is harder than negotiating with a foreign power!") In the budget-passing process in
Parliament, this member saw his colleagues as ignorant bystanders
and himself as a client of enlightened bureaucratic interest.

Among the bureaucrats, an official in the Department of Finance
had even less regard for Parliament. Not only had the DPR wiped
out his job in the 1950's by abolishing the land tax as a colonial
holdover—he had until then been helping to administer it—but
also, when he met with members of the current Parliament on
financial matters, he found them uninformed and uncreative. Once,
at his invitation, the political parties had sent representatives to his
office to give the parties' views on fiscal policy, but he found the
meeting useless; the politicians, he recalled, had nothing to suggest
about what should be done. Another administrator estimated that
about half the DPR members were "incompetent."

The legislators' lack of information and the administrators' disdain appeared to be mutually reinforcing, the ignorance of the one
group being both a cause and a consequence of the indifference of
the other. As one legislator complained in 1968 during the final
debate on a taxation bill, his earlier attempt to find out from the
government how much money the proposed taxes could be expected to yield had never been answered, and how could the DPR
intelligently vote a tax without knowing how much revenue it
would generate?[12] The bill passed anyway.

The absence of voting was a fourth reason for the ineffectiveness of the DPR. The diversity of viewpoints and interests represented often combined with the body's drawn-out process of
consensus-seeking to delay legislative action. Accordingly, precisely the more controversial (and often crucial) issues often fell
to the executive by default; in the 1960's, for example, four different bills addressed the delicate question of allocating central subsidies among large and small, wealthy and poor, producing and
consuming provinces. On each occasion the DPR failed to reach
agreement, leaving the executive free to continue allocating funds
by its own lights. Nor did the DPR ever pass legislation on either

12. Speech by the late Sahat Nainggolan (Murba), not a sample member,
as reported in the uncorrected *Risalah Resmi*, 1968–1969, first session, Sept.
27, 1968, p. 8.

the First or the Second Five-Year Plan.[13] The DPR was not inactive—in its 1967–1968 session, for example, eleven laws and five resolutions were adopted[14]—but its diversity and nonvoting procedure limited it and made it amenable to executive control. As one legislator put it, the DPR only had influence when it wanted to do something the government wanted done; another member doubted that the DPR would ever come into its own until it could review the implementation of those bills it did manage to pass.

Several bureaucrats were critical of their own institution. One spoke of the corrupting effect on government of the 1955 elections, which had given rise to office gossip against officials like himself as suspected "bourgeois intellectuals"—especially those who belonged to the liberal anticommunist Indonesian Socialist Party (Partai Sosialis Indonesia, PSI). In the 1950's, he complained further, the rapid succession of ministers had disoriented the professional civil service by leaving behind a chaos of contradictory rules and regulations. Another official recalled how, in 1963, he had tried to fire certain employees beneath him whom he judged unqualified or lazy; how the government workers' association had prevented him from doing so; how, because of politics, there had been no controls over corruption and ineffectiveness; how wags had renamed the 1961 civil servants' pay regulation (PGPN) Pinter Goblok Pada Nasibe (the smart and the stupid have the same prospects). A third bureaucrat said that if the government were to be truly effective, between a third and a half of all civil servants would have to be fired; but of course, he quickly added, "that's

13. In early 1974 the proposed Second Five-Year Plan was submitted to Parliament for discussion, but not for amendment or ratification; nor was there a general plenary debate. Instead, a twenty-three-member Special Committee was set up to have a "dialogue" with the government on the subject, the plan itself being promulgated as a presidential decree. Thus the DPR had the right to legislate the annual budget but not the plan whose priorities the budget was supposed to reflect. See Yuti [Sayuti Melik], "Parlementaria (I)," *Suara Karya*, Jan. 15, 1974.

14. Of the eleven laws, nine were on economic questions, including the 1968 budget, cooperatives, banking, investment, and Indonesia's membership in the International Development Association; the other two were on minor matters of health and administration. Of the resolutions, three were on foreign affairs (ex post facto support for the normalization of Indonesian-Malaysian relations, for example), one supported General Suharto as acting president, and one endorsed the latter's independence day message to the DPR. Antara, *Warta Berita*, July 1, 1968, B.

impossible." Another recommended that the Departments of Information and Religion, which he considered overstaffed and useless, be abolished.

However, unlike the legislators, all but a few of the officials felt that their talents were being used. Most had some training for the work they were doing, and some, through experience or education, had become experts on the matters that crossed their desks. All could understand the purpose of the institution in which they held office: to govern. By comparison, the purposes of Parliament, especially an appointed one, were much less clear. Even the one official who admitted he would rather be a DPR member than a high-level administrator qualified his preference with the proviso that the DPR be elected, not appointed.

A final institutional difference worth noting is that administrators had easier access than legislators to prestige through international travel. Occasional DPR delegations were sent overseas, but their infrequency made participation in them a hotly contested honor; one legislator recounted an incident some years earlier in which two parliamentarians had actually come to blows over which of them was entitled to a ticket to go abroad. By comparison, exposure to foreign countries was much more common among administrators. Of the bureaucrats, 65 per cent had substantial foreign experience, measured by frequency of trips and length of residence overseas; 20 per cent had been abroad at least a few times; and only 15 per cent had never been outside Indonesia. Among legislators, the equivalent percentages ran in the opposite direction, being 20, 30, and 50. On this last dimension, too, the officials were the more cosmopolitan group.

Summary

The first part of the institutional hypothesis has been supported. The socialization, recruitment, and historic dominance of the bureaucratic elite have made it more homogeneous, more cosmopolitan, and more powerful than its counterpart in Parliament. Table 8 summarizes much of the evidence. A pure "cosmopolitan" bureaucrat was an older son of a strong-impact father who had worked in the public sector; the son had obtained a higher, secular education, and had traveled widely or lived overseas. Of the administrators who could be classified, slightly over half displayed at

Table 8.   Summary of distinctive experiences

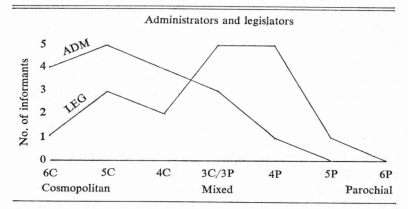

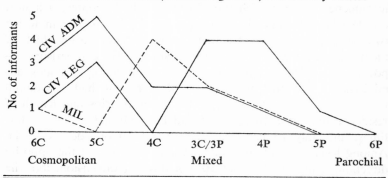

Note: The two syndromes are clusters of the opposite values of six dichotomous variables: travel and residence abroad (more-less), educational secularity (secular-religious), educational level (higher-secondary), father's
impact (strong-weak), father's occupational sector (public-private), and birth
rank among brothers (older-younger). If the first named attribute in each
of these six pairs is labeled "C" and the second "P," the pure "cosmopolitan"
type had all six C's (noted "6C") while the pure "parochial" type had all
six P's (noted "6P"). Horizontal axes locate each informant between these
two extremes: for example, "3C/3P" means any combination of three cosmopolitan and three parochial attributes. Six individuals had to be omitted;
four of these could not be classified on one or more variables because of
inadequate information and two could not be classified on the dichotomous
birth rank variable because they were median sons. The thirty-four persons
included in the table consist of seventeen administrators and seventeen legislators, of whom four in each category were military men.

least five of these six cosmopolitan attributes. Members of Parliament, on the other hand, tended toward an opposite, "parochial" pattern in which each of these particulars was reversed. By conforming more closely to the pure cosmopolitan type than the legislators did to the extreme parochial profile, the bureaucrats showed greater homogeneity of social background. Only one member of Parliament had five of the parochial characteristics; none had all six.

The military's recruitment and socialization, though skewed toward the cosmopolitan end of the spectrum, offered a pattern intermediate between the civilian bureaucrats and legislators. As well as penetrating the two civilian institutions, the officers bridged them in social background. The advantage the military elite has as a political force in Indonesia may lie not only in its monopoly of the means of coercion but also in its social origins and its experience as a set of leaders cosmopolitan enough to rule a modern state in tandem with secular civilian technocrats yet not so uniformly cosmopolitan as to be isolated from less urbane sectors. A number of the officers interviewed would probably endorse this view. But the difficulties these officers experienced in adjusting to relatively flaccid or ostensibly egalitarian institutions in which command styles of leadership were not always appreciated, and their clear prior loyalty to their own armed service, would appear to complicate their adaptation and limit their receptivity to civilian feedback.

On the first part of the cultural group hypothesis—that the experiences of ethnic and religious minorities in the elite sensitized them to disadvantaging cultural differences and strengthened their group identities—the evidence is mixed. Most members of the elite became aware of ethnic and class stratification early in life as they were socialized, on playing fields and in subnationally defined associations, into the structure of a plural colonial society; their sensitivity to religious differences tended to appear only later and in more political contexts. Ethnicity as a factor in cultural politics was less controversial than religion, and religious divisions in politics were more adult creations than social givens learned in childhood. The santri-abangan rift, for example, smacked of adult politics, whereas in the childhoods of a number of Javanese Muslims in the samples these cultural types were two faces of the same coin.

But the ethnic and religious identifications of cultural minorities were stronger than those of cultural majorities; the smaller the ethnic group, for example, the deeper its religious commitment. Their response to being outnumbered was not assimilation but retrenchment and intensification. Such minorities appeared to be self-conscious about their position in relation to the secular-abangan Javanese majority. And although the officers were not more Javanese than the civilians, their social backgrounds were more secular-abangan, suggesting that in religious politics the military leadership would favor an anti-santri stance.

The bureaucratic elite lay at the confluence of two cultural majorities: Javanese ethnicity and abangan religion. Parliament, by contrast, was the home of minorities, of affiliation, intensity, or both. If content is to be inferred from context, it might be expected that greater disaffection would be found among legislators than among administrators, whether for reasons of the former's paltry influence and weak institutional identity or because of their perceived cultural isolation and disadvantage. Does the evidence confirm such an expectation? Did the bureaucratic elite, compared to the legislators, have a more positive, less distrustful view of its social environment, and were cultural minorities more defensively negative than their counterpart majorities? These questions—which express the orientational parts of the two hypotheses: the extension of experience into outlook—will guide the inquiry in the next chapter.

CHAPTER 5

ORIENTATIONS

This chapter relates content to context in elite political culture. Content is limited to five kinds of outlooks that are relevant to problems of cultural politics: perceptions of social anomie, perceptions of conflict, orientations toward authority and leadership, support for empathy as a social priority, and eclectic religious tolerance.[1] (For information on scale construction and questionnaire administration, see the appendix.) The contexts used to explain these outlooks are institutional and cultural, in accordance with the two hypotheses that have structured the analysis so far. Contextual variables are introduced only insofar as they are helpful in accounting for the orientations; variables that do not discriminate significantly between elite outlooks are omitted. The findings are summarized in a final section as part of an overall assessment of institutional and cultural differences in elite political culture.

Anomie and Conflict

On a scale of perceived anomie—in which, following Finifter,[2] normlessness and powerlessness were combined—the institutional

1. As noted in the introduction, I do not claim to have explored dimensions of personality. That is why I refer to perceived anomie rather than alienation, to support for deference to authority rather than authoritarianism. In exploratory cross-cultural research it seems wiser not to assume the projective power of one's instrument. Nor is it necessary to do so, since political culture is, by definition, a more superficial construct than political personality.

2. Ada W. Finifter, "Dimensions of Political Alienation," *American Political Science Review*, 64 (June 1970), 389–410. Compare my "Bureaucratic Alienation in Indonesia: 'The Director General's Dilemma,' " in R. William Liddle, ed., *Political Participation in Modern Indonesia* (New Haven: Yale University Southeast Asia Studies, 1973), pp. 58–115.

hypothesis was supported. As shown in Table 9, which also lists the four statements about which respondents were asked to express an opinion, the administrators had a more positive view of their

Table 9. Perceived anomie

	Low (1)	(2)	(3)	(4)	High (5)	Mean scale score ($\overline{X}$)
Administrators	5	5	3	3	2	2.5
Legislators	3	3	4	4	4	3.1
Totals	8	8	7	7	6	2.8

Constituent dimension	Percentage agreement in each sample		Scale item and item no.
	Adm.	Leg.	
Perceived normlessness	17	33	Nowadays most people who do good are really only trying to conceal the evil things they did previously. (19)
	17	28	In our society today evil people have more influence than good people. (31)
Perceived powerlessness	61	72	So weak and limited are a man's capacities that most of his goals won't be realized in his lifetime. (27)
	39	61	Times are changing so fast these days that there isn't a single person who knows his own fate. (22)

Average interitem correlation = .53

Note: Each respondent on each of the items was scored on a scale running from 1 through 5 depending on whether he Disagreed, slightly disagreed, was neutral, slightly agreed, or Agreed with the item in the direction of the scale (here, increasing perceived anomie). Each respondent's item scores were then summed to obtain a raw scale score, which was divided by the number of items in that scale to obtain an individual mean scale score. These individual mean scale scores were summed and divided by the number of people in the sample who completed the questionnaire to obtain a mean scale score $(\overline{X})$. The column headings (1) (2) (3) (4) (5) represent ranges of individual mean scale scores, with each range eight units wide except for the middle (column 3) range, which was allocated nine units to maintain symmetry $(.8 + .8 + .9 + .8 + .8 = 4.1$, which covers the scale distance from a score of 1.0 [Disagree] to 5.0 [Agree] inclusive). For example, the five administrators who showed the lowest perceived anomie (column 1) had individual mean scale scores falling between 1.0 and 1.7 inclusive. In this and the next six tables, when percentages refer to agreement (Agree + slightly agree), higher scores and column headings mean more approval for the opinion(s) expressed in the scale; when percentage disagreement (Disagree + slightly disagree) is given, higher scores and headings mean less approval. Of the forty men interviewed, thirty-six completed the questionnaire (see the appendix), and half of these were bureaucrats, half politicians; the number of men in each sample who could be located on any scale is therefore eighteen. Item numbers refer to the order in which the statements appeared in the questionnaire and are listed for ease in reading the interitem scale correlations presented in the appendix. An interitem or average interitem correlation, as above, is given in the tables for each scale containing two or more items; the higher the figure (to a limit of 1.0), the more internally consistent the scale.

social environs than the legislators. At the same time, taken as a whole the elite was not particularly anomic in outlook; the mean score for all thirty-six individuals who completed the questionnaire fell close to the midpoint of the scale. Reference to some of the comments made by these men in responding to these and related statements should clarify the reasons for the institutional difference.

Politicians were more inclined than bureaucrats to read political content into the two normlessness items, relating the statements to the instability and upheavals of political life. In addition, the legislators felt themselves personally more exposed to the risks of politics, to the inconstancy and damage potential of political friendships. Several of them lamented the dissolution of revolutionary comradeship. In those days, recalled an older Sundanese politician, —a man would join the guerrilla movement, leave his family behind, climb up and down mountains. Maybe his home would be destroyed; maybe he'd have to destroy it himself. But now, waking up from the dream, what does he see? His old comrades-in-arms chasing money and jobs. They say they're filling [giving content to] independence, but really all they're filling is their own pockets! Before they were friends fighting together. Now they fight one another.—

Others in Parliament, proud of their revolutionary credentials, resented the current prestige of senior bureaucrats who, they felt, had not proven themselves loyal in 1945–1949. A politician in his mid-fifties from the outer islands, who had had only some post-primary vocational training, complained that those who had cooperated with the Dutch, former colonial civil servants especially, were the ones now in power; those who had loyally fought and sacrificed to defeat the Dutch had been overlooked and thrust aside. It was unfair. The bureaucrats, on the other hand, tended to view their environment more favorably from the greater security of their educationally, socially, and politically advantaged positions. Some bureaucrats did indeed see social and political injustice and dislocation. One told of how he had confided to his best friend in the office his opinion that if more anticommunists had supported Sukarno the president would not have been so influenced by the PKI, and of how the "friend" had promptly reported him to certain higher-ups as a Sukarnoist. But generally the administrators did not appear so personally affected by shifting political winds as the legislators did.

A related statement, "nowadays it's rare to find a person one can trust," divided the two samples dramatically along these lines. Among legislators, 61 per cent felt that trustworthy people were rare; among administrators, 67 per cent felt that they were not. Again, legislators tended to read political content into the statement, whereas officials saw trust more as a nonpolitical matter.

The legislators also politicized and personalized the notion of powerlessness. As Table 9 shows, although both samples tended to agree that a man's capacities are sorely limited, the legislators generally saw a connection between the pace of social and political change and the unpredictability of a man's fate that the bureaucrats did not. For most of the bureaucrats, a man's fate was in any event unknowable, and sudden changes were seen as affecting only the most involved minorities—that is, people other than themselves. As an official in the Department of Finance put it, sketching his thoughts on a notepad as he spoke: —Let's say that during the Old Order the pattern was A-B-C, with the A's actively supporting Sukarno, the B's uninvolved, and the C's against him. In those days, of course, the A's were in official favor and the C's were not. In 1965–1966, the pattern flipped over. The A's, the ex-Sukarno-ites, were out of favor, and the C's, his former critics, were in. But only a few people were affected because only a few were ever really "Old Order" or "New Order"; most remained in the middle where they'd always been. When A-B-C became C-B-A, the B's stayed put. If they were involved before, they were only carrying out orders, which is all they're doing today. So I don't agree that a rapid change affects a man's fate. At least not for most people.—

The politicians were more likely to have been A's or C's, to have committed themselves publicly for or against the regime while the civil servants were "only carrying out orders" in government offices. Among the members of Parliament, many owed their seats to the reversal of political fortunes in 1965–1966, and several others were anxious retroactively to put as much distance as possible between themselves and the ruins of the Old Order; none was indifferent. In this instance, among bureaucrats, Purwoko was an exception. He felt keenly the link between rapid political change and personal uncertainty; his own ministry had been affected more deeply than Finance, for example, by the shock of the attempted coup and its anticommunist aftermath. But, in general, the politicians felt more acutely and personally the unsettling effects of rapid social and, especially, political change.

According to the cultural hypothesis, members of religious and ethnic minorities should be more anomic in their perceptions than members of majority groups. Is this true? A first religious variable is affiliation. Because there were only four Christians in the samples, differences between them and the thirty-two Muslim respondents can be no more than suggestive. But the finding that Christians, on the average ($\overline{X}$), scored higher on perceived anomie ($\overline{X} = 3.4$) than the large Muslim majority ($\overline{X} = 2.8$) supports the hypothesis. (These mean scale scores were calculated as indicated in the note to Table 9, but using religious groups instead of samples.) A minority religious group, as the Christians are in Indonesia, appears to be more likely to perceive anomie than a religious majority. Such a pattern is certainly logical; members of an outnumbered group might be expected to show greater dissatisfaction with dominant group norms and a greater sense of powerlessness to effect change than members of a majority.

But while the Muslims constitute a majority in quantitative terms, qualitatively, in terms of commitment and practice, they do not. If the Christians as a quantitative minority were more anomic than the Muslims as a numerical majority, might it not be expected that the practicing adherents of any faith would be more anomic than its nominal adherents, insofar as the former are a minority and the latter a majority within that faith? The reasoning behind such an expectation is that the majority constitutes the norm, and the norm is unsatisfying to the committed minority because it implies religious laxity. The result might be called "anomic piety," the product of both a deep sense of (religious) community and a sense of being bypassed or threatened by (secularizing) change. This was, in fact, the observed result. Generally speaking, the stronger a person's religious affiliation, the more likely he was to perceive anomie in the society around him. Sample members with stronger affiliations averaged a higher scale score ($\overline{X} = 3.2$; $N = 16$) than sample members with weaker affiliations ($\overline{X} = 2.5$; $N = 20$). (N is the size of the group to which the mean applies.) Nor did this difference disappear or change direction when Muslims and Christians were separated.

A third religious variable, secularity of respondent's schooling, yielded a parallel result. Persons whose educations were wholly or partly religious in auspices and content were slightly more inclined toward anomie ($\overline{X} = 3.1$; $N = 13$), that is, toward a view of human beings as impotent and deceitful and society as unjust, than those who went through purely secular schools ($\overline{X} = 2.7$; $N = 23$). But these figures conceal some subtle differences. Consider the statement, listed in Table 9, that a man's capacities are insufficient to the realization of most of his goals in his own lifetime. Agreement with this proposition rose from 57 per cent for those with secular, to 83 per cent for those with Christian, to 86 per cent for those with Islamic educational experiences, and from 55 per cent, to 75 per cent, to 88 per cent among respondents with weak, moderate, and strong religious affiliations, respectively. But the quality of Islamic and Christian reactions to this statement, as revealed in oral comments of the respondents, differed. Both groups dealt with the item from two frames of reference simultaneously: secular and religious. For Muslims, agreement suggested disaffection from the secular success ethic, according to which any man who works hard enough can realize his goals, but was integrative in relation to the religious idea of human impotence before Allah. The difficulty lay less in the perception itself than in the fact that, in the activist-cosmopolitan atmosphere of elite society in Jakarta, the religious idea was so unfashionable. As a result, their rationale for personal impotence integrated these Muslims not outwardly into society but inwardly, back into the pious core of the surrounded—according to some, the besieged—community of Islam. Several of these men admitted feeling that their pesantren schooling had held them back in their attempts to get ahead, by secular standards, in the modern world. (Usman was an exception, for his pesantren experience had been a springboard to status that he could not otherwise have hoped to attain.) The Christian-schooled also tended to accept the notion of personal impotence, and by the same two standards of judgment, but with reversed consequences. Christian education was socially integrative by secular standards; its products took pride in it because its high quality, they felt, had equipped them well to realize their life-goals in a secular world. In religious terms, however, the experience was comparatively disaffecting, for those who were Christians because it inducted them into the norms of a minority religion, for the Muslims because it tended to create pressure against their prior familial commitment to majoritarian Islam.

The cultural minority hypothesis is supported, but it appears to work in different ways for different minorities. Specifically, far from feeling disadvantaged by their Christian education, the Christian minority, and even those Muslims who had gone through Christian schools, valued the experience as having been a good preparation for getting ahead in secular society. The minority of pious Muslims with Islamic educational backgrounds were the ones who felt disadvantaged on these terms, although, by the same token, their sense of belonging to a surrounded ummat was strong. In terms of cultural politics, the presence of the anomic orientation appears to matter less than the reasons why different groups hold it and the different positions they occupy in the social and political structure.

Cultural politics flows from the interaction between cultural identity and political position, and the latter aspect should not be slighted in favor of the former. In Parliament, members divided neatly in their relative disaffection along the scale of perceived anomie into a group made up of PNI men ($\overline{X} = 3.5$; $N = 4$) and members of religious parties ($\overline{X} = 3.3$; $N = 7$) on the one hand, and the government coalition of intellectuals and professional men and officers ($\overline{X} = 2.7$; $N = 7$) on the other—that is, roughly, into the more pessimistic political "outsiders" and the more optimistic "insiders." Members of the Development Group and the armed forces found it easier to be positive about the system they were helping to maintain. The political parties, by comparison, were under considerable pressure from the government, either because of previous leftist associations with the Sukarno regime or because of still earlier rightist links to militant Islam. Among politicians, anomie was a consequence not merely of piety in a secular urban society but also of political disfavor under a military-technocratic regime. And when anomie rested simultaneously, as it did for the pious Muslims in the Islamic parties, on cultural isolation and political impotence, religious and political minority statuses were reinforcing.

The cultural minority hypothesis was also supported in terms of ethnic groups. The Javanese ($\overline{X} = 2.7$; $N = 20$) and Sundanese ($\overline{X} = 2.5$; $N = 6$) were, on the average, more optimistic in outlook than were the small ethnic minorities (the nine outer islanders and one Jakartan in the sample [$\overline{X} = 3.4$]). Members of these minorities, rather than linking themselves positively to an integrated superculture in the capital city, tended instead to relate negatively to what they saw as a dominant Javanese culture. A young politician from one of the eastern islands was especially outspoken. He found the vaunted politeness and indirection of the Javanese merely hypocritical and a cause of government malfunction; just as Javanese families always serve a guest the very best food, food they never buy for themselves, he said, so do the Javanese only tell officials what the officials want to hear.

Ibrahim Lubis, a Sumatran administrator, also criticized insincere indirection and authoritarian deference as Javanese traits. If a non-Javanese in a government office wanted to go overseas, said Lubis, he would simply list his reasons: experience and information to be gained, benefits in improved policy, and so on. If a Javanese wanted to go, he would not put his name forward but, rather, stay quietly in the background. And the superior, being Javanese, would award the trip to the more self-effacing of the two: the Javanese, who had not offended the superior's sense of necessary humility. —The Javanese,— generalized Lubis, —work more by feelings than intelligence.— In dealing with his own subordinates around the conference table in his office, Lubis said, he had long ago learned that the way to involve a non-Javanese was to appeal to his pride by telling him to speak first; a Javanese, by contrast, would rather be invited to speak only after others had had their say. Lubis also complained that Javanese subordinates were less self-reliant, more dependent on others. —With a non-Javanese [Lubis meant especially people from Sumatra, Kalimantan, Ambon, and Sulawesi], you give him a schedule of things to do every day and he'll keep it without your having to remind him, but a Javanese has to be told over and over again.— (A Javanese bureaucrat, on the other hand, was no less critical of what he saw as the tendency of some outer islanders in government to form nepotistic cliques from which Javanese were excluded.)

The stereotypical nature of these impressions was betrayed by Lubis' refusal to distinguish at all among Javanese—for example, between those from the north coast and those from the interior, or between those from central and eastern Java—and by the highly selective nature of his evidence. At one point he said that throughout government the real movers were non-Javanese, and he mentioned two names. When I noted that one of the names was Javanese, Lubis said, "Yes, but he's been in Kalimantan so long, he's really a Banjarese." (Also noteworthy is the fact that both of the individuals Lubis mentioned were army officers.)

The cultural minority hypothesis held up when tested against the strength of ethnic affiliation. Respondents whose ethnic identities were strongest were decidedly less optimistic about person-society interaction ($\overline{X} = 3.6$; $N = 6$) than those with a moderate ($\overline{X} = 2.8$; $N = 14$) or weak ($\overline{X} = 2.6$; $N = 16$) sense of ethnicity.

The samples also yielded support for a regional version of the minority hypothesis. Respondents born on the outer islands were markedly more anomic in outlook ($\overline{X} = 3.5$; $N = 8$) than the Java-born majority ($\overline{X} = 2.6$; $N = 28$), a difference illuminated by the preference expressed by several of the outer islanders for what they saw as the egalitarian structures and styles of their home regions compared to the hierarchical patterns of Java, and by their concern that the outer islands' export economies be given more in return for their productive resources. Several of them appeared anxious that the central government's location on Java should not lead to Indonesia's political economy being Javanized.

These cultural differences create a stock of available tension below the surface workings of elite-level politics. Insofar as I could pinpoint the objects of anomie in the interviews, minorities of affiliation—Christians and outer islanders—appeared to be most fearful or critical of an Islamic or a Javanized state.[3] But these spectres were related less to abstract majorities of affiliation (Muslims in general, Javanese in general) than to minorities of intensity within those majorities ("fanatic" Muslims, Javanists). And these anxieties, particularly the religious ones, were reciprocated: practicing Muslims worried not only about the low-intensity majority of nominal Muslims within their own religion but also about the high-intensity minority of evangelical Christians outside it. In the event of crisis, the stereotypes these groups used could become terms of blanket opprobrium.

At the same time, an important difference in quality was evident in the respondents' comments about ethnic as compared to religious identity; generally, ethnic judgments were offered more lightly, with less emotional force. These men were conscious of the ethnic dimension, but it was less deeply or freshly divisive than religion.

The interplay of differences between minorities of religious affiliation and minorities of religious strength suggests that the impact of secularization, at least in the short run, will not be to mitigate these tensions but rather to shift the type of minority involved. Whereas secularization can bring relief to the members of an outnumbered faith by isolating and attenuating an opposing minority of intensity, for the latter it becomes an additional threat. This is one reason why the Christian minority in Indonesia has tended generally to welcome secularization, the practicing Islamic minority to oppose it. The Christian idea of separated church and state and the Islamic idea of unity between mosque and state have served to rationalize each side's concrete stake in the argument.

3. For an extreme illustration of ethnic fear, see Kahar Muzakar, "Down with the New Madjapahitism!" circulated illegally in 1960 and republished in Herbert Feith and Lance Castles, eds., *Indonesian Political Thinking 1945–1965* (Ithaca: Cornell University Press, 1970), pp. 330–335. Born in Sulawesi, Muzakar led a revolt there against the central government in the 1950's.

The relationships between these independent, contextual variables of institutional, religious, ethnic, regional, and (within Parliament) organizational affiliation or strength and the dependent variable, anomic orientation, collectively support the institutional and the cultural hypotheses. Other independent variables—age, sibling rank, father's impact, educational level, and civilian-military status—did not vary significantly according to whether outlooks were more or less anomic. What is more, the cultural and institutional dimensions overlap. The more anomic viewpoint of the politicians reflects in part the greater representation of cultural minorities in Parliament than in the bureaucracy. The less anomic stance of the administrators reflects their socially more advantaged (cosmopolitan) backgrounds in an institution that, compared with Parliament, is at once politically dominant and culturally more homogeneous and majoritarian.

Very broadly speaking, two patterns of discontinuity have been revealed: one in which cultural minorities of affiliation and intensity face one another in Parliament, another in which these minorities face the basically secular-abangan Javanese bureaucratic elite. It appears that in Indonesia national institutions can be either culturally representative or politically powerful, but not both. The long-run success of the overarching military institution will depend in part on the validity of its claim to be the exception to this rule.

On the basis of the evidence so far, findings for perceptions of conflict might be expected to parallel those for perceptions of anomie. Conflict too is a product of men and the situations in which they find themselves. If legislators and cultural minorities are less trusting of their social environments, they might be expected to see social conflict as a product of aggressive natures in winner-take-all circumstances, that is, to take a pessimistic view of conflict as ineradicable and extreme.

Table 10, however, does not uphold the institutional hypothesis; legislators and bureaucrats did not differ significantly in their views of conflict. Furthermore, as in the case of perceived anomie, the samples as a whole were not especially pessimistic. Several members of Parliament spoke of the possibility of mutually beneficial politicking; several bureaucrats pointed out that investments could enlarge the size of the economic pie for all; and a majority in both

Table 10. Conflict perceived as immutable and zerosum

	Mutable-nonzerosum				Immutable-zerosum	Mean scale score
	(1)	(2)	(3)	(4)	(5)	$(\overline{X})$
Administrators	5	3	3	3	4	2.9
Legislators	7	1	4	2	4	2.7
Totals	12	4	7	5	8	2.8

Percentage agreement in each sample		Scale item and item no.
Administrators	Legislators	
50	39	Warring and fighting with his own kind are unchangeable characteristics of man. (17)
39	39	In our society, an increase in the wealth of one person means a decrease in the wealth of another. (33)

Interitem correlation = .45

Note: Zerosum here describes a conflict situation in which one person's gain $(+)$ equals another's loss $(-)$, the sum of the two being zero, whereas, in a variable-sum situation both parties can gain. Other things being equal, conflict is logically more extreme in the win-lose than in the potentially win-win case.

institutions shared the view of the high-ranking officer who commented as follows on the statement that conflict is an inherent part of human nature: —Clausewitz also says man is nothing but a wolf, a bird of prey. But that just isn't true.—[4]

4. This finding contrasts with James Scott's generalization from a sample of Malaysian bureaucrats that the "constant pie" assumption—material goods are nonexpandable and scarce—is widespread among Third World elites and that it correlates inversely with economic prosperity (James C. Scott, *Political Ideology in Malaysia: Reality and the Beliefs of an Elite* [New Haven: Yale University Press, 1968], chs. 5 and 6, pp. 94 and 128, and appendix C). The finding that the outlook of the Indonesian elite as I sampled it was not markedly pessimistic would not be expected if prosperity were the determining condition; Malaysia had, when Scott wrote, and still has, a much higher standard of living than Indonesia. Possible attenuating

The cultural minority hypothesis, however, did receive support. Compared to those with weaker religious affiliations ($\overline{X} = 2.6$), respondents with stronger ties to a religion were more inclined to see conflict as immutable and zerosum ($\overline{X} = 3.0$); and the minority with some religious schooling also had a more pessimistic view of conflict ($\overline{X} = 3.0$) than the majority without ($\overline{X} = 2.6$). These differences were smaller than those obtained for anomie but coincided in suggesting pessimism among religious minorities. Percentage agreement with the notion that one person's gain entails another's loss, for example, declined from 63 among those with strong religious ties, to 50 among the moderately committed, to only 25 among the weakly affiliated. (N's are 8, 8, and 20, respectively.) Along the variable of religious schooling, the men who had gone to Muslim schools were the most pessimistic about conflict ($\overline{X} = 3.2$; $N = 7$), while those with Christian schooling ($\overline{X} = 2.8$; $N = 6$) were almost as optimistic as those with secular educational backgrounds ($\overline{X} = 2.6$; $N = 23$).

Why should the more strongly religious and the Muslim-educated favor the darker view of conflict? The answer does not appear to lie in religious ideology, for Islamic arguments were used to defend opposing views. A young Muslim politician, for example, Agreed with the statement that man would always be in conflict with his fellows, on the grounds that only in heaven was there real peace and no temptation; here on earth in the very beating of a man's heart could be heard the sound of the devil knocking to get inside and turn him against his neighbor. But Usman explained his Disagreement with the statement by citing the Islamic doctrine that asserts the purity of the newborn. Another haji agreed that there would always be war, because "the Koran says that's the way man is born."

The explanation appears to lie instead in the structural position

---

variables may include higher levels of intercommunal tension in Malaysia in 1967–1969, the relative abundance of unexploited natural resources in Indonesia, the greater size of Indonesia and the "growing room" afforded by her underpopulated outer islands, Indonesia's wider elite-mass gap, and the nonredistributive, growth-promoting economic policies of the Indonesian government in 1969. The causes and contents of "constant pie" thinking clearly beg for disaggregation.

of the religiously committed and the Muslim-educated as minority groups in the secularizing society of metropolitan Jakarta, a society which they tended at best to view as uncongenial and at worst to fear as a possible future for Indonesia. Anomie and sharp conflict were mutually supporting images of external reality. Through the comments of several of these men, for example, ran a sense of regret that people in Jakarta, especially younger people, were not more disciplined and restrained, the implication being that the city's highly secular life style was partly to blame. Their experience in confessional schools had led these Muslims to entrench themselves in their religious community and increased the distance between them and what they tended to see as a comparatively immoral, Western-penetrated elite milieu around them. Again, Usman was a partial exception. He was both religious and pesantren-trained, but his success as an entrepreneur led him to reject the immutable-zerosum view, as he cited savings, investment, and the cooperative nature of man. Islamic minority status in a secularizing plural society appears merely to make pessimism more likely for a given individual; variations in actual experience can moderate or even cancel its realization. As for the Christian-schooled minority, again they fell more toward the optimistic end of the scale, and again the explanation is basically structural. Compared to the Muslim-trained, their schooling had equipped them for higher status in more advantaged positions in secular society, positions from which they could afford the more benign view.

The cultural minority hypothesis was also supported by ethnicity and region of birth. Members of ethnically non-Javanese minorities ($\overline{X} = 3.2$; $N = 16$) were more pessimistic about conflict than the Javanese ($\overline{X} = 2.5$; $N = 20$), and the minority born off Java was more pessimistic ($\overline{X} = 3.4$) than the Java-born majority ($\overline{X} = 2.6$). (Previously given N's are not repeated.) A few Javanese respondents used cultural models to elaborate their views; especially common was a sense of sharing and collaboration, values they imputed to Javanese village life. As compared with the Javanese, ethnic outer islanders were less predisposed by their home cultures to endorse models of minimal conflict and consensual action; the Sumatrans and most of the eastern islanders were more individualistic and accepting of conflict than the average Javanese in the samples. The relative optimism of the Javanese would probably have seemed unrealistic to these non-Javanese.

But a structural explanation is also possible. All three of the outer islanders (ethnically and by birth) at the extreme pessimistic end of the scale were politicians, and all three saw themselves in Jakarta trying to enlarge their regions' claims on scarce resources controlled by the center. One lived in government housing, exclusively with other persons from his province. He had come to Java, he said, to get help from the central government to develop his home area, which he saw as poverty-ridden and backward. Another, living in very modest quarters far from the center of town, was sensitive to the contrast between his undeveloped province and the facilities of metropolitan Jakarta. This awareness of economic scarcity and inequality made the zerosum image of conflict more appropriate in their eyes. They talked more, too, about obtaining larger subsidies from the center than about stimulating autonomous local initiatives in their regions, and this sense of dependency on the bureaucracy for a slice of a limited pie probably reinforced their either-or understanding of conflict. Whatever their cultural predispositions toward conflict, the political position in which they found themselves made the more extreme model plausible.

Two other variables bear brief mention. First, bureaucrats in the cultural-social-communications sector (the Departments of Religion, Education and Culture, Information, Transmigration and Cooperatives) were more pessimistic about conflict ($\overline{X} = 3.8$; $N = 6$) than their counterparts in the economic sphere (Finance, Trade, Agriculture, Industry; $\overline{X} = 2.6$; $N = 7$) or the political sphere (Defence, Home Affairs, Foreign Affairs; $\overline{X} = 2.2$; $N = 5$). Very roughly speaking, the more prestigious or influential and the less overstaffed or party-penetrated the ministry, the more optimistic its incumbents' outlook on conflict. Just as the structural position of opposition groups in Parliament helps explain their stronger perceptions of anomie, so the hierarchy of departments (by secular, cosmopolitan standards) tends to reflect the distribution of immutable-zerosum images of conflict among administrators. Second, sibling order correlated negatively with optimism about conflict; oldest siblings were more pessimistic ($\overline{X} = 3.9$; $N = 7$) than middle ($\overline{X} = 2.6$; $N = 14$) and youngest siblings ($\overline{X} = 2.3$; $N = 12$).

With some exceptions, oldest brothers shouldered responsibilities at an earlier age than did middle or youngest brothers. Again a hierarchy of position and experience parallels the distribution of the orientation. All other variables—father's occupation and impact, military-civilian status, and so on—showed a weak relationship or none at all with different outlooks on conflict.

In sum, the analysis of this second orientation dovetails with the findings for the first. In both cases cultural minorities were more pessimistic, and both explanations emphasized not merely cultural predispositions but also structural hierarchies of position and influence. Religious variables were especially evident, and an Islamic pattern emerged in which pious Muslims and the Muslim-educated showed the greater disaffection. For perceived anomie, the institutional hypothesis that legislators would be more pessimistic was also supported.

Tolerance and Empathy

The evidence so far points to a potential for hostility on the part of other groups toward the abangan Javanese majority and also between the Christian and the strongly Muslim minorities. But two orientations could lessen this potential in that they would indicate communication and understanding across cultural cleavages: religious tolerance in particular, and empathy in general. Before generalizing further about cultural tensions in politics, it will be helpful to see whether cultural minorities and members of the weaker, less cosmopolitan institution (Parliament) are also relatively less tolerant of others' religious beliefs and less inclined to see a need for empathic understanding in society.

Purwoko and Usman, it will be recalled, had different notions of religious truth. To Purwoko, one truth—the existence of a Deity—underlay all religions. To Usman, one religion—Islam—encompassed all truth. In 1945, the constitutional debate over the relationship between religion and the state involved a clash between the syncretic abangan world view of much of the administrative elite, shared to a degree by certain nationalist politicians, including Sukarno, and the absolutist viewpoint of Islamic leaders; as already noted, the same issue arose again in the Constituent Assembly in the late 1950's and the MPRS in 1968.

The difference in outlook between Purwoko and Usman held

Table 11.   Eclectic religious tolerance

	Low (1)	(2)	(3)	(4)	High (5)	Mean scale score ($\overline{X}$)
Administrators	2	–	1	1	14	4.4
Legislators	6	1	1	2	8	3.3
Totals	8	1	2	3	22	3.8

Percentage disagreement in each sample		Scale item and item no.
Administrators	Legislators	
83	56	Among all the religions in the world, there is only one true religion. (39)

for the full samples. As Table 11 shows, the bureaucrats, many of whom had secular-abangan world views, cosmopolitan experiences, and priyayi origins, were much more inclined to believe in multiple paths to religious truth than the legislators, who were more parochial and had, on the whole, deeper religious commitments.

In its English translation in Table 11, the statement used to measure religious tolerance compares all religions in the world according to how true they are. Thus the "one true religion" is that religion with the only accurate (truthful) understanding of God and man's relationship to Him. In English, the sentence taps the empirical dimension only, leaving open the possibility of a religion that is scientifically invalid but morally good, but in its Indonesian form it does not allow such distinctions. Goodness and validity both are implied by the Indonesian word for true (*benar*).

Their comments made it clear, however, that none of the eight least tolerant respondents actually disparaged another religion. They stressed instead their belief that their own religion (for seven of the eight, Islam) was above, had come after, and encompassed all other faiths. Several of these men spoke in a defensive tone. Rather than treating the statement as self-evident, and confidently espousing Islam as the one true religion, they took pains to explain why they had to Agree. Placed as they were in Jakarta in a more or less secularized, polyconfessional atmosphere, this minority of absolutist respondents felt under pressure to conform to the relativist position; by defending Islam as the only true faith they might seem fanatic or intolerant toward other faiths.[5]

In contrast, 83 per cent of the administrators took the relativist view. Several of the relativists inferred from Islamic precepts a supra-Islamic perspective; after all, Allah had instructed mankind to believe in and uphold His word, including not just the Koran but also the Torah and the Old and New Testaments. The books were many, but God was one; like the roads to Rome, it mattered not which one you took, the destination was the same. The relativist majority included Christians too.

The tolerance of the majority was mainly cognitive. It did not necessarily imply emotional tolerance toward those who believe deeply and completely in only one religion. In my conversations with the bureaucrats, extreme believers were sometimes called "fanatics," just as the Dutch had termed them decades earlier. Ironically, cognitive tolerance could and did coexist with emotional intolerance in the outlooks of a number of respondents. The opinion that all religions are theologically true, for example, did not prevent an abangan administrator from sharply criticizing one of the five pillars of Islam, the pilgrimage to Mecca, as a drain on the nation's foreign exchange.

By comparison, the minority's commitment to Islam as the one true religion was marked by a certain protectiveness, in which the empirical and moral meanings of benar were fused, as if the respondents feared that in separating the two levels of meaning they might weaken the efficacy of their defense. Within elite political culture in Indonesia today, Islam is not an aggressive but a defensive force. Likewise in cultural politics: Acculturated into pre-existing systems of belief, isolated by the Dutch, defeated in the PPKI, driven to acts that only reinforced the colonial-priyayi image of its fanaticism, political Islam had retreated steadily, from the

---

5. I do not think the defensiveness of these respondents was merely the result of my presence. By the time they answered the questionnaire, my friendships with them were deep enough and both my agnosticism regarding Christianity and my respect for Islam were evident enough that they were not, I think, unduly inhibited. On the atmosphere of the interviews, see the appendix.

Darul Islam uprising to the last-ditch campaign to keep the Jakarta Charter alive.

Given the religious content of eclectic tolerance, it is hardly surprising to find it closely linked to religious variables. The stronger a respondent's religious affiliation, the more likely he was to believe that his religion had a monopoly on religious truth ($\overline{X} =$ 2.5, compared to $\overline{X} = 4.9$ among the less committed). Trichotomizing the independent variable, mean tolerance ran from 1.6, through 3.4, to 4.9 as religiosity decreased. Similarly, those with secular educations showed much more eclectic religious tolerance ($\overline{X} = 4.6$) than those who went to religious schools ($\overline{X} = 2.5$); and within the latter group, the Muslim-educated were, on the average, much less willing ($\overline{X} = 1.7$) to allow for multiple religious truths than were the Christian-educated ($\overline{X} = 3.3$).

When matched against political party affiliations, religious tolerance reproduced the abangan-santri split—though in an Indonesian, not a purely Javanese context—as a perfect polarity. All four PNI politicians were at the syncretic or eclectic end of the scale ($\overline{X} = 5.0$); all five Muslim party members were at the pure or monopolist opposite extreme ($\overline{X} = 1.0$). Religious tolerance distinguished one political group from another far more sharply than any other single orientation. Between the PNI and the Islamic politicians came the New Order coalition ($\overline{X} = 4.0$ for the Development Group [N = 4] and the military [N = 3] combined, and also for each separately) and the Christian parties ($\overline{X} = 3.0$; N = 2). Neither Sukarno's rhetoric nor the presumed integrative effects of mass communications and social interpenetration had blurred the clarity with which a basic religious difference, between syncretic tolerance and absolute faith, was maintained in the labels of elite partisanship. Members of the governing military-civilian alliance were the only legislators who moderated their reactions by selecting one of the three intermediate response categories.

Ethnic and regional variables also proved to be strongly related to differences in this orientation. The Javanese ($\overline{X} = 4.1$) and Sundanese ($\overline{X} = 4.3$) were highly tolerant when compared to the ethnically outer island (including the one Jakartan) respondents ($\overline{X} = 3.0$). Men born on Java ($\overline{X} = 4.1$) were much more tolerant than those born on other islands ($\overline{X} = 2.8$). If the degree of religiosity, the ethnic group, and the regional origin of a member of the elite were known, therefore, his conception of religious truth would not be hard to predict. Also, persons born in urban communities—defined as at least 100,000 in size according to the 1961 census—were more tolerant ($\overline{X} = 3.9$; $N = 7$) than the rural-born ($\overline{X} = 3.4$; $N = 29$).

These findings extend the notion of an Islamic factor in elite political culture. Just as pious Muslims and the Muslim-schooled showed greater disaffection on the dimensions of anomie and conflict, so were they less willing to entertain visions of religious truth other than their own. The institutional difference also recurred, between a more cosmopolitan, more tolerant bureaucratic elite and the more parochial and intolerant legislators. Within the DPR— the more diversely recruited and variously oriented of the two institutions—the Islamic factor was reflected in the Muslim politicians' much less eclectic religious outlook in comparison with the members of the government grouping and, even more, the mainly abangan PNI. At the same time, the finding that ethnic and regional minorities had more absolute religious views further illustrates the degree to which cultural cleavages at the elite level tend more to reinforce than cut across one another.

Before inferences can be drawn from these findings about the future of cultural politics in Indonesia, it must be determined how far this intolerance extends. How did the men in the samples react to the issue of social empathy in general? In principle, the exclusive truth of one's own religion can be affirmed even while society's need for people willing to put themselves "in the other person's shoes" is endorsed. Were the minorities who showed low tolerance also less inclined to support empathy as a social priority?[6]

The answer, for religious minorities, is yes. An Islamic pattern of low support for empathy distinguished Muslims ($\overline{X} = 4.0$), the

6. On the importance of empathy in Third World societies, see Daniel Lerner, *The Passing of Traditional Society: Modernizing the Middle East* (New York: Free Press, 1958), and Cesar A. Portocarrero and Everett M. Rogers, "Empathy: Lubricant of Modernization," in Everett M. Rogers in association with Lynne Svenning, *Modernization among Peasants: The Impact of Communication* (New York: Holt, Rinehart and Winston, 1969), pp. 195–218.

Muslim-schooled ($\overline{X} = 2.9$), and members of Muslim parties in Parliament ($\overline{X} = 3.0$) from Christians ($\overline{X} = 4.8$), the Christian-schooled ($\overline{X} = 4.8$), and members of Christian parties ($\overline{X} = 5.0$). A politician whose religion, education, and party were all Islamic flatly Disagreed with the statement (Table 12) that people are needed who can see things from the other person's viewpoint. "We Muslims," he said, "already have a viewpoint. For example, we oppose the group that calls itself the 'modernizing' group" (referring to the Western-trained intellectuals in the civilian wing of the governing alliance in Parliament).

Table 12.   Support for empathy as a social priority

	Low (1)	(2)	(3)	(4)	High (5)	Mean scale score ($\overline{X}$)
Administrators	1	2	–	6	9	4.1
Legislators	2	2	1	3	10	3.9
Totals	3	4	1	9	19	4.0

Percentage agreement in each sample		Scale item and item no.
Administrators	Legislators	
83	72	What our society needs a great deal nowadays is people who always try to see things from the other person's point of view. (14)

Once more, the reasons for these consistent differences appear to involve a group's structural position in addition to the formal content of its norms. Content is important insofar as it encourages group members either to empathize subjectively with others or to recognize an objective need for empathy with others, and Christian ideology in Indonesia probably encourages that capacity and that perception more than Islamic doctrines do. The Christian idea of loving one's enemy and turning the other cheek has no counterpart in Islam, where the ummat's boundary marks members of the faith off from unbelievers. The closest equivalent to empathy in Islam is *uchuwah*, a term more accurately translated as solidarity and one that applies strictly to interaction within the ummat. But Christians in the samples also saw a greater objective need for empathy in Indonesian society simply because the minority status of their religious community made it vulnerable. More than the Muslims, they tended to identify with the "other person" in the statement and to argue that Muslim politicians should try to understand the Christian minority's point of view. Contemporary incidents, in which crowds of Muslims expressed anger at the relative wealth and evangelical success of the Christian minority by burning churches, only underscored the need for empathy in the Christian's eyes. Committed Muslims, on the other hand, tended to see little reason to adopt the viewpoints of others, since they already had their own.

Two other religious minorities who were less tolerant were also less inclined to see a need for empathy in general: respondents with some religious education ($\overline{X} = 3.8$), compared to products of secular schooling ($\overline{X} = 4.2$); and those with stronger ($\overline{X} = 3.8$) as opposed to weaker religious affiliations ($\overline{X} = 4.2$). In parallel fashion, the rural-born were less inclined to support empathy ($\overline{X} = 3.9$) than were those with urban backgrounds ($\overline{X} = 4.4$).

The range from least to most support for empathy ran from stronger Muslims ($\overline{X} = 3.3$), through weaker Muslims ($\overline{X} = 4.1$), to weaker Christians ($\overline{X} = 4.7$), and stronger Christians ($\overline{X} = 5.0$). What this ordering suggests—the N's (7, 25, 3, and 1, respectively) are too small to warrant a stronger term—is that Muslim and Christian minorities of intense religious affiliation may carry the views of their less deeply committed coreligionists toward opposite extremes. Speculating further—for change over time cannot strictly be inferred from evidence gathered at one point in time—elite secularization, in the sense of reducing the identification of an individual with his religion, may not shift opinion uniformly in one direction or another but may instead reduce the extremes and build up consensus around the center. If this is true, then, insofar as Muslims become less intensely (and less defensively) Islamic, they should find it easier subjectively to empathize with non-Muslims; and the less intensely identifying the Christians become, the less they should feel an objective need for empathy on the part of others toward themselves. And these effects would be interactive; a decline in the number of "fanatic" Muslims, or in the intensity of their beliefs, would be seen by Christians as ameliorating the situation that gave rise to the stress on empathy in the first place, while a similar decline among "aggressively" proselytizing Christians would facilitate empathic understanding on the part of Muslims. The escalatory converse would also be true.

The institutional hypothesis found little support; legislators were only trivially less likely to support empathy than bureaucrats (Table 12). Overall, in both samples, support for empathy was remarkably high. It cannot be concluded from this, however, that the individuals in the samples were themselves empathic. Again, respondents' comments illuminate their outlooks. First, for many, agreement with the statement reflected not so much support for empathy, in the sense of putting oneself in the other person's shoes, as support for tolerance, in the sense of respecting the other person's views without necessarily accepting them. The notion of adopting another's point of view, even temporarily, was essentially strange to most of these men. Mutual understanding and respect were said by many to be desirable. But each side would maintain its own opinion. The point, these men felt, was not to erase the intersubjective gap but, rather, to recognize it and make sure that communication across it was relatively clear and not unnecessarily hostile. Some respondents modified their agreement or actually disagreed with the statement because they felt that to act on its premise could mean abandoning their own viewpoint entirely—an unacceptable, if not incomprehensible, option.

Second, respondents interpreted the statement in an exclusively cognitive mode. There was no question of emotional empathy; none mentioned interpersonal rapport as a social priority. In part, this reflected the metaphor of seeing (rather than feeling) used in the statement itself. But clearly cognitive tolerance was something that could be comprehended and recommended by the respondents more easily than full-fledged emotional empathy could.

The statement was both a prescription and a diagnosis. The large majority of respondents (more than three-fourths) who agreed that there should be more empathy also agreed that condi-

ere tense enough to warrant it. In this, the respondents ap-
both realistic at a cognitive level and constructive at an
ve one. But the limited meaning empathy had for them
must be kept in mind.

In short, the impacts of Islamic identity and rural origin were
parallel for both of these orientations. Muslim politicians, the
Muslim-schooled, and the rural-born were simultaneously less tolerant of alternative religious truths in particular and less inclined
to support empathy in general. Religious tolerance characterized
the mainly abangan bureaucrats in comparison with the legislators
and, within Parliament, the abangan-secular political groups.

Authority and Leadership

So far, broadly speaking, a certain pessimism—a view of the
social environment as relatively untrustworthy and conflict-ridden
—has been identified as characteristic of certain religious, ethnic,
or regional minorities and, the conflict orientation excepted, of the
members of a broadly recruited but politically disadvantaged legislature. Approximately the same minorities and legislators were also
relatively intolerant and/or disinclined to support empathy as a
social priority. The cultural hypothesis and the institutional hypothesis have found support.

A final step can now be taken toward isolating the implications
of elite political culture for cultural politics by introducing the
question of authority. The meaning for political change of a comparatively disaffected and encapsulated Islamic factor in elite political culture, for example, can only be assessed with a knowledge
of Muslim attitudes toward authority. The more support they give
to authority in general, and political leadership and the central
government in particular, the less likely they are either to speak
against existing authority themselves or, insofar as they are a part
of its upper structure, to accept criticism from below.

The men making up my two samples were mainly raised before
World War II, in a period when generalized deference to parental,
school, and state authority was widespread and still relatively un-
challenged save in anticolonial contexts. They experienced the upheavals of occupation and revolution and were exposed, directly or
indirectly, to Western libertarian ideas. Later they heard Sukarno
attack liberal democracy and individualism as inappropriate to

Indonesian conditions, and they lived under his authoritarian regime. How much would the cultural minorities among them value deference, and to what kinds of authority?

Table 13.   Support for deference to authority

	Low (1)	(2)	(3)	(4)	High (5)	Mean scale score ($\overline{X}$)
Administrators	1	5	6	4	2	3.1
Legislators	5	2	3	2	6	3.1
Totals	6	7	9	6	8	3.1

Percentage agreement in each sample		Scale item and item no.
Administrators	Legislators	
94	78	The best youth is the youth who obeys his parents, obeys his teacher, and respects those who hold high positions. (42)
56	50	A leader's orders must always be obeyed. (23)
39	50	Only the leaders of the state are capable of determining the meaning of the "national interest." (37)
17	33	A good school is one where the teacher teaches and his pupils listen and take notice without asking a lot of questions. (2)

Average interitem correlation = .44

In Table 13, which gives the scale of support for deference to authority in general, the institutional difference is irrelevant; administrators and legislators supported deference to equal degrees. The two distributions do, however, reflect the more varied social makeup of the DPR. Roughly a third of the members of Parliament stood at each of the two extremes of antideference and prodeference on the scale, inverting the pattern of bureaucratic clustering around the point of neutrality in the middle. To illustrate, one member of Parliament, a civilian who was neither older nor Javanese nor Muslim, Disagreed with all four statements; he was proud to come from a region that had no kings, let alone what he termed the extreme feudalism of the Javanese. Another legislator —an officer who was older, Javanese, and a Muslim—no less emphatically Agreed with all four statements. More homogeneous in age, ethnic origin, and religion, and perhaps more judicious for being more highly educated and cosmopolitan, the bureaucrats included no one with such extreme views.

As for the cultural hypothesis, elite minorities of religious, ethnic, and regional identity were more inclined to reject deference to authority than were their majoritarian counterparts. The four Christians ($\overline{X} = 2.5$) were less prone to support deference than the Muslims ($\overline{X} = 3.2$).[7] The ethnic outer islanders and the one Jakartan ($\overline{X} = 2.5$) were less prone than the Javanese ($\overline{X} = 3.3$) or the Sundanese ($\overline{X} = 3.5$). Finally, respondents born on the outer islands were also less accepting of deference ($\overline{X} = 2.5$) than was the Java-born majority ($\overline{X} = 3.1$)—a finding that is consistent with the outer islanders' greater propensity to see anomie and conflict in society.

When Christians and respondents born, or from ethnic groups, outside Java visualized leaders at the national level they tended to

7. Usman Agreed that pupils should silently absorb their teacher's wisdom, whereas Purwoko Disagreed, and the difference was typical of those with strong and weak religious affiliations and with Muslim as opposed to secular or Christian educations. Going from weaker to stronger affiliations, the means increased from 1.9 to 2.1 to 3.0; the Muslim-educated respondents supported pupil deference the most ($\overline{X} = 2.9$), the secular-trained came next ($\overline{X} = 2.1$), and the Christian-schooled endorsed it least ($\overline{X} = 1.7$). In their comments, the Islamic-educated tended to recall the deferential pesantren format, while the Christian-schooled remembered the premium placed on independent inquiry in their classroom experiences. On rote learning in the pesantren, see the account, admittedly written from a reformist (Muhammadiyah) perspective, in Amir Hamzah Wirjosukarto, *Pembaharuan Pendidikan dan Pengadjaran Islam jang Diselenggarakan oleh Pergerakan Muhammadijah dari Kota Jogjakarta* (Yogyakarta: Penjelenggara Publicasi Pembaharuan Pendidikan/Pengadjaran Islam [1962]), pp. 34, 74–75, and 81. Djajadiningrat, *Kenang-kenangan*, p. 26, refers to one type of pesantren instruction (*sorogan*) in which the santris do ask questions of the kiyai, but a more recent account (Asjari, "Kedudukan Kjai," p. 130) describes the same method as straight dictation.

see them as coming from majority groups—as being Muslims, Java-born, and ethnically Javanese or Sundanese. For these minorities, deference was likely to require a crossing of cultural lines and was, for that reason, rarer than among majoritarian respondents, who could more easily accept the idea of obedience to leaders because the leaders were likely to be akin to themselves. (The Sundanese members of the samples also showed support for deference, a fact that reflects their close cultural proximity to the majoritarian Java-nese and perhaps, too, the importance of the Sundanese governor of Greater Jakarta, who in 1969 was one of the most popular men in the capital.)

An important negative finding was that strongly ethnic or reli-gious respondents were not more prone to reject authority than the weakly ethnic or religious. The strong Javanese, among them Surjowidjojo, were convinced supporters of deference. They had internalized the value of deference in Javanese culture to a marked degree. But the proudly ethnic non-Javanese, who constituted a doubled minority of intensity and affiliation, were vigorous in re-jecting deference. Similarly, in the case of religious intensity, there was considerable support for deference among the committed Mus-lims; believing that the Islamic community took precedence over the secular state, they envisioned Muslim leaders worthy of an ummat that would gladly obey them. But the strong Christians were highly egalitarian. Here is further evidence for the proposi-tion, introduced to explain the distribution of support for empathy, that especially intense commitment to the values and norms of an ethnic or religious group exaggerates the orientation that is char-acteristic of that group. Insofar as religiosity is weakened by secularization, and ethnic commitment by national integration, one may speculate that political culture will become not less deferential but more consensual, through a diminution of the extremes of acceptance and rejection of authority that in 1969 appeared to characterize, respectively, the strongly Javanese/Muslim and the strongly non-Javanese/Christian members of the elite.

Another variable that proved helpful in explaining support for deference to authority was political affiliation. Earlier, PNI poli-ticians were seen to be most anomic, religious party members only slightly less so, and the governing alliance of officers and techno-crats, as represented in Parliament, least anomic (most optimistic) in outlook. The same progression occurred on the authority scale. The most willing to accept authority were the PNI members ($\overline{X} = 4.0$); then came the religiously affiliated legislators ($\overline{X} = 3.4$); lastly, the government grouping was by far the most likely to reject the idea that leaders should always be obeyed, that only leaders can know what is in the nation's interest, and that the model youth or pupil is one who obeys his superiors and does not bother them with a lot of questions ($\overline{X} = 2.3$).

The pattern of acceptance of authority shown by PNI members is not surprising. Their party had been a mainstay of the Old Order. Of the four PNI men in the legislative sample, two were older men who followed traditional styles of leadership, building out of Javanese and Sundanese proverbs the familial images of authority that they found most congenial. Both had been teachers, and one had also had a long career in the pamong praja. Deference to leaders was for them an article of faith. The other two, however, were younger men; their support for deference rested less on cultural models than on the images they had of themselves as having exercised vigorous leadership in the past. Both recalled in great detail their roles as local guerrilla commanders during the revolution. One of them had played a rather audacious part in a local conflict between the PNI and the PKI before the attempted coup in 1965. Their support for complete or near-complete deference was linked to an ideal of active charismatic command.

The category "religious parties" conceals a sharp difference between the two Christian party politicians, whose average score was only 2.3, and the five Islamic party members ($\overline{X} = 3.8$); the Muslim party representatives were almost as approving of deference as the PNI members. Among Islamic party delegates, the four NU legislators, with a mean of 4.3, were even more prone to support deference than the PNI representatives, while the Parmusi member, with a mean of 1.8, was one of the men least ready to accept authority in the parliamentary sample. Officials in the two departments where the PNI and the NU were most heavily entrenched, Information ($\overline{X} = 3.8$; $N = 2$) and Religion ($\overline{X} = 3.7$; $N = 2$), also showed the highest support for deference to authority of any department in the bureaucratic sample.

Like the PNI, the NU cooperated with Sukarno within the

framework of the Old Order. Several NU members had a heavily state-dependent view of their party as essentially an earner of patronage for the ummat. Several justified their support for deference with Koranic equivalents of the proverbs favored by the PNI respondents. Parmusi, however, was a post-Sukarno version of Masyumi, which Sukarno banned in 1960 as being a threat to the state, and the Parmusi informant did not hide his contempt for unreasoning obedience to authority. At the time I interviewed him, abangan generals in power under the New Order were interfering in his party, promoting one group of leaders at the expense of another.[8]

As for the legislative bloc most clearly identified with Suharto's government, namely, the alliance between the military (ABRI) and the professional men in the Development Group, its members, on the average, approved of deference the least of all ($\overline{X} = 2.3$). But again the summary mean conceals an important gap. Within the alliance, the officers in ABRI were much more inclined toward deference ($\overline{X} = 3.2$) than were the civilians in the Development Group ($\overline{X} = 1.7$). Indeed, one of the latter, a student leader studying for an advanced degree, rejected all four statements as inappropriate to the kind of modern democracy he wanted Indonesia to become. Like him, the more highly educated members of the elite were generally less accepting of authority ($\overline{X} = 2.8; N = 22$) than those who had not gone beyond secondary school ($\overline{X} = 3.6; N = 14$).

These findings reflect in miniature the predicament of the three major groups (the military, the parties, and the nonparty civilians) in New Order politics in the late 1960's. The military shared with the nonparty civilian elite an antipathy to the discredited Old Order parties; but in its support for deference to authority (*its* authority, to be sure), the military shared the hierarchical orientation of the Old Order politicians in contrast to the nonparty civilians, particularly the more vocal remnants of the "1966 generation," who were critical of authority. If their social backgrounds enabled the officers to bridge the cosmopolitan bureaucracy and the more parochial legislature, their outlook on authority likewise placed them in a position intermediate between the university-

8. On these events, see Samson, "Islam in Indonesian Politics."

hnocrats and the politicians. In that central position,
remained politically indispensable to the institution
er side.

erences conceal one important common characteristic:
uency to personalize authority. The statements that leaders
must always be obeyed and that only leaders of the state can know
the national interest were rejected by one group of respondents for
sounding dictatorial. But the point this group made was not that
the gap between leaders and led should be narrowed in order to
ensure more control by the latter over the former. On the contrary,
these men took the existence of such a gap for granted; their solution was to ensure that leaders would be morally superior persons—
although they never explained how this could be done. Two of
them cited Hitler. They did not object to his great power; leader-
led relationships were necessarily unequal. What they minded, and
what they cited in rejecting the statements mentioned, was Hitler's
morally debased personality, which had made him incapable of
using his power for good ends. Another respondent criticized Sukarno in similarly personal terms.

Another group, generally in agreement with both the statements
rejected by the first group, did not assume an unbridgeable gap
between leaders and led but believed that leaders could and should
narrow, even eliminate, the distance between themselves and the
common people. But, like the first group, they stressed the personal
qualities of leaders rather than procedures either for democratically
selecting them or for constraining them and rendering them ac-
countable to the public once in office. The psychic union of leader
and led would obviate the need for a structural solution to the
problem of authority.

Illustrating the view of this second group was the story told by
the Javanese politician Surjowidjojo about Abubakar, the second
head (after Muhammad) of the first Islamic state. One day Abubakar was walking and came upon a widow boiling stones in a pan
of water. She did not realize he was the head of state.

"Woman, why are you boiling those stones?" asked Abubakar.

"Because I have no rice," she replied. "I must cook stones for
my children instead."

"But they cannot eat stones."

"True," she replied, "but the sound of the boiling stones is like the sound of boiling rice, so at least they will think we still have food and will not cry."

"Why don't you tell the head of state of your need?"

"Why?" she answered. "He should know that we suffer and are in need without our making any report to him at all." Abubakar was so embarrassed to hear this that he went home and returned with enough rice to feed the widow and her children.

A Westerner might assume the moral of the story to be that leaders are not the only ones capable of knowing what is in the popular interest; not until the widow told him did Abubakar know of her need. But Surjo drew a different lesson: Abubakar *should have known.* Although the story was Islamic in origin, its point, Surjo explained, could be summarized in the Hindu-Javanese belief in *kawula-gusti,* the unity of ruler and ruled. A Westerner would identify this concept as a purely normative ideal. But for Surjo it transcended the artificial (Western) categories of ideal and real. Accordingly, he could cite Abubakar's ignorance of the widow's plight to justify his emphatic Agreement with the statement that only a country's leaders know the national interest—and see no contradiction between his evidence and his conclusion.

For both these groups, the personal characteristics of a leader justified deference to him. The important thing was the leader's spirit and style. In citing particular leaders, whether Koranic or contemporary, these men stressed the "spirit of self-sacrifice," the "lionheartedness," the "noble soul" of the leader as the attributes that made him deserving of obedience and respect. Melodramatically, but along just such personalized lines, one informant recalled his grief at the death of John F. Kennedy and how he had hidden his tears behind sunglasses in the office that day. He had met Kennedy a few years earlier and been deeply impressed, not with anything the man had done, but with what he was. Significantly, in all the discussion of authority the statements triggered, not one respondent referred explicitly to a leader's performance as the primary basis for obeying him.

The capacity of the elite in Indonesia to democratize the system in which it enjoys prestige and power thus appears to be limited both structurally and culturally. Having been recruited into elite positions by executive appointment—directly in the case of the administrators, indirectly in the case of the politicians—the members of the samples tended, with several exceptions, to accept as legitimate the top-down administrative polity. This was true even for many of those who disagreed with the assertions that leaders should be obeyed and are the only ones privy to the national interest. These men knew they depended for their jobs not on popular mandates but on patrons. Structurally, there was no incentive for them to want to reverse the flow of enabling authority. Culturally, again with several exceptions, their models of leadership had more in common with the example of Rama's good character that the king had asked Purwoko's father to emulate than with criteria of success in solving problems or improving conditions. The kawula-gusti assumption renders irrelevant all mechanisms of accountability except the conscience of Abubakar. The structural democratization of Indonesia's polity, if it is to occur, seems unlikely to enlist the active cooperation of such men as these.

To summarize, overall the respondents were neither deferential nor egalitarian in outlook. They tended to personalize authority. The institutional hypothesis was not supported as an explanation of the variation among respondents, but the cultural hypothesis was. Minorities of religious and ethnic affiliation and regional minorities held more egalitarian views than their counterpart majorities. Minorities of religious and ethnic intensity, on the other hand, appeared to exaggerate, in opposite directions, the orientations toward authority that characterized the larger groups of which they were a part. This finding suggested that secularization, in the sense of weakening religious and ethnic identities, might further consensus by reducing extreme views. In Parliament, the nonparty civilians were a stronghold of egalitarian attitudes, but their allies, the military, firmly supported deference. In this respect, while it worked with the nonparty civilians to undercut the parties' influence, the military shared the tendency of the Old Order party members to accept authority. Finally, higher (secular) education appeared to encourage egalitarianism.

The tendency of some respondents to personalize authority and to speak less of concrete responsibilities than of personal rapport between leader and led points to the importance not only of deference to leaders but also of trust in them. Asked to choose between two different postures toward leaders, one of trust and one of suspicion, nearly two-thirds of the elite preferred the trusting stance (Table 14). They were themselves leaders, of course, and they related the statement to their own positions in government. Compared to the legislators, bureaucrats were more trusting and expected more trust from others. Typical among administrators was the Javanese from the Department of Transmigration and Cooperatives who explained that a leader's personal authority and the trust of his followers were inextricably linked; withdrawing the latter would damage the former and should therefore be avoided at all costs. He saw the leader-led relationship in symbiotic terms similar to those used by many others when reacting to the statements on deference to authority. The politicians, by contrast, were sharply divided; their responses formed a distribution even more steeply U-shaped than in the case of support for deference (compare Tables 13 and 14).

Table 14. Support for trust in leaders

	Low (1)	(2)	(3)	(4)	High (5)	Mean scale score ($\overline{X}$)
Administrators	1	3	1	5	8	3.9
Legislators	6	2	–	3	7	3.2
Totals	7	5	1	8	15	3.5

Percentage disagreement in each sample		Scale item and item no.
Administrators	Legislators	
72	56	It is better to suspect a leader than trust him. (29)

Along almost every cultural variable, respondents were distinguished into relatively trusting or suspicious groups. In accord with the cultural hypothesis, minorities of religious affiliation and intensity were both comparatively reluctant to place their trust in leaders: Christians ($\overline{X} = 2.8$) were more suspicious than majoritarian Muslims ($\overline{X} = 3.6$), and respondents with stronger religious affiliations ($\overline{X} = 3.1$) were more suspicious than respondents with weaker ties ($\overline{X} = 3.9$). The results were similar for ethnic variables: the outer island minority (including the one Jakartan)— comparatively anomic, pessimistic about conflict, and opposed to deference—were more suspicious of leaders ($\overline{X} = 2.6$) than the Sundanese ($\overline{X} = 3.5$), who in turn were less trusting than the majoritarian Javanese ($\overline{X} = 4.0$). The most strongly ethnic were more suspicious ($\overline{X} = 2.8$) than those who identified with their ethnic groups moderately ($\overline{X} = 3.4$) or weakly ($\overline{X} = 3.6$). Again, by affiliation and intensity, minorities were the most disaffected. Similarly, by region of birth, the minority of outer islanders proved much more suspicious ($\overline{X} = 2.5$) than those born on Java ($\overline{X} = 3.8$).

On this orientation, political groups in Parliament reversed the order of their distribution on the scale of support for deference; the PNI showed by far the least inclination to trust leaders ($\overline{X} = 2.0$), followed by the religious parties ($\overline{X} = 3.3$), and the government grouping ($\overline{X} = 3.7$). The reason for the shift is that, whereas the first scale measured support for deference to various kinds of authority, including parental and pedagogic authority, this statement was interpreted by most respondents to refer specifically to political authority.

One PNI politician who Disagreed with the statement did give it cultural referents. Had not the prophets been shepherds and mankind the sheep? Then leaders today must be trusted in the same way, as sheep trust their shepherds. But the other three PNI members all Agreed with the item, and their references were specific, political, and contemporary. Their comments revealed an attitude that compartmentalized authority as something culturally legitimate but politically suspect.

Again, a political-structural explanation must supplement the cultural one. The members of the government coalition in the DPR were in a position opposite to the PNI's; they were involved in and supported a specific political authority—Suharto's alliance of military and technocratic leaders—but had been socialized out of the matrix of culturally authoritarian norms in which the PNI members' attitudes were still embedded. Again, however, there was a sharp division between civilian and military elements in the coalition. Just as the civilian intellectuals and professionals showed themselves much less prone to accept deference than the officers, so were they much less trustful of leaders ($\overline{X} = 3.0$, compared to the officers' extremely high 4.7). Similarly, in the samples as a whole, military men were much more trusting ($\overline{X} = 4.4$) than civilians ($\overline{X} = 3.3$).

In the grouping of religious parties, which fell between the PNI and the government alliance, there was again a considerable difference between the five Islamic party members, who were on the whole trusting ($\overline{X} = 3.6$), and the two Christian party members, who on the average were not ($\overline{X} = 2.5$). The cultural and political minority of Christian party delegates both rejected deference and were suspicious of leaders, that is, they were culturally and politically disaffected.

Minority groups were once again likely to see a leader as belonging to a majority group; hence their greater suspicion. Institutional and cultural hypotheses were reinforcing: the bureaucrats were more inclined to trust leaders, and, as leaders, to expect trust from others, because of the deferential content of Javanese culture, the majority position of the abangan Javanese, and the hierarchical structure of the bureaucracy as a prestigious institution. Even the bureaucrats were not strikingly authoritarian in outlook; a good number of those who disagreed with the proposition that leaders should be suspected rather than trusted did so not because they believed the opposite—that all leaders should be trusted—but because they found blanket suspicion simply too extreme. But the combination of their own cultural and institutional milieux did seem to predispose administrators away from suspicion of leaders and toward trust.

If the bureaucracy was culturally majoritarian, the legislature was culturally fragmented, and the striking lack of consensus among politicians on the question of trust reflects their varied origins. Even within political groupings there were sharp differences: for example, between officers and civilians in the government alliance over the question of deference to authority.

Finally, the greater relative suspicion among members of Parliament was related to their readiness to read political meaning into the statement that leaders should not be trusted and to their ability to keep separate questions of general deference to culturally sanctioned models of authority (teachers, kings, and parents, in the old Javanese formula) and of trust in specifically or purely political leaders. Legislators were less ready than bureaucrats to support both kinds of authority. It may be that the more insulated an institution is from partisan politics the easier it is for its incumbents to generalize their deference from cultural to political authority, and that, conversely, the more exposed an institution is to partisan politics the less the spillover from the one type of orientation to the other.

This expressly political aspect of the legislators' perceptions and rationales further marks their responses to a statement on central versus regional authority. Given an unspecified issue on which the center (that is, the central government) and the regions held different positions, who should prevail? It might be expected that the administrators, who worked for the central government, would have given the center priority over the regions, while the politicians, many of whom lived in Jakarta only when called from the regions to attend sessions of Parliament, would have placed the regions first. Instead, the bureaucrats were almost equally divided between those who would give priority to the center and those who would not, and nearly half the legislators Agreed that the interest of the center should come first (Table 15).

The politicians' answers illuminated this result. Many legislators who favored the central government did so while citing the same kind of symbiotic imagery they had used when speaking of leaders and followers. Center and region were like the two sides of the betel leaf, said one, different yet the same. Others recited a dictum commonly invoked against center-regional conflict: "The center belongs to the regions and the regions belong to the center." The point about these formulae is that they did not mean equality but were instead denials that a conflict of interest between the center and the provinces could even exist. These answers were appropriate to a protagonist of the unitarian republic against regionalist demands. The four PNI members, for example, who all Agreed that the center should come first, felt very much heirs to the nationalist rhetoric of unity in 1945. Had not the revolution, one of them argued, been fought against the federalist idea of the recolonizing

Table 15. Support for central authority

	Low (1)	(2)	(3)	(4)	High (5)	Mean scale score ($\overline{X}$)
Administrators	3	6	1	6	2	2.9
Legislators	2	5	2	1	8	3.4
Totals	5	11	3	7	10	3.2

Percentage agreement in each sample		Scale item and item no.
Administrators	Legislators	
44	50	In the event of differing standpoints between center and region, the center's interest should take priority. (26)

Dutch? Some of the comments of these men carried unmistakable echoes of the debates and struggles of 1945–1950.

Others who opted for the center did so because of the reality of state preponderance. A member of NU preferred a metaphor of meat and fire. The regions were the meat being roasted by the center's fire. All energy lay with the fire; passive and dependent, the provinces could no more hope to influence the central government than meat could hope to become fire. This respondent came from outside Java and was too young to have fought in the revolution. His mild agreement that the center should come first signaled not so much approval as resigned acceptance of things as they were and as they were likely to remain. He felt that the central government had slighted and ignored his region, but fire was fire and meat was meat and the natural superiority of fire was incontestable. His fellow NU members, all older and Javanese, easily Agreed with the statement; for them it was a description both of the real situation and of the ideal unitarian republic for which they had fought in the revolution.

Memories of the effort on behalf of a single, unified republic also surfaced in the remarks of the administrators. One, a military man, took evident pleasure in recollecting a long discussion he had had with the nationalist Muhammad Yamin not long after the 1945 constitutional convention. They had both agreed how absolutely essential it was to have a strong central government to defend Indonesia and advance her historic role as one great independent nation. Both of them, this informant recalled with a smile, had been caught up in the secular nationalist mystique. Now he could see the costs of a unitarian system, its top-heaviness, the way it had enabled clique parties in Jakarta to "sink their claws," as he put it, into the regions. Yet the formative impact on him of the revolution to which he had so passionately committed himself had not been cancelled by his more prosaic experiences since 1949, however disillusioning those latter events should logically have been. The working out in practice of the unitarian ideal led him to reduce his support for the central authority by only one notch, from Agree to slightly agree.

For the few administrators and politicians who actually Disagreed with the idea that Jakarta's standpoint should come first, more recent experiences of arbitrary and unresponsive rule by the center were decisive. And one reason why the administrators were more critical of the idea of central priority was that, on the whole, they did not have such vividly positive memories of the unitarian revolution as did the politicians. Drs. Sujoso was one of the bureaucrats who favored the regions. He recounted at length his experience as a ranking official in a province outside Java in the period immediately before the attempted coup in 1965. In this area, Islam was strong, and the PKI had no roots. Yet an instruction came from his ministry in Jakarta that a large number of local and regional bodies were to undergo "NASAKOMization," that is, their executive positions were to be divided equally between nationalist (NASionalis), religious (Agama), and communist (KOMunis) members in a kind of ideological troika. This directive made no sense to Sujoso, who knew the religious anticommunism of the local population. He could not oppose the order, but he tried to lessen its effect by involving the anticommunist army command as much as possible in its execution. Because so few bona fide PKI members were available, Sujoso recalled, some persons sought and obtained positions under the KOM quota who were not party members at all. Nor did the fact of the misnomer save them from drowning when the tide turned in 1965.

Another bureaucrat, Sumarno, who also rejected the statement, told a tale of central government interference in the interisland rice trade in the 1950's. The region to which he had been assigned could barely feed itself, yet it had been ordered by Jakarta to provide for its neighbors as well. Sumarno related with some pride how, in trying to win from the center the lowest possible export quota for his province, he had been able to halve the tonnage originally demanded. The responses of this critical minority were not bound up in the heroic achievement of republican unity. Nor did they assume the fact of overwhelming central advantage to be irrevocable. By dealing in concrete instances that they had themselves experienced while serving in the regions since independence and that they felt illustrated their success in at least attenuating the damage of Jakarta's intervention and ignorance, they reversed the revolutionary perspective and apathetic resignation of the majority.

There is a further reason for the institutional difference. Not only were the legislators ideologically heir to the 1945 tradition of revolutionary unity, they operated in a tradition, dating back to the Volksraad, of bodies legislative in name but administrative in reality. All the members of the DPR in 1969 had been approved by the Suharto government and some had been proposed by it as well. Despite their organizations' membership figures and claims to rural representation, they were beholden to the executive fire that roasted the legislative meat, or to the sunward face of the betel leaf.

The institutional difference concealed an extremely sharp contrast between, on the one hand, the perfectly centralizing PNI contingent ($\overline{X} = 5.0$) and the distinctly centralizing religious party members ($\overline{X} = 4.1$) and, on the other, the markedly decentralizing government bloc ($\overline{X} = 1.9$). Ironically, the PNI, ostensibly an opposition party, unanimously preferred central to regional authority, while the officers, professionals, and intellectuals whose collaboration sustained the central government looked more favorably on regional interests. By comparison to the government alliance, members of the PNI and NU ($\overline{X} = 4.8$) were prisoners of a simplistically unitarian revolutionary paradigm, as cherished as it was unrealistic. This is not to deny the persistence of centrifugal forces in present-day Indonesia. On the contrary: precisely in trying to respond to such forces, the kind of reflexive, unconditional, and essentially rejective paradigm of unity developed in the struggle of an anticolonial movement becomes more of a hindrance than a help. For those in both samples who retained this extreme or automatic centralist perspective, the lessons of the revolution had been overlearned.[9]

The PNI and the NU were also fundamentally statist parties; to their leaders, politics was mainly a contest for bureaucratic position. And although in this competition the NU, unlike the PNI, at least had a base outside government—in the networks of rural pesantrens and kiyais—Islamic schooling appears to have facilitated among NU spokesmen the same view of the center as properly predominant. The informant who represented Parmusi, the Islamic reform party, was more urbane, widely traveled, and Western-educated than his NU coreligionists, and unlike them he disagreed that the center should come first. His views also echoed the struggle for regional autonomy that Parmusi's predecessor, Masyumi, had waged in the 1950's.

Religious minorities were, on the average, more centralist in outlook than religious majorities. This held true for persons with religious educational backgrounds ($\overline{X} = 3.3$) compared to those without ($\overline{X} = 2.7$), for those with stronger ($\overline{X} = 3.4$) rather than weaker religious affiliations ($\overline{X} = 3.0$), and for Christians ($\overline{X} = 3.8$) compared to Muslims ($\overline{X} = 3.1$). Among all these groups, only the secularly schooled were on the average actually decentralist.

The greater average preference for central authority among Christian respondents is not hard to understand. The movement for an Indonesia-wide Islamic state had been defeated by leaders at the center who had defended the constitutional idea of a state "based on belief in One God" against any confessional interpretation. Conversely, the closest to reality the concept of a Muslim state had come in Indonesia had been in the regions, notably

9. This argument is developed at greater length in my "Students and the Establishment in Indonesia: The Status-Generation Gap," in W. Howard Wriggins and James F. Guyot, eds., *Population, Politics, and the Future of Southern Asia* (New York: Columbia University Press, 1973), pp. 259–295.

Aceh.[10] Christians were solicitous of the center because by and large it had protected them.

The findings relating to religious intensity and religious schooling are harder to explain. In the civil conflict Indonesia underwent after independence, rebels against the central government favored religious and regionalist appeals. The Islamic-secessionist uprisings of the 1950's are a case in point. But the religious and religiously schooled minorities in my Jakarta-based samples were not especially disturbed about the preponderance of central over regional authority. The three respondents who were both more religious and most centralist were all members of NU and had been educated in Islamic schools. In the religion to which, compared to the others, they adhered more devoutly, the ideal state was thoroughly sacralized, religio-political power being indivisible in Islam. Their pesantren education may have promoted a view of central (sacral) authority as necessary if the natural tendency of men toward greed and struggle with their fellows was to be curbed. (The more religious and the religiously schooled, it will be recalled, were also the more anomic and held more pessimistic views of man's capacity for conflict.)

Somewhat less speculative is the possibility that the religious content of their education and their strong piety inhibited the resocialization of these respondents out of the revolutionary paradigm and into a more shaded and flexible view of center-region authority. Roughly speaking, the more a respondent believed that the center should prevail, the more flatly axiomatic was his expression of that view. If, as Takdir argued, reflexiveness as opposed to nuanced, critical thinking is promoted by rote learning at the feet of the kiyai in the pesantren, and if strongly held religious commitments encourage simplistic or absolute judgments, then these devout Muslims would seem least receptive to resocialization out of a centralizing perspective—one appropriate to a period of warfare against a divisive colonial enemy—into more qualified and less dated views of center-region relations.

Other evidence supports this argument. Although those with (secular) higher education were only trivially more critical of central authority than the secondary-trained, they were much more nuanced in their responses; whereas about four-fifths of the better

10. See Boland, *Struggle of Islam,* pp. 68–75 and 174–185.

educated chose a qualified or intermediate answer category, about four-fifths of those who never went beyond secondary school took an extreme position. And the rural-born ($\overline{X} = 3.3$) preferred the centralizing paradigm more than those born in cities ($\overline{X} = 2.6$).

The attributes of rural origin, religious education, and piety recall the parochial backgrounds of the legislators. If a respondent with these characteristics acquired a centralist outlook in 1945–1949, they apparently inhibited its later moderation. Parochialism apparently worked to rigidify orientations toward authority, not only in the case of individuals but also institutionally, as is reflected in the more centralizing stance of the less cosmopolitan legislative elite. The structural dependence of the main Old Order parties in Parliament—and of Parliament itself—on the central executive further promoted in their members a recognition of central supremacy. And if it is true that secularization, in the sense of education, urbanization, and weakening religious ties, promotes greater sensitivity to regional interests, then the problem for cultural politics of Jakarta-based elite politicians may be not that they mirror subnational sentiment but that they are too likely to ignore it. Once again the picture of an elite whose divisions are defined by the pattern of cleavage among the general populace appears inaccurate. On the contrary, the closer by social background a member of the elite is to the rural mass, the more deeply his structural dependency on central authority may influence him—so that he becomes, so to speak, more royal than the king—and, conversely, the further removed (that is, more cosmopolitan) he is from that rural mass, the more responsive he may become to its interests.

Similar logic accounts best for the otherwise surprising finding that whereas officers were more likely than civilians to endorse trust in leaders, they were less inclined to favor the center's interest over the regions' ($\overline{X} = 2.4$, compared to 3.4 among civilians). At first glance, this pattern seems inconsistent. Military leaders in Jakarta play a powerful centralizing role and the armed forces pride themselves on their defense of the nation against regionalism; the officers in the samples might have been expected both to endorse trust and uphold the center. Consistency appears instead in the attitudinal company these military men kept. Three other important segments of the elite shared the officers' views: relatively ready to trust but decentralist were two religious majorities, of affiliation (Muslims, compared to Christians) and intensity (the less pious, compared to the devout), and the dominant institutional elite (bureaucrats, compared to legislators). The military component in the elite lay, on balance, closer to the mainstream abangan cosmopolitanism of these three groups (Muslims, the less pious, the bureaucrats) than to the minoritarian outgroup intensities of their counterparts (Christians, the more pious, the politicians). Again, a structural explanation stressing political and cultural advantage is helpful. Dominant, urbane majorities who control the center can afford to be at least symbolically magnanimous toward the regions, whereas underdog minorities in a centralizing state may either look to it for protection, identify with it as the source of power and patronage, or lack the secular education to recognize and criticize its drawbacks.

Three main observations follow from this analysis. First, cultural minorities (of religious, ethnic, and regional affiliation and, to a lesser extent, of religious and ethnic intensity) gave less support than cultural majorities to deference in general and trust in leaders in particular—just as the disaffected minority hypothesis predicted. This does not mean, however, that these minorities supported the regions against the center. The Christians particularly felt that they could get a better hearing in Jakarta than in the regions, especially in the most exclusively Islamic ones.

Second, among political parties, the two main survivors of the Old Order—the PNI and the NU—leaned sharply toward acceptance of authority, both in their approval of general deference and in their support for the central government. In comparison, the government coalition in Parliament was at the opposite—the egalitarian and the regional—end on both scales. Were Indonesia ruled by a combination of abangan- or santri-based parties, prospects for decentralization might be even worse than they are under Suharto's military-technocratic regime. As for prospects in reality, the military's views are too ambiguous and too contextually integrated to infer from the evidence of their orientations a distinctive policy bias. On the one hand, officers appeared more decentralist than civilians in the elite. But insofar as deference to authority implies regional deference to central authority, contrary evidence is provided by the gap, noted earlier, within the government's legis-

ce between civilians criticizing and officers defending
The military's willingness to agree that the center's in-
not always override the regions' may, of course, apply
but not political interests; the tentative steps toward
economic decentralization introduced under the Second Five-Year
Plan (1974–1979), unaccompanied as they are by political decentralization, illustrate this distinction.

Third, most of the men in the samples personalized authority
and leadership. None used performance criteria; many stressed
charisma and feeling. The problem of securing a responsive authority was seen as a problem of finding good men, not of creating or
reforming institutional arrangements to promote simultaneously
democratic and effective government. Whether their views were
realistic or not in the circumstances of Indonesia—a matter of
debate—these men could not be expected to try to democratize the
nation's government structurally.

Summary

The second, orientational parts of the two hypotheses have been
supported. Cultural minorities were generally more defensively
negative than their counterpart majorities, as can be seen in summary Table 16. Compared to cultural majorities, they were less
inclined to trust leaders or tolerate alternative religious truths,
more inclined to see extreme conflict and anomie in the social
environment, and less likely (Christians excepted) to support empathy as a social priority.

Religious minorities, and particularly Islamic minorities of religious intensity, were more disaffected than ethnic or regional minorities. An unassimilated Islamic factor persists in elite political
culture and is likely to remain a potential source of tension in
cultural politics. If any single cultural group considered itself outside the ambience of the cosmopolitan elite in 1969 it was the
Islamic group. The Parmusi politician in Parliament spoke with
unconcealed bitterness about what he considered the anti-Islamic
policies of the Suharto regime and the Christian "assault" on Indonesian Islam; others, including the NU members and Department
of Religion officials, were less defiant. But knitting together the
commentaries of most of the committed Muslims in the samples
were feelings of malaise. Islamic discontent was neither so spe-

Table 16. Summary of distinctive orientations

	Empathizing	Centralist	Trusting	Anomic	Tolerant	Conflictful	Deferential
Religious minorities							
More strongly religious	less	more	less	more	less	more	
Having religious, especially Muslim, schooling	less	more		more	less	more	
Christians	more	more	less	more			less
Ethnic and regional minorities							
Non-Javanese			less	more	less*	more	less*
Born off Java			less	more	less	more	less
More strongly ethnic			less	more			
Institutional outgroups							
Members of Parliament		more	less	more	less		
Party members in Parliament, especially PNI and NU		more	less	more			more
Officials in less powerful or prestigious, more party-penetrated ministries						more	
Other groups							
Rural-born	less	more					
Civilians		more	less		less		
Elder siblings						more	
More highly educated						more	less

* Sundanese excepted.

Note: The group for comparison is implied in each row heading; for example, the more strongly religious were less empathizing than the less strongly religious. Column headings summarize each orientation in a single word, for convenience; exact renderings —for example, "support for empathy as a social priority"—are given in the appropriate tables.

cifically focused nor so violently expressed as to suggest a repetition of the religio-political rebellions of the 1950's. Instead, the Muslims' discontent appeared to be a kind of underground reservoir of available but latent opposition. Insofar as Islamic issues were mixed up in other conflicts and alignments, the reservoir might be tapped for one purpose or another, but its waters appeared unlikely to surface unaided. If the regime were blatantly and publicly anti-Muslim, if it made of the many Islamic groups a common enemy, then Muslim grievances could rise to flood proportions; but only then.

At the elite level, the more centralist orientation of the committed Muslims probably inhibited action. Especially among the NU members, but also in the commentary of the Islamic-schooled, a recognition of the center's supremacy, whether regretful or approving, probably helped keep this disaffection from spilling over into protest behavior. But the potential was there.

As for the orientational part of the institutional hypothesis, it too was supported, in that members of Parliament were less trusting of leaders or tolerant of other religious truths and tended to see more injustice and evil in their social surroundings than did bureaucrats. The reasons appear to be partly political and partly cultural, a matter of structural position and prior socialization. The legislators were not only more likely to be members of a cultural minority than were the mainly abangan Javanese bureaucrats, but also—especially the party delegates—located to their structural disadvantage outside the counsels of the regime. Members of the Muslim parties constituted both a cultural minority (of intensity) and a political outgroup; compared to them, the legislators in the government coalition had a more optimistic view of society, more trust in leaders, less generalized deference to authority, greater sensitivity to the regions, and more tolerance of other faiths. And, with the exception of general deference, on which the two samples did not differ, the administrators as a whole, nearer as they were to the cockpit of the regime, also showed greater optimism, trust, sensitivity, and tolerance.

In one sense, these results are encouraging. The ruling nonparty elite in Indonesia in 1969 was not strikingly authoritarian, insensitive, or narrow-minded—compared, that is, to its potential opposition, the surviving Old Order parties. Men with the views this group held appeared capable of compromise in cultural politics. Nor did the abangan majority appear to be about to force its philosophy on the country at large. These findings, however, are only partial clues to behavior in cultural politics, as the next chapter shows.

The most striking negative finding is that the military as a group differed from the civilians on only two of the seven orientations. Although their views were marked by a symmetrical vigilance, against the communist left and the Muslim right, officers in the Indonesian elite did not constitute a distinct orientational subculture within elite political culture. Structurally, of course, they had the upper hand; but their outlooks, at least as measured by my scales, overlapped too much with civilian viewpoints to suggest unambiguously how officers would use that advantage: on the one hand they were more decentralist than the civilians, but on the other they endorsed trust in leaders more. These views did, however, appear to link the military with the members of the elite's cosmopolitan mainstream who shared them. If, in terms of their social background, the officers served as a bridge between more and less parochial (that is, between legislative and bureaucratic) institutions (Table 8), their views, insofar as they could be isolated at all, were more akin to those of civilian officials than civilian politicians. The army leadership's choice of a bureaucratic, nonparty partner to join it in building the New Order could be a behaviorial expression of this affinity.

Singling out the three youngest informants in the samples, their trust in leaders was the lowest of all ($\overline{X} = 1.7$). A large gap in years divided these three from other respondents; in addition, they were all civilian members of Parliament, non-Javanese, and identified fairly strongly with their religions, two of them actually representing religious parties. The comments of these young men made it clear that their lack of trust in leaders was especially marked because so many of the possible grounds for distrust were relevant for them: from their perspective, Indonesia's leaders looked older, more secular, nonparty if not antiparty, and Javanese. The more such cleavages coincide, the greater the disaffection produced. If these junior members of the elite can be made for a moment to stand for the youthful mass outside it, their critical views are a challenge to the nation's leadership as a whole to avoid lining up on the same side of too many coextensive divisions—generational, cultural, political, or economic.[11]

Within the elite, mutually implicating imbalances raise the dilemma of institutionalizing democracy in a plural society. In multicultural Indonesia, where the bureaucracy constitutes a relatively homogeneous, majoritarian, and cosmopolitan subculture of similarly socialized individuals, where the legislature is by contrast more diversely and parochially recruited, and where executive structures have long held sway over representative ones, the growth of disaffection, mistrust, and intolerance among higher civil servants has been inhibited. Conversely, the same conditions have tended to breed disaffection, mistrust, and intolerance among legislators. The dilemma is this: to shift the center of political gravity from the bureaucracy to Parliament is to risk the divisions and instability of policy-making without consensus. But to allow the bureaucracy to continue to pre-empt the representative function is to risk a different kind of fragility: that of an artificial, imposed consensus. In the next and last chapter, through a case study of official responses in the 1970's to the danger of reinforcing cleavages and to this dilemma of institutional imbalance, the policy questions with which this book began are reintroduced and tentatively answered.

11. See my "Students and the Establishment."

CONCLUSION

CULTURAL POLITICS AND
THE INDONESIAN ELITE

The contrasting lives of Usman and Purwoko yielded two main hypotheses, one about cultural groups, the other about political institutions, and both having to do with orientations shaped by experience. With evidence from the full samples, these propositions have been explored, refined, and supported. Compared to cultural majorities, ethnic, religious, and regional minorities (Christians and Sundanese partly excepted) have been led by experience to hold a darker view both of the surrounding society and of the culturally majoritarian figures who wield political authority. The cultural homogeneity, social advantages, and political influence of the bureaucratic elite have rendered its perspective more benign than that of the legislative elite. These findings overlapped, in that cultural minorities were better represented in the politically weaker institution.

As noted in the introduction, major ethnic and religious cleavages cut across one another: the Javanese are religiously divided, and Islam is transethnic. This pattern is culture's great boon to Indonesian nationalism. For if the Javanese were Muslim and the non-Javanese adhered to other faiths, or if both called themselves Muslim but only the non-Javanese took their religion seriously, the history of the archipelago would have been written differently. Above all, the promise of political unity—implied in the colony's borders as drawn by the Dutch, furthered through a lingua franca that belonged to no major group, realized in the struggle to make Indonesia, and defended against secession after independence— would have proven far harder to achieve. Cross-cutting cleavages give meaning to the nation's motto: Bhinneka Tunggal Ika (unity in diversity).

A main finding of this book is that within the elite, ethnic, religious, organizational, and institutional differences are much more nearly parallel. The representative body is at once culturally and politically disadvantaged. Legislative groups were distinguished one from another more by their degree of religious absolutism than by any other orientation examined. In Parliament, an Islamic factor reflected both the impotence of the institution and personal disaffection from secular-abangan norms prevailing in the capital city; by virtue of their personal and institutional advantages, the bureaucrats were much more at home in the atmosphere of Jakarta, Purwoko's nostalgia for the village notwithstanding.

To make these cultural and political cleavages less coincident, the regime could either empower the representative body or diversify the executive. In fact it has done neither. This book ends, therefore, with an attempt to answer four questions about the current state of, and prospects for, cultural politics in Indonesia. First, what are the problems of cultural politics as they appear in the mid-1970's? Second, will the patterns of elite experience and outlook sketched in this book be more likely to help or hinder their solution? Third, what is the regime doing, or not doing, to solve them? Fourth, what could happen in the future?

In the 1970's, the Jakarta press popularized a new term, *sara*,[1] standing for the kinds of groups between which conflict could prove most dangerous to Indonesia's development and unity: *s* for *suku* (ethnic groups), *a* for *agama* (religions), *r* for *ras* (races), and *a* for *antar golongan* (referring to conflict "between groups"). The fourth term is intentionally ambiguous, for it covers two especially sensitive divisions, between military men and civilians and between higher and lower classes. In the foregoing discussion, these cleavages have been linked to elite opinions expressed in 1969; in this last chapter, they are illustrated in relation to elite behavior four years later, in 1973–1974. The shift of focus should yield a judgment about how useful the generalizations developed from this study of political culture are in understanding, if not predicting, the dynamic phenomena of cultural politics. Four incidents are discussed, three briefly and one in detail.

1. See, for example, the editorial in *Kompas*, July 15, 1974.

One night in April 1973, in the central Javanese city of Yogyakarta, where students from all over the country come to study at
the nation's largest university, a Javanese pedicab driver became
involved in an argument with three youths from the provinces of
West Sumatra and Central Sulawesi. The dispute ended in the
death of the driver, who was apparently stabbed by one of the
non-Javanese youths. The latter were soon arrested, but the other
pedicab drivers in the city were not mollified; that night and the
following week they massed in front of dormitories housing university students from outside Java to protest the killing. "Destroy
Sumatra!" cried the drivers.

This they could not do, but they could and did attack West
Sumatran (ethnically Minangkabau) student quarters, killing two
students, smashing windows, setting fires, and badly wounding a
Minangkabau tailor who happened to be in the building. To avenge
these deaths, a mass of students went on a rampage along the city's
main street, breaking store windows and setting pedicabs on fire.
The violence ended there, but not before a local police officer had
speculated that former political prisoners with communist connections were behind the affair. A newsweekly wrote that the violence
showed just how explosive ethnic differences could become when
combined with "socioeconomic dissatisfaction," a reference to the
gap in status between students and drivers.[2]

Less serious but also revealing is the case of the high school
teacher in Ujung Pandang, South Sulawesi, who organized a poetry-
reading contest among the school's pupils. One of the poems to be
read, written by a Javanese, contained the statement that "the
Javanese are lazy about praying and fond of mysticism." One of
the school's pupils, also a Javanese, took offense at the line and
showed it to his father, who took still greater offense. The father
attended the contest, waited until it was over, and then seized the
mimeographed copies of all the poems read and ordered the organizing committee to report to a local military authority; he could
do this because he was an officer in the army's military police.
During interrogation, the teacher was asked about his earlier membership in a PNI cultural organization and given a form to fill out
regarding possible complicity in the "G30S/PKI." (This official

2. For this interpretation, and on the incident itself, see *Tempo*, May 5,
1973.

term for the September 30th Movement [Gerakan 30 September] that kidnapped and killed the generals in 1965 was meant to leave no doubt about the communists' role in those events.) He was not arrested, but the military authorities ordered him to report to their office every Monday. As in the Yogyakarta case, the authorities appeared eager to blame the affair on communists. The incident illustrates, too, the slight grounds on which officers could question civilians and restrict their freedom in the name of order and security.[3]

Earlier the same month, August 1973, in West Java's capital city of Bandung, a bullock cart and a Volkswagen grazed each other. Three young Indonesians of Chinese descent got out of the car and beat up the driver of the cart. Inflamed by a false rumor that the bullock-cart driver had been killed, mobs of young people, including a number of pedicab drivers, began turning over cars and setting them on fire. Chinese-owned stores and homes were broken into and their contents looted and burned in a replay of the anti-Chinese violence that had occurred in the same city in 1963 and 1966. Although the racial character of the flare-up was unmistakable, interpretations of the event's other dimensions varied. Government officials, mainly military men, charged that "remnants of the G30S/PKI" were responsible; the wife of a PKI-linked political prisoner in the Bandung area was arrested just after visiting her husband, and other suspects were picked up at the house of a man previously jailed for his leftist associations. A Muslim party representative in Parliament suggested that the real cause of the affair was the growing gap between the haves and the have-nots, implicitly drawing a comparison between the Chinese-blood Indonesians who dominate the country's commerce and the economically less active and poorer majority of racially indigenous citizens. After the incident, the military authorities, doubtless worried at the prospect of Muslims lining up against Chinese for combined economic and religious reasons—as happened in 1911, when an Islamic Trade Association (Sarekat Dagang Islam) quickly turned into the colony's first mass movement (Sarekat Islam)— cautioned mosque officials against mentioning the event in their Friday sermons. One such sermon was cancelled by the authorities

3. On this event, see *Tempo,* Sept. 1, 1973.

minutes before it was due to be given by a former Masyumi leader to a large crowd in Surabaya.[4]

These incidents, occurring in different cities in the same year, substantiate the concern shown in this book over the dangers of cumulative cleavage in cultural politics. In Yogyakarta, ethnic, regional, and class differences coincided in a lopsided confrontation between Javanese pedicab drivers and non-Javanese university students. In Ujung Pandang, ethnic, religious, and military-civilian differences were superimposed in such a way that a Javanese army officer could act against a presumed anti-abangan slur—and illustrate, incidentally, the pro-abangan bias of the military noted in chapter 4. In Bandung, a combination of racial and class differences multiplied the explosive force of a protest against Chinese merchants and automobile owners, leading the military to take steps to ensure that religious differences between indigenous Muslims and Chinese non-Muslims (mainly Confucian-Buddhists and Christians) did not make matters even worse.[5] In all three instances, spokesmen for the government added to these lines of cleavage a political division between the New Order and putative leftist subversion.

The events in Bandung and Yogyakarta involved violence, but the hottest controversy in cultural politics in 1973 surrounded a proposed national law on marriage. The affair is worth recapitulating at some length because it spotlights the Islamic factor and because in its resolution the relative strengths of Parliament, Golkar (the official contender in the 1971 elections), and the armed forces are clearly revealed; it affords a test in the policy sphere of

4. On the Bandung incident, see *Tempo,* Aug. 11 and Sept. 29, 1973. According to official estimates, one person (a Chinese merchant) died as a result of the riot, 64 were hospitalized, and 130 cars, 175 motorbikes, and 1,520 buildings were destroyed or damaged (*Kompas,* Dec. 17, 1974). *Pedoman,* Aug. 15, 1973, described the arrest of suspected leftist perpetrators. The socioeconomic interpretation was reported by *Berita Buana,* Aug. 8, 1973. *Tempo,* Aug. 18, 1973, cited the ban on Muslim speeches about the event.

5. That the first and third incidents began in street traffic is no coincidence. Ethnoeconomic conflict in Jakarta between Batak bus and Javanese pedicab drivers could also be cited (*Harian Kami,* March 23, 1972). Traffic in Indonesia's major cities is a pattern of forced social interaction involving a great variety of vehicles, each one signaling the status of its owner or user and all competing for street space; the exclusive recruitment of one ethnic group to one kind of job heightens the likelihood of violence.

the overlapping cultural and institutional hypotheses that have shaped this inquiry. The controversy can be treated as a behavioral extension of some of the elite experiences and opinions already mapped; several of the men I interviewed four years earlier played key roles in the affair. If political culture contains rival visions of the future and cultural politics is the process of reaching an authoritative choice between them, the dispute over the marriage law shows concretely how the ideals of different groups are lost, won, or compromised.

In 1969 when I interviewed members of Parliament, among their pending business was a draft law on Muslim marriage and divorce. Introduced in 1967 by the Department of Religion and backed by the Muslim parties, the bill would have enforced Islamic marital law, with sanctions applicable to all Muslims. Whereas in the Constituent Assembly in the late 1950's the Muslim parties had struggled to secure official enforcement of Islamic law in general, in the late 1960's they were trying to realize the Jakarta Charter piecemeal, first in marital law, later perhaps in some other field.

In 1968, secular, abangan, and non-Muslim religious leaders, including some of the men in my samples, considered this bill to be a clear threat; for one thing, it mentioned the Jakarta Charter. To draw its sting, the Department of Justice submitted to Parliament a second draft statute that approved the idea of a separate marriage law for each religious community but went no further than laying down basic principles, postponing details to future legislation. To neutralize one bill by submitting another, on the same topic, whose general provisions were conveniently left to future specification, was a standard maneuver. In this instance, the Department of Justice, whose purview was secular law, tried to head off the Islamic-law project of the NU-oriented Department of Religion, and the DPR merely served as an arena where the bureaucracy's competing designs could be fought out. Just as one of the members of the DPR sample played proxy for the Department of Finance in budget debates, so were there Muslim party representatives eager to defend Religion's draft against Justice's.

Neither bill attracted a consensus, and Parliament, true to form, would not vote. Deadlock ensued. The Catholic party's objections to any attempt by a state organ to enforce, or even recognize, religious law were especially vehement; when the two bills were discussed in committee, Catholic party members boycotted the sessions. Abangan Javanese have nothing equivalent to Islamic law, and their marriages were generally already conducted under formally Islamic auspices; for them, therefore, the threat of the 1967 bill was less that they would no longer be able to do things they had done in the past than that they could in the future become punishable under Muslim law for not living up to its tenets. Supporters and opponents alike saw Religion's bill as the thin end of a wedge. The DPR's inability to act merely extended the status quo.[6]

The stalemate was broken in August 1973 when the government withdrew both earlier bills and substituted new draft legislation prescribing uniform secular rules—for marriage, divorce, and such related matters as engagement and adoption—enforceable in the secular courts. Significantly, the Department of Justice submitted the new text, not the Department of Religion. If the first bill had frankly promoted Islamic legal aims, and the second had at least catered to Muslim sensitivities by remaining general and recognizing religious law in principle, this third piece of proposed legislation was comprehensively and specifically secular.

The new draft law on marriage (Rancangan Undang-Undang tentang Perkawinan, RUUP) would have curtailed political Islam in two domains, the institutional and the legal. Institutionally, it would have reduced the role of the Muslim court system, as coordinated by the Department of Religion. Marriages conducted according to the draft law's provisions would need only to be registered to become legally binding. Religious courts were mentioned by name only once, in an appended "clarification" that left their role unclear; allusions to them in the body of the bill appeared contradictory. Enforcement of the bill's provisions was assigned to the

6. The Jakarta press covered these events in successive waves, from late May 1967 and from early September 1968. On the floor of the house, DPR members alluded to the Justice Department's maneuver to neutralize Religion's bill (*Risalah Resmi* [uncorrected], 1968–1969, first session, Sept. 6, 1968, p. 31, and Sept. 10, 1968, p. 2). The Catholic position is given in H. M. Rasjidi, *Kasus R.U.U. Perkawinan dalam Hubungan Islam dan Kristen* (Jakarta: Bulan Bintang, 1974), pp. 32–39. Hasbullah Bakry, *Pengaturan Undang-Undang Perkawinan Ummat Islam* (Jakarta: Bulan Bintang, 1970), is a useful historical overview; see also *Tempo,* June 30 and Sept. 9, 1973, and Boland, *Struggle of Islam,* pp. 166–168.

secular courts, and even the word religion occurred only twice in seventy-three articles.

In the legal sphere, the bill's secular precepts collided with those of Islam in several respects. The RUUP declared religion to be no obstacle to marriage, meaning that bride and groom need not share the same faith. Islam, as Muslim leaders angrily pointed out, did not permit its women to marry outside the ummat. The RUUP gave adopted children equal rights with natural children in the same family and required a break between the adopted child and his blood parents. Under Islamic law, adoption was a purely social act without legal consequences, and Muslim spokesmen speculated that denying a child knowledge of his true parents might result in his marrying his own mother without knowing it. Muslim leaders also objected to articles in the bill recognizing engagement before marriage, providing for the legitimation of children born out of wedlock, and requiring a man to marry his fiancée at her request if he has impregnated her, on the grounds that these rules would encourage both nonmarital sex, which the Koran forbids, and entrapment by scheming women. Other provisions, concerning marriageable age, polygamy, and remarriage for widows and divorcees, were also rejected as unacceptable to the ummat. Muslim critics found as many as twenty-six points on which they felt the RUUP conflicted with Islamic law.[7]

Before August had ended, Muslim opposition to the bill had begun to snowball. Among Jakarta newspapers, *Abadi,* a former Masyumi mouthpiece once silenced by Sukarno and in 1973 the only Muslim daily left in the capital, led the attack on the RUUP and quickly became the proposed new law's most scathing critic. In 1973, Golkar's contingent in Parliament was chaired by a Catholic, a fact that rendered especially ominous in Muslim eyes his reported statements that Indonesia, as a modern, nontheocratic state, needed the RUUP, that the country could not afford to follow religious teachings on marriage and divorce if progress was to be achieved, and that Golkar was ready to pass the law by voting if necessary. (Successor to the Development Group whose members

7. *Tempo,* Sept. 8, 1973, summarized the main Muslim objections. For other criticism, see *Abadi,* Aug. 13, 24, 28, and Oct. 16, 1973; *Indonesia Raya,* Aug. 28, 29, and Sept. 19, 1973; *Harian Kami,* Aug. 27, 1973; *Tempo,* Sept. 1 and Oct. 13, 1973.

I interviewed in 1969, Golkar in 1973 held an absolute majority of all the seats in Parliament.) *Abadi* replied, in an editorial headed "Golkar is Hostile to Religion," that Golkar leaders were apparently using their overwhelming victory in the 1971 elections as a weapon against religion; a young NU militant later claimed that the reported Golkar statements "square with the communist doctrine that regards religion as poison." The fundamentalist Muslim, Rasjidi, who had been Indonesia's first minister of religion, denounced the RUUP for allowing marriage between followers of different faiths; this, he said, would erase "the limits of religion [that is, the critical line around the ummat]." In his view, for all its trappings of national law and modernization, the bill was nothing but an attempt to Christianize the "ninety per cent" among Indonesians who were Muslims. On the day that *Abadi* published Rasjidi's charge, the army officer serving as vice-chairman of the DPR warned members of Parliament not to make hasty or inflammatory comments on the bill, in the light of the Bandung riots just two weeks before. To this, one Muslim representative replied that legislators were not civil servants, to be ordered about by superiors —an unintended echo of the objection twenty-three years earlier by another DPR member, Muhammad Yamin, to being treated as a mere government employee.[8]

Another fundamentalist Muslim leader, Hamka, condemned the RUUP as an outright attack on Islam. The Muslim community, he wrote, was extremely weak, politically, economically, in every field. All Muslims had left was their faith, and now "they" would take that away too. For here was a bill that would "force the majority Muslim group in this country" to exchange its own religious marriage law for a law "intended to destroy utterly the basic principles of Islam." Earlier "they" had been able to silence the Muslim group, lest its leaders even mention the Jakarta Charter, whose phrase "with the obligation to carry out the laws of Islam for the adherents of Islam" had been "intentionally erased" from the preamble to the constitution in 1945. Nowadays, "if you even mention

8. Sources for this paragraph, each preceded by the number of the sentence it refers to, are (2) *Abadi,* Aug. 13, 1973 (one of many examples); (3) *Jakarta Times,* Aug. 13, 1973; (5a) *Abadi,* Aug. 16, 1973; (5b) *Tempo,* Aug. 25, 1973; (6, 7) *Abadi,* Aug. 20, 1973, reprinted in Rasjidi, *Kasus,* p. 14; (8) *Abadi,* Aug. 22, 1973; and (9a) *Harian Kami,* Aug. 22, 1973. For Yamin's exact words (9b), see pp. 61–62 above.

this you can be accused of being an 'extreme rightist'—or even 'G30S!' " So the Muslims were silent; they no longer spoke of the Charter. Moreover, there were still many in the Muslim community who did not want to observe Islamic law. Seeing the Muslims thus helpless, wrote Hamka, "they" had gone "one step further," putting forward a bill that said marriage was not a religious act at all, that would let you marry your own sister, that would legalize free sex as advertised in pornographic magazines, that would allow bastards to inherit property through adoption, that would make a widow wait 306 days before marrying again—all things that violated Islamic law.

"So you must throw out Islamic law," Hamka concluded sarcastically. "That's it. You are forbidden to practice the rules of Allah and the Prophet." He went on to warn the government that if the RUUP were forced on the Muslim community, if it were voted into law in a show of force by Golkar's legislative majority, the Muslim community would not revolt—they were too weak—but they would refuse to obey the law. Islamic teachers would declare it forbidden by Islam; if a Muslim were to marry according to its provisions, he would become in Muslim eyes an infidel.[9] The renegade, Hamka seemed to say, would be cast out of the ummat, expelled across its critical boundary line.

Several critics, writing in *Abadi,* drew ironic parallels between the ummat's treatment at colonial hands and under an Indonesian government. In the late 1930's, wrote one, the Dutch had tried to get a secular marriage law passed in the Volksraad declaring monogamy to be a basic principle of marriage—whereas Islam allows up to four wives in certain circumstances. He concluded that because the RUUP made this same anti-Muslim point, the New Order must wish to attack the ummat just as the colonial order had done. Another writer comparing the two governments even praised the colonial regime: the 1937 regulation had been discussed first among various social groups and, because of their opposition, had not been submitted to the Volksraad at all; not so the RUUP.[10]

9. Hamka, "Dari Hati ke Hati: RUU Perkawinan yang Menggoncang-kan," *Harian Kami,* Aug. 24, 1973.
10. See the articles by M. Yunan Nasution, S. Djalal Soeyoeti, T. Jafiz-ham, and E. Saifuddin Anshari in *Abadi,* Aug. 24, 29, 31, and Oct. 16,

Charges flew. The RUUP would lead to "atheistic marriages."
It would "castrate the Department of Religion." To thus "sabotage
Allah's will" could destroy Indonesian unity and trigger the growth
of religious states within the state. Islamic organizations in Jakarta
and the regions held meetings and cabled protests, to Parliament
and to President Suharto, warning of dark consequences. Compared to the comments of spokesmen for the fundamentalist Parmusi and like-minded groups, NU criticism was softer; but NU,
too, rejected the bill. A series of lectures on the RUUP at NU's
religious headquarters in East Java was broken up and banned, for
fear that local sentiments would be inflamed—which is just what
the authorities' action achieved. Time and again, in press releases,
articles, and telegrams, Muslim advocates cited Islam's "ninety per
cent" of the population.[11]

In September, deeds accompanied words. Young Muslim militants were arrested in front of the DPR for passing out leaflets
attacking the RUUP. Then a group of some 500 Muslim young
people staged a demonstration inside Parliament, interrupting a
defense by the government of the marriage bill and forcing sus-
pension of the session. For a little more than two hours, the youths
occupied the main hall of the building, denouncing the RUUP,
screaming the takbir just as Usman and his fellows had during the
revolution. Five tanks and seven trucks of soldiers and police
were needed to clear the hall. In October, the Islamic bloc in
Parliament threatened to boycott further deliberations on the bill.
In November, another echo of Usman's revolutionary Army of
Allah was heard when the members of an East Java Islamic Community Action Command wrote a letter to Suharto swearing their

1973, respectively; the paper later reprinted Nasution's article as a pamphlet
for wider distribution. Jafizham was the one who tried to make the Dutch
look good by comparison.
    11. In order, the quotes are from *Pedoman*, Aug. 27, 1973, citing DPR
member and Parmusi spokesman H. M. Sanusi; T. Jafizham, "Rancangan
Undang2 Perkawinan," *Abadi*, Aug. 31, 1973; and Anwar Harjono, "Ada
'Jurang' Dalam RUU Perkawinan," *Harian Kami*, Aug. 28, 1973, citing
Hazairin, *Demokrasi Pantjasila* (Jakarta: Tintamas, 1970), pp. 48–49. For
accounts of protest meetings and telegrams, see *Indonesia Raya, Harian
Kami*, and *Abadi* from late August onward. *Abadi* reported the incident in
East Java on Aug. 28, 1973; the same day, *Indonesia Raya* cited a telegram
to President Suharto from "2,000" members of a Muslim educational organization who opposed the RUUP because it would contravene the religion
of "90 per cent" of the population.

readiness to die as syahids in defense of their faith. In December, young Muslims gathered once more in front of Parliament to demonstrate against the draft law, and again they shouted the takbir.[12] The critical line had become a barricade.

By this time, however, a search for a compromise was well under way. In October-November, army leaders and Muslim spokesmen reached a private understanding in direct negotiations outside Parliament. Working from this agreement, a legislative committee with an equal number of representatives from the armed forces, Golkar, the Muslim faction, and a fourth faction composed of the PNI and the Christian parties (in other words, a committee that did not reflect Golkar's absolute majority in Parliament) revised the bill to meet, or at least appear to meet, all major Muslim objections. The committee made over thirty changes in the wording of the draft law, and most of these were in line with the army-Muslim understanding.[13]

So far as the institutional aspect of the issue was concerned, whereas the first draft would have entrusted enforcement of the law's provisions to the secular courts, the new version gave this task to the religious judiciary, that is, to the Islamic court structure under the Department of Religion. As for the kind of law that would be applied, the revised draft stated that a marriage would be legally valid if it were conducted according to the laws of the bride and groom's religion or "belief"; civil registration of the marriage was made to seem like a mainly administrative convenience. Although the bill provided that decisions of the religious judiciary would somehow be "strengthened" by the secular courts; although the addition of the term "belief" was not welcomed by Muslim leaders (for reasons discussed below); and although some of the new draft's "clarifications" muddied the meaning of the bill —at least the Muslims had averted the disaster of the initial ver-

12. On the distribution of leaflets, see *Pedoman* and *Abadi,* Sept. 20, 1973; on the larger demonstration, *Tempo,* Oct. 6, 1973; on the boycott threat, *Indonesia Raya,* Oct. 5, 1973; on the letter from East Java, *Abadi,* Nov. 28, 1973; on the December demonstration, *Nusantara,* Dec. 7, 1973.

13. See *Abadi,* Dec. 5 and 10, *Kompas,* Dec. 7, and the Jakarta press generally, December 19–22, 1973. Changes were enumerated by comparing the original draft bill, as published in *Sinar Harapan,* Sept. 3–6, 1973, with the text of the law actually passed, as printed in K. Wantjik Saleh, comp., *Himpunan Peraturan dan Undang-Undang tentang Perkawinan* (Jakarta: Ichtiar Baru-Van Hoeve, 1974), pp. 85–116.

sion. And at best they had won a victory; for if the new bill passed, and if it were not then reinterpreted and implemented in ways unfavorable to Islam, Muslim legal institutions would have even more authority than before.[14]

Compared to Muslim spokesmen, Christian leaders had been noticeably more moderate in their comments on the first draft—understandably, given the bill's separation of church and state, the Christian minority's awareness of the issue's explosive potential, and their reluctance to risk Muslim reprisals. The two Christian-oriented Jakarta dailies, *Kompas* (Catholic) and *Sinar Harapan* (Protestant), reported the facts of the controversy and, when they embarked on comment, editorialized with far less vehemence than *Abadi*. When the needle swung toward Islam, however, Christian, and also secular-nationalist, voices were raised in support of the view that, as an Indonesian Young Generation Action Committee put it in mid-December, public authorities "must not oblige the followers of a particular religion to observe its norms and laws" in marriage or in any other matter.[15]

On December 21, 1973, the national Catholic students' organization issued an eleventh-hour appeal to Parliament to put off a decision on the new draft; there was by then no hope of its being rejected. On December 22, *Kompas* warned that the adoption of the revised bill would prove that Indonesians were still unable to come together "in true unity as citizens of one nation" (with one marriage law for all); that, after more than twenty-eight years of independence, Indonesia had actually "regressed" from the goals and spirit of the preamble to the constitution of 1945 (which made no mention of any "obligation to carry out the laws of Islam for the adherents of Islam"); and that the DPR was still not able to function "independently, with authority, and effectively." But the bill passed the same day—"by acclamation," to cover up the real division in the house.

These extraordinary events in 1973 illustrate at least three themes from the foregoing study of elite political culture in 1969: the Islamic factor, the bridging role of the military, and the weak-

14. See Anwar Harjono, "Undang2 Perkawinan: Sebuah Tanggapan," *Abadi*, Jan. 14, 1974, and the Department of Religion's expectations as reported in *Kompas*, Feb. 19, 1974.

15. *Sinar Harapan*, Dec. 12, 1973; also see the issues of Dec. 17 and 19.

ness of Parliament. Unless the controversy is examined along these three dimensions—this chapter's next task—it is hard to understand how organized Islam could achieve so much when its political position had never been weaker.

That political Islam was feeble could not be doubted. As noted previously, the July 1971 elections gave the mainly secular-abangan Golkar absolute numerical control of the DPR. Westernized professionals and intellectuals were strongly represented in the new parliamentary bloc, which included a former member of the Development Group whom I had interviewed in 1969. In September 1971, Suharto broke an eighteen-year tradition of NU influence in the Department of Religion by appointing as minister a politically unaffiliated "religious technocrat," H. A. Mukti Ali, who then set about dismantling NU's empire and inserting secular vocational subjects into the curricula of Islamic schools. Suharto's choice to head the Department of Social Affairs was a moderate Muslim whom the regime had earlier installed in the leadership of Parmusi, H. M. S. Mintaredja. Not coincidentally, in a book written on the eve of the elections, Mintaredja advocated abandoning the struggle for the Jakarta Charter, labeled the Muslim political claim to 90 per cent of the population as "nothing but an empty slogan," urged that the old ideological warfare be ended in favor of economic development, and supported the fusion of the existing parties[16]—opinions that also belonged to the generals in Golkar and the army.

Under mounting pressure through 1972 to regroup after their electoral defeat, NU, Parmusi, PSII, and Perti finally came together, in January 1973, in a new Unity and Development Party (Partai Persatuan Pembangunan, PPP). At the same time, the PNI and the Christian parties merged to form the Indonesian Democracy Party (Partai Demokrasi Indonesia, PDI). These acts of consolidation followed a period when all of the major and some of the minor parties had felt, at least once, the manipulating touch of the generals around Suharto—especially whenever the time came to elect new party leaders. Mintaredja himself was made general chairman

16. H. M. S. Mintaredja, *Renungan Pembaharuan Pemikiran Masjarakat Islam dan Politik di Indonesia* (Jakarta: Permata, 1971), passim; the quotation is from p. 35.

of the PPP over the opposition of several Muslim spokesmen who disdained the new party as an artificial creation of the regime.[17]

In this simplified system there remained only four recognized political forces in the country: the armed forces (ABRI), Golkar, the PPP, and the PDI. The PPP's and PDI's constituent organizations, acting in their own names, were permitted to play only nonpolitical roles. No reference to Islam was made in the name of the PPP; similarly, Christian labels were buried in the PDI. A younger PPP legislator from NU looked to the day when political compartmentalization by cultural identity would disappear altogether; and PPP leader Mintaredja declared, rather extravagantly, that the party was already open to non-Muslims.[18] With only these four forces competing, the government hoped that the 1977 elections would become the first in Indonesia's history in which no organization could raise a religious banner to political ends.

The defanging of fundamentalist Islam and the proportions of Golkar's electoral success made it possible for the government to unite the Muslim parties into one body without threat to itself. At the same time, the generals around Suharto sought to balance Islam as a religious force by organizing and legitimizing the abangan alternative. In 1970–1972, a number of Javanese mystical sects for which the abangan outlook was not a gloss on Islam but a world view in its own right were brought together under a Joint Secretariat for Beliefs (Sekretariat Bersama Kepercayaan) similar in name and structure to Golkar (Sekretariat Bersama Golongan Karya). The head of the new grouping was a practicing mystic and former minister of education, Wongsonegoro, who had been responsible in the constitutional debates of 1945 for inserting the phrase "and beliefs" in an article guaranteeing the freedom of all citizens to follow their own "religions and beliefs." The amendment provided a rationale for elevating the abangan outlook to a status equal to that of the four world religions, Islam, Christianity, Hinduism, and Buddhism. It remained basically an unused weapon,

17. IPKI and Murba also joined the PDI, but they were by then paper organizations only, for they had won no seats in 1971. On army manipulation of Parmusi, see the references in ch. 1, n. 51. Examples of Muslim criticism of the PPP can be found in *Harian Kami*, Feb. 14, 1973, and *Sinar Harapan*, Feb. 15, 1973.

18. Zamroni, cited by *Kompas*, Jan. 9, 1973; Mintaredja, cited by *Nusantara*, Jan. 11, 1973.

however, until, in November 1970, a Symposium on Beliefs held in Yogyakarta under Wongsonegoro's stewardship took it up to justify a demand for official recognition of the beliefs of the nation's (mainly Hindu-Javanese) mystical associations and their equal treatment alongside the four established religions. Subsequently, although it has still not been given such status by the Department of Religion, the abangan alternative accumulated recognition and legitimacy, obtaining time on public radio and television equal to that already made available to each world religion, publishing (since April 1972) its own monthly magazine, and holding its second national congress in December 1974 with material and moral support from President Suharto. Its greatest symbolic victory came in March 1973 when, over the objections of Muslim spokesmen, the phrase "and belief" was added after "religion" throughout the Broad Outlines of State Policy that the MPR laid down to guide Suharto's government through 1978. (This MPR was the People's Consultative Assembly originally named in the 1945 constitution; it had replaced the wholly appointive Provisional People's Consultative Assembly [MPRS] after the 1971 elections.)

The rising political influence of secular-minded Golkar intellectuals and Javanese religious relativists helps to explain why the marriage law controversy occurred in the first place. (A third important factor, the women's movement, is slighted here as less directly related to issues of cultural politics.) In February 1972, at a mass gathering in Jakarta held to celebrate the Javanese New Year, after a word of encouragement from President Suharto, read by Major General Sudjono Humardani, the most deeply abangan of the president's advisers, Wongsonegoro as chairman of the Joint Secretariat for Beliefs urged the government to adopt a national marriage law that would be valid for all Indonesians regardless of their religion or belief. A month later there appeared among the resolutions of an Indonesia-wide working conference of Golkar one calling for a national marriage law that, although not infringing a person's right to marry according to his own religion or belief, would apply to everyone.[19] A year later, in an action

19. On these two events, see M. Hadi Soesastro, ed., *Indonesia dan Dunia Internasional 1973: Ringkasan Peristiwa* (Jakarta: Yayasan Proklamasi, Centre for Strategic and International Studies, 1973), pp. 57 and 36, respec-

virtually unnoticed at the time, the MPR appeared to prepare the way for such a universal statute by including in the Broad Outlines of State Policy a call for the codification and unification of law "in certain sectors." More than a year after that, the RUUP was submitted to Parliament over Suharto's name.

Angry Muslim observers blamed the RUUP mainly on three groups: Golkar, Christians, and abangan Javanese. It is hard to measure the truth in these accusations, but they were fervently believed, and in them different cultural and political distinctions can be seen coinciding, lining up the same groups on the same side of the resulting divide. The fact that Golkar's chairman in Parliament at the time was a Catholic, and that *Abadi* attacked him and Golkar for supporting the bill, has already been noted. Rasjidi, in his statements, first blamed evangelical Christians but later concluded "that the whole problem has arisen because a handful of people from the Javanese ethnic group . . . think that *kejawen* or Javanism is a religion," that it is "indigenously Javanese," and that "Islam is from the Arabs." These people do not realize, wrote Rasjidi, that Islam is a universal religion, kejawen just a remnant of Hinduism.[20] In kejawen, religion and ethnicity are reinforcing —although Rasjidi is himself a Javanese.

Another explanation circulating privately among Muslim leaders at the time placed a triple stigma on those presumed responsible for the RUUP. In this version, as told to me by a devoutly Muslim non-Javanese well known for his defense of the ummat (but not a member of either of my samples), a Catholic priest in Central Java had planned the affair with key Catholic leaders in the government in order to Christianize Indonesia. The priest talked to a

tively. Although the Joint Secretariat for Beliefs has tried to portray itself in national terms by involving non-Javanese groups, it remains fundamentally abangan. At the Javanese New Year ceremony in 1973, although some 100 girls from different regions participated in a symbolic representation of beliefs around the country, the cultural core of the event was an all-night wayang kulit performance (*Suara Karya*, Feb. 2 and 6, 1973).

20. For *Abadi*'s charge that Golkar had fallen under Catholic influence, see—in addition to the previously cited editorial ("Golkar is Hostile to Religion," Aug. 16, 1973)—Mustakim Ali's strongly worded "Isi R.U.U. Perkawinan Melanggar dan Memperkosa U.U.D. '45 dan Pancasila," which the paper published on Oct. 24, 1973. According to one rumor circulating among Muslims at the time, the Catholic Golkar chairman's wife originated the idea of the bill. Rasjidi's remarks are taken from his *Kasus*, p. 21, but were first made public by *Abadi*, Nov. 29, 1973.

Chinese Catholic politician in Jakarta, who passed the plan on to two other Chinese, who influenced two abangan Javanese generals in favor of the plan, who, in turn, planted the idea in the president's mind through his wife. This chain of conspiracy imaginatively linked three of the four evils of sara—religion (Catholics and abangan Muslims), race (Chinese), and ethnicity (Javanese), in order of decreasing importance to my informant—in a composite portrait of the enemy.[21] The ethnic label mattered least to him, but the combined Christian-abangan-Chinese threat was vividly real.

In these conspiracy theories, the Islamic factor is clearly visible. As a cultural minority of intensity, deeply committed Muslims tended to distrust leaders from the abangan-secular majority (let alone from other supposedly hostile minorities, such as Christians and Chinese), to see little need for social empathy (as the young NU politician in my DPR sample told me in 1969, "we Muslims already have a viewpoint"), and to see conflict as extreme. A controversy of cultural politics like that over the marriage law, which appeared to involve the ummat's right to follow the precepts of its own religion in one of life's major rituals, could activate the Islamic factor in elite political culture with deadly effect. Already predisposed to mistrust outgroup leaders and to polarize conflict on any matter involving the necessary barrier separating Muslim from unbeliever, and seeing attempts to empathize across this barrier as only likely to weaken it, committed Muslims in the elite quickly dug in, defining deep lines of cleavage around the ummat on the other side of which they could see an unholy alliance of secular Golkar intellectuals, abangan generals, Chinese politicians, and Christian priests preparing for a final assault. These strongly identifying Muslims did not themselves engage in violence—they were, after all, part of the elite and to have done that would have meant giving up too much—but they helped create an atmosphere of frustration and anguish that legitimated the ancient call to jihad.

To ask why major violence did not in fact break out is to juxtapose political culture and cultural politics in still another way. To recapitulate the evidence gathered in 1969, officers differed from civilians in the elite in six important ways. First, they enjoyed, on

21. Interview, April 2, 1974.

the average, higher standards of living in childhood; most over-represented among the officers' compared to the civilians' fathers, for example, were businessmen, the single wealthiest category (see Table 1). Second, officers were more likely than civilians to be nominal or abangan Muslims. All of the military men in my samples were Muslims, but none was strongly religious (among the civilians, by contrast, one-third were pious Muslims); and all four Javanese officers were strongly abangan, their bias invigorated by remembered participation in the suppression of Islamic revolts from the time of the revolution onward. Third, still in terms of social background, the officers tended to fall between, and so to diversify, the bureaucratic and legislative institutions: more parochial than the civilian bureaucrats but more cosmopolitan than the civilian legislators, the military bridged the two institutions while penetrating them (see Table 8). Fourth, the officers' primary loyalties were to the armed forces, especially the army, with which they identified much more strongly than civilian legislators or administrators did with their institutions; the military career as a shaper of identity was revealed, for example, in the command-oriented leadership styles of these men (see Table 7 and accompanying text). Fifth, compared to the civilians, although less strongly in favor of central authority, officers believed that leaders should be trusted (see Table 16). (Aside from these differences no uniquely military outlook within elite political culture as a whole was found.) Sixth, between officers and civilians in the government coalition in Parliament, officers were strikingly more ready to accept deference toward authority and trust in leaders; one civilian in the Development Group (later Golkar), a student leader, rejected both attitudes as inimical to the modern (Western-style) democracy he wanted Indonesia to become.

Just as the marriage bill controversy laid bare the Islamic factor, the resolution of the crisis can be seen as a behavioral consequence of these elite military attributes. Ignoring existing institutions, the military compromised directly and authoritatively with the Muslim group to avoid public violence. Among the conditions leading to this response were, first, that the top military leaders were distinct from and politically superior to Golkar, regarding it as a vehicle of convenience. Army generals did not originate the RUUP; rather, some of them allowed and supported the initiative taken by mainly civilian, Golkar-related groups: Christian politicians, women's organizations, and secular intellectuals. As early as August 1973, military leaders, both in the DPR and outside, were making conciliatory statements in deference to Muslim sensitivities;[22] and, as the crisis progressed, they disassociated themselves more and more from Golkar's campaign. The apparent threat by the Catholic civilian head of Golkar in Parliament to bring the issue to a vote—one that his group would obviously have won—was countermanded in October by the general chairman of Golkar (an abangan general), who promised that Golkar would do no such thing. In September, in a private meeting in the palace, President Suharto assured the PPP that Indonesia's laws could include no statute contrary to the teachings of any religion recognized by the government.[23]

Second, the army command was sufficiently diverse in composition and spread widely enough across civilian institutions to register the explosive potential of the situation as it got rapidly out of hand. Though they were politically inconsequential, a small minority of generals even identified with Islam. General Nasution, for example, once army head but a peripheral figure in the New Order, characterized, in a sermon given in a Jakarta mosque in August, the ummat's secular-abangan challengers as "self-styled modernizing intellectuals" and people who held absurd "beliefs" about the nature of God.[24] One of the officers in my legislative sample in 1969 had been named to Parliament in part because of his good Muslim contacts; army leaders, despite their great power, were not eager to burn bridges to the ummat unnecessarily. This same officer, a non-Javanese, was still in the DPR in 1973, still playing the

22. See, for example, *Abadi,* Aug. 22, 1973, reporting comments by a police brigadier general and vice-chairman of the DPR Commission on Religion and Education, who in turn cited earlier speeches by Suharto to the effect that conflict between secular and religious law would be avoided.

23. *Kompas,* Oct. 9, 1973, carried the general chairman's promise. As for the president's statement, *Abadi,* on Sept. 27, 1973, compared it to "the sound of a gong" (as in the musical accompaniment to a wayang performance) heard by the delegates with a sense of relief, a "king's decree" that the newspaper hoped would be implemented fully with regard to the RUUP. *Abadi's* relief was doubtless sincere, but its language satirized the abangan kraton culture that the editors felt surrounded the president and his advisers and set them apart from the ummat.

24. *Abadi,* Aug. 27, 1973.

go-between role. The fact that army officers did not constitute a distinct subset of opinion within elite political culture, combined with their diversity and dispersion across so many pressure points in society, gave them flexibility as a stabilizing force.

Third, the officers' weak identification with the extramilitary institutions in which they held office, their sense of internal discipline, their top-down command orientation, and their sense that leaders (like themselves) should be trusted and obeyed were all factors encouraging them to short-cut the political process and impose a solution on Parliament. The chief victims of this maneuver were Golkar and the DPR itself. As the daily *Pedoman* put it on December 22, the day the revised bill was passed, Golkar legislators had turned into "faceless men"; in *Kompas'* words of the same day, the new law had been written "silently outside the DPR." Had the revised draft been subjected to a free vote in Parliament strictly on its content, it would almost certainly have been defeated. Parliament served well as a signaling device and a lightning rod, registering opinion and absorbing protest. Once it had done that, however, the army command felt obliged to bypass it altogether, as an instrument inappropriate to the finding of an actual solution to such a sensitive issue. The function of a safety valve is to relieve pressure to allow repairs, not to effect the repairs itself. Legislative diversity, although less in 1973 than in 1969 because of Golkar's induced landslide at the polls in 1971, was still sufficient to make Parliament a forum for the clash of opinion, but for that reason the army felt compelled in the end to pre-empt the legislature's law-making function.

Fourth, the mainly abangan coloration of the military component of the elite—all four Javanese officers in my samples fit this description, and the two legislators among them were still in Parliament in 1973, one of them playing a key role in the negotiations over the marriage law—can be seen in a facet of the outcome of this affair that is still widely ignored. Compared to the original RUUP, the revised law was not only a victory for the Islamic group but also advanced abangan claims to legitimacy. Because those on the army side most closely involved in the compromise were abangan Javanese, it was natural that they should seek to balance Muslim demands, not with the kind of secular universalism Golkar intellectuals desired, but with the abangan alternative, couched in the highly elastic term "belief." Whereas the RUUP mentioned "belief" only once, and then merely in specifying that different beliefs were no obstacle to marriage, abangan army negotiators borrowed Wongsonegoro's addendum "and belief" from the 1945 constitution and the 1973 Broad Outlines of State Policy and inserted it after a number of key references to religion in both the body of the bill and its clarification.

Aside from the behavioral expression in cultural politics of the Islamic factor and the position of the military to be found in the marriage law controversy, the bill's fate illustrates another theme traced in this book: the overshadowing of legislative by executive power. To conclude a law with a note that its implementation will be regulated by government decree is standard procedure in Indonesia. In this way, the substance of the law can be reinterpreted by the executive without hindrance from the legislature. The executive is also given a means of appearing to support a law while indefinitely postponing the issuance of the regulations necessary to its implementation. Although the marriage law proclaimed itself to be in effect from January 2, 1974, when President Suharto signed it, the minister of religion observed more accurately that so long as an implementing decree had not been issued it would not be enforced. When asked whether any of the provisions in the original bill that were taken out at the Muslims' request might reappear in the executive regulation, the minister replied, with striking candor, "We'll see. It's still too early to say."[25]

More than fifteen months after the bill passed Parliament, the implementing decree was issued; another six months elapsed before, on October 1, 1975, the law finally went into effect. A product of intensive negotiation between the Departments of Justice, Religion, and Defense and Security, the decree represented, in essence, a decision to instruct the legal structures of the ummat to protect its women.[26] To please secular civilian Golkar elements, especially women's organizations, divorce and polygamy among Muslims were made more difficult through a long series of restrictions. To satisfy Muslim leaders, those restrictions were to be applied by the Islamic courts under the Department of Religion. To accommodate the abangan group, "belief" was reaffirmed

25. *Kompas,* Dec. 27, 1973.
26. For the text of the decree, see *Surabaja Post,* April 10–12, 1975.

alongside the main religions as a legitimate spiritual alternative whose followers could be married or divorced outside Islam. As for Christians, Buddhists, and Hindus, cases involving them would continue to be handled by the secular legal apparatus of the Department of Justice. At the end of the long struggle, no group could claim exclusive victory or complete defeat.

The aftermath of the affair is also revealing. The evolution of the army's role in these events was associated with a shift of influence between two pairs of army generals: Suharto's close political advisers, Ali Murtopo and Sudjono Humardani, on the one hand, and, on the other, his chief security officials, Sumitro and Sutopo Juwono. As Islamic protest became more and more obviously a threat to stability and public order, Murtopo and Humardani, who had allowed or encouraged the RUUP, gradually gave way on the matter to Sumitro and Juwono, who intervened not out of sympathy with Islam but because, as heads, respectively, of the Command for the Restoration of Order and Security and BAKIN (the intelligence body), they were concerned lest events get out of hand.

Their concern was appropriate, for in the second half of 1973 unrest was building rapidly on another front. Students in Jakarta and other cities were criticizing the government in increasingly large numbers and harsh terms for neglecting the widening gap between wealthy and poor people and for depending on foreign "aid" and investments that were making the gap still wider. Chief among student targets were Generals Murtopo and Humardani. The army move to negotiate directly with the Muslim leaders of the PPP may thus also have been motivated in Sumitro's case by a desire to outmaneuver these two rivals. In any event, Sumitro's group succeeded in hammering out the compromise bill and getting it accepted.

The "soft line" taken by Sumitro in negotiations with the Muslims did at least put a respectably ambiguous end to the legislative phase of the affair; although no one was exactly happy with the result, no one's ox was obviously gored either (save that of the Golkar civilians behind the original bill). Perhaps Sumitro thought he could repeat this success with the demonstrating students. Perhaps, alternatively, he wanted to use the campus protests to eliminate his rivals. Whatever the reason, in November he set out to placate the students, listening to their criticisms, urging "two-way communication" between rulers and ruled, and even suggesting that Indonesia needed a "new style" of leadership.[27] Whether or not these remarks implied ambition for higher office is unclear; what is clear is that he fell victim to subsequent events.

After a meeting with Suharto on December 20 to report on the marriage law controversy, Sumitro and Juwono publicly pledged themselves to take the best possible precautions for security during the planned visit to Indonesia in mid-January of Prime Minister Tanaka of Japan. (Japan's presence in Indonesia was already a prime target for student demonstrations.) Many interpretations are possible of what happened next. One is that Sumitro was planning a coup against the Murtopo-Humardani group, or even against Suharto himself.[28] Another is that Sumitro was simply trapped by his own pledge when his "soft line" failed to dampen student protests. For on January 15 and 16, 1974, Jakarta suffered the most damaging riots in its history: the students' themes of nationalism and social justice—the first decrying exploitation by Japanese businessmen in league with army officers and Indonesian Chinese, the second denouncing gross class inequities—were articulated in flames and blood as buildings and cars burned, eleven persons died, and more than a hundred were injured.[29]

Sumitro was sacked and Juwono shunted off to Holland as ambassador. As for Murtopo and Humardani, the president dissolved his advisory staff, a move that lessened these two men's visibility but left their access to the president not obviously impaired. In the ensuing crackdown, all newspapers whose reports or editorials had been critical of or embarrassing to the government were closed down for good—among them *Abadi*. Hundreds of people were arrested; hundreds more feared arrest.[30]

27. See *Tempo,* Nov. 24 and Dec. 8, 1973.

28. It would be interesting to know whether or not Sumitro met secretly with General Nasution in Magelang on January 11 to discuss the student protests and their implications (see the small item in *Kompas,* Jan. 14, 1974), and if so what they said—especially in the light of Nasution's identification with Islam. Another general, Sarwo Edhie, was also in Magelang on that day, but later denied taking part in secret discussions; by 1975 he had been sent off to Pyongyang as ambassador to North Korea.

29. See *Tempo,* Jan. 26, 1974. By one official reckoning, damage was done to 807 cars, 187 motorbikes, and 146 buildings (*Berita Buana,* Jan. 24, 1974).

30. On Sumitro's resignation, see *Berita Yudha,* March 22, 1974; on Sut-

For the elite, the main lesson of the happenings of 1973–1974 is that the accumulation of cleavages should be avoided, lest the resulting gulf be unbridgeable. Had a compromise not been reached on the marriage bill, the violence of January 1974 could have gone well beyond the already serious proportions it actually reached. Had infuriated Islamic groups joined the mob in Jakarta to oppose a regime seen not only as pro-Japanese, pro-Chinese, and antipopular, but also as anti-Muslim, the riots could have spread to the regions, turning disaster into holocaust; out of the chaos might possibly have emerged a nationalist-populist-religious contender for power with partial army backing. That such was not the result, that by compromising with the Muslims Suharto managed to avoid a fight on two fronts, is a credit to the president's tactical skills. But what of the political culture of the larger elite? How appropriate will it prove to the solution of problems of cultural politics in years to come?

The New Order in Indonesia has sought to depoliticize cultural conflict in several ways: by trying to harness public attention and energy to the fulfillment of a series of economic development plans; by driving sara-related issues out of such open forums as Parliament and the press, lest they be used there to incite the general public; by merging, manipulating, and coopting political organizations with a view to eliminating their cultural distinctiveness; and by weighting the abangan side of the Javanese coin to offset its santri obverse in politics. Though partly successful, these efforts have contributed to a fresh conflict, one that falls under the heading of the final a in sara, namely, conflict between classes.

Economic development in the post-Sukarno period has unques-

---

opo Juwono's ambassadorial appointment, *Sinar Harapan,* April 17, 1974. In August 1974, Murtopo and Humardani received presidential awards for outstanding service to the state; at the time, Murtopo was BAKIN deputy head for operations and Humardani an inspector general for development (*Sinar Harapan,* Aug. 15, 1974). Among the casualties of the press crackdown were six dailies (*Abadi, Harian Kami, Indonesia Raya, Jakarta Times, Nusantara,* and *Pedoman*) and four weeklies (*Mahasiswa Indonesia, Pemuda Indonesia, Wenang,* and the news magazine *Ekspres*); all were permanently banned. According to the armed forces commander, 775 persons were arrested (*Berita Buana,* Jan. 24, 1974). Thirty-nine persons were reported still under arrest two months later, including four members of Parliament (*Kompas,* March 15, 1974). Over the next year and a half, a few of these detainees were released; others were tried and sentenced to prison terms of up to six years.

tionably benefited the wealthy more than the poor,[31] and among the wealthy are some of the targets of the demonstrations and riots of January 1974: the Chinese- and Japanese-linked generals who were burned in effigy on the streets of Jakarta. In 1973, in addition to the riots in Bandung and Yogyakarta, a number of small, local confrontations occurred in some of the towns and villages of Java. In the subdistrict of Jatiroto, East Java, at least thirty-nine peasants refused to rent their land to the local state sugar plantation at rental rates that were considerably below what they could have earned by keeping the land and growing rice on it for sale. The holdouts were arrested; twenty-five managed to last a week in detention without giving in, until the local army commander broke their will by smashing a peasant's jaw in their presence to show what would happen if they persisted in withholding their land. The

---

31. Evidence of rural poverty and sharpening inequality on Java is rapidly accumulating. See, in reverse chronological order: Dwight Y. King and Peter D. Weldon, "Income Distribution and Levels of Living in Java, 1963–1970," unpublished paper, Jakarta, January 1975; Lembaga Penelitian Ilmu-ilmu Sosial, "From Peasant to Farmer: Suatu Perkembangan yang Memperluas Gejala Proletarisasi di Daerah Pedesaan (Sawah) di Jawa Tengah," *Cakrawala*, 6 (March-April 1974), 493–503; "Choice of Technique in Rice Milling," a comment by William L. Collier, Jusuf Colter, Sinarhadi, and Robert d'A. Shaw, and a reply by C. Peter Timmer, *Bulletin of Indonesian Economic Studies*, 10, 1 (March 1974), 106–126; Willard A. Hanna, "Indonesian Projections and the Arithmetic of Anxiety," *American Universities Field Staff Reports* (Southeast Asia Series), 22, 3 (March 1974); Richard W. Franke, "Miracle Seeds and Shattered Dreams," *Natural History*, 83, 1 (Jan. 1974), 10–18 and 84–88; Penny and Singarimbun, *Population and Poverty;* William L. Collier, Soentoro, Gunawan Wiradi, and Makali, "The Limits of Involution: Tebasan, HYV's, and Rural Change in Java," research report, Agro–Economic Survey of Indonesia, Nov. 1973; Roger Montgomery, "Employment and Unemployment in Jogjakarta" (Ph.D. dissertation, Cornell University, 1973); Richard W. Franke, "The Green Revolution in a Javanese Village" (Ph.D. dissertation, Harvard University, 1972); A. Buddy Prasadja, *Pembangunan Desa dan Masalah Kepemimpinannja: Suatu Penelitian di Desa Gegesik, Kabupaten Tjirebon, Djawa Barat* (Bogor: Lembaga Penelitian Sosiologi Pedesaan, IPB, 1974); Paul R. Deuster, "Rural Consequences of Indonesian Inflation: A Case Study of the Jogjakarta Region" (Ph.D. dissertation, University of Wisconsin, 1971). Less factual but also relevant is Rex Mortimer, ed., *Showcase State: The Illusion of Indonesia's "Accelerated Modernisation"* (Sydney: Angus and Robertson, 1973); compare the counterargument by H. W. Arndt, "Development and Equality: The Indonesian Case," *World Development*, 3, 2–3 (Feb.-March 1975), 77–90, and the reviews of Mortimer's book by H. Feith and G. F. Papanek in the *Bulletin of Indonesian Economic Studies*, 10, 2 (July 1974), 114–125.

victim was a former "PKI" political prisoner who could thus easily be blamed for instigating the farmers' resistance—even though, from fear, he had surrendered his land at the outset. In Cibadak, West Java, poor people reportedly invaded a state forest to collect wood despite an official ban on doing so. In Sukabumi, street vendors reportedly organized a demonstration against official moves to clear them from the roadsides. In Majalaya, also in West Java, small-scale Indonesian textile manufacturers reportedly organized a meeting to protest against Japanese competition and strongly criticized a Japanese-linked general when he came to speak to them. In the wake of the Bandung riots, tensions reportedly ran high between Chinese and non-Chinese Indonesians in Purwokerto and Tegal in Central Java.[32] These rural stirrings did not amount to much. But they could easily recur and spread. The dividing line between Java and the outer islands so important for cultural politics during the republic's first two decades may have already been superseded in importance and violence potential by class lines stratifying the huge, partly desperate population on Java.

In the January riots in Jakarta, the burning of Proyek Senen, a huge multistory shopping center built by the city's governor (a general in the marines) in a densely populated market area, was a clear case of destruction across the class gap. In trying to make the capital a showcase metropolis, the governor had catered more to middle class comforts than to the needs of the poor. Around Proyek Senen, petty retailers were driven off the small plots of ground where they had been accustomed to spreading out their few wares; they could not afford to rent space in the shopping center, and local police would round them up in periodic razzias if they tried to return to open-air selling on their old plots. (Just a few days before Proyek Senen burned, shopkeepers in the Kramat Bundar area facing it, some of whom had been there for a decade or more, were also moved out.) It seems likely that some of these petty traders were among the mob that on the night of January 15 set fire to the building that had displaced them.

32. *Tempo*, Aug. 11, 1973, covered the Jatiroto case. None of the other incidents, to my knowledge, was covered in the press; by "reportedly" I refer to oral reports about these events obtained from reliable journalistic and scholarly sources, in Jakarta and Central Java, on March 29 and July 12, 1974. In the wake of the Jatiroto affair, the local military commander was reassigned; he retired from the army soon after.

By increasing the significance of class issues, "showcase modernization" may prove a self-undermining solution. So long as the Chinese minority retains its commercial influence and the door to foreign capital stays open, economic inequality will be subject to interpretation in racial and nationalistic terms. Making the PKI a universal scapegoat may also prove self-defeating in the long run, for it contradicts the regime's goal of depoliticizing Indonesian life. Charges of PKI responsibility align a variety of cleavages—social, economic, and cultural—with the political divide that isolates the pariah left. As a tactic designed continually to discredit the PKI and repress conflicts by renewing the fear of being called a communist, a policy of blaming the party may work in the short run, if only because the left is too bloodied and others too intimidated to resist. But in the farther future, if inequalities worsen, a resurrected left may thank Suharto and his generals for enhancing its potential appeal and power base by laying so many grievances at its door.

Cumulating cleavage can be seen, too, in the institutional imbalance between Parliament and an executive that is at once more powerful and more abangan-secular and Javanese. Yet how can one recommend empowering a Parliament that includes a set of cultural minorities and political outgroups many of whose outlooks are relatively untrusting, anomic, intolerant, unempathic, centralist, and conflictful (see Table 16) as compared to the outlooks of the politically dominant, culturally mainstream bureaucratic elite—an institution, in short, whose very representativeness spells potential disruption?

An answer to the problem of a weak but representative legislature—where minorities continued to have a voice, albeit a smaller one, after Golkar's triumph in 1971—is suggested by another finding of this study: that the social and political position of a group is as important as its cultural origins in shaping the outlooks of its members. Christians, being fairly highly placed in the cosmopolitan social structure of the Jakarta-based national elite, viewed their surroundings much less anomically than might have been the case had their status as a cultural minority disadvantaged them socially. Because of its high secular quality and the status it could bestow, Christian education reduced even its Muslim graduates' propensity toward anomie. Conversely, Muslim-schooled and strongly religious minorities favored darker views of conflict, not—or not only—because of doctrinal bias in their religions but also because they were outgroups in secular elite society.

Summarizing other structural evidence, ethnically outer island politicians were more pessimistic about conflict because they came from regions disadvantaged in the struggle for scarce resources controlled by the center. Opposition groups in the DPR were more anomic in outlook and trusted leaders less than the government coalition did; the latter's power advantage encouraged confidence. Between institutional elites, the greater optimism, trust, tolerance, and empathy of the bureaucrats could be attributed not—or not only—to their shared origins in a cultural majority but to their favored position in Suharto's administrative state.

These results suggest two things. First, irresponsible positions encourage irresponsible views. By controlling and constraining Parliament, the regime allows outgroups to remain almost comfortably disaffected insofar as they are denied the need to broaden their appeal through coalition with others. Imposed coalitions such as the PPP and the PDI seem unlikely to reduce the disaffection of their member groups. In that they isolated these outgroups even more—in a sense driving them from Parliament just as poor people have been driven off Jakarta's streets—the 1971 elections were a step backward. Even if the DPR were to be given more power, the Golkar group could use its absolute majority to roll over the remnants of opposition. Ironically, the compromise of 1973 was a direct consequence of the 1971 victory at the polls; the regime had accumulated so much power that it could not, when the time came, use it.[33]

Second, the kind of issue Parliament debates affects the way it is debated. A symbolically charged topic invites a resentful cultural minority to project its discontent. The highly charged question of religious versus secular marital law was submitted to Parliament to decide, yet complex, mundane matters that have little sloganistic appeal but that relate directly to the activity of development, in which the goverment has invested so much of its energy and prestige, are kept away from the legislators as being too important to entrust to them. Development plans are written by technocrats and

33. Compare B. R. O'G. Anderson, "The Idea of Power in Javanese Culture," in Claire Holt, ed., *Culture and Politics in Indonesia* (Ithaca: Cornell University Press, 1972).

implemented by bureaucrats without Parliament's approval at all; annual budgets, though formally subject to legislative review, have never been amended by Parliament under the New Order in even the slightest particular.[34] Yet these are the kinds of issues on which responsibility can make the views of those who are allowed to exercise it more realistic and more open to compromise. Development planning and budgeting are unlikely to raise the critical barrier around the ummat. The generals have also found it easier to condemn the subversive potential of cultural politics than to remedy the political imbalances strengthening that potential. In December 1973 certain student leaders decried the impotence of Parliament, but when the commander of the armed forces addressed the DPR a month later, he spoke not about institutional reform but about the evils of sara.[35] That in the interim unchanneled frustrations boiled over into violence in Jakarta underscores the need for the elite to redefine the problem of cultural politics before it can expect to solve it.

Redefinition may not be easy for this generation of leaders. Returning to the question with which this book began, elite political culture in Indonesia hampers creative resolution in cultural politics in several ways. First, it fosters an elite view of cultural politics that is at best obsolete, at worst dangerous. The 1945 revolution was fought not over social justice but for national unity; its memory three decades later could not help solve the former problem, which had become acute. Army officers for whom the revolution remained a keystone experience were ready again to rescue the na-

34. In January 1974 a PPP legislator asked the government whether Parliament in fact had the right to make changes, since in the New Order it had never done so (*Berita Buana,* Jan. 21, 1974).

35. In October 1973 the Bandung Institute of Technology Student Council wrote an open letter to Parliament politely questioning whether it was able to channel popular aspirations and whether the existing distribution of power between legislative and executive arms of government was proper (*Harian Kami,* Oct. 11, 1973). In December, Hariman Siregar, chairman of the University of Indonesia Student Council and a key figure in the student demonstrations that preceded the January riots, stated flatly that "the DPR is impotent; it cannot function" (*Sinar Harapan,* Dec. 28, 1973). Earlier the same month, a prominent lawyer, Yap Thiam Hien, also criticized Parliament's ineffectiveness (see ch. 4, n. 11). Siregar and Yap were both arrested in the crackdown after the January riots. The warning against sara delivered to Parliament by the armed forces commander, a Christian Batak, was reprinted in *Berita Buana,* Jan. 24, 1974.

tion from communist or Muslim subversion, as they remembered having done before. When secular but noncommunist urban students and intellectuals also became a target, because they seized the issue of social justice and used it against the regime with devastating consequences in January 1974, the military establishment did not attempt to understand the protest on its own terms—the terms of a postrevolutionary generation sensitive to foreign exploitation and the income-skewing side effects of state capitalist development. Instead, the affair was blamed on the PSI, Indonesia's tiny socialist party, and Masyumi, banned by Sukarno back in 1960. A confidential white paper on the January violence—blatantly entitled "Why are the PSI-Masyumi so Fond of Coups?"[36] —was circulated at cabinet level to encourage government spokesmen to repeat this explanation in answer to questions about the affair. The paper's anonymous author ignored the social dimensions of the riots, preferring instead to rehash the vendettas of Jakarta politics since the 1940's. Because among the many arrested after the January explosion were a few older critics of the regime who had once been associated with the PSI, the party's ghost could take the blame. Links to Masyumi were even harder to find. Perhaps the influential abangan general who sponsored the paper meant to imply that, by protesting against the RUUP, fundamentalist Muslims had encouraged the students to protest against Tanaka's visit; but even if that were true, it hardly proves treason. In fact, Muslim student organizations were careful to abstain from the demonstrations against economic and social inequalities in order to concentrate on the more important marriage bill. When Tanaka arrived, Muslim leaders appeared anxious not to provoke the generals for fear of endangering the compromise second draft of the RUUP negotiated only a few weeks before. The PSI-Masyumi "explanation" of the affair would be laughable were it not for its official source.

The second limitation concerns the question of where problems of cultural politics should be solved. In 1974, decentralization was still anathema to many in the elite. These men remembered at-

36. Anon., *Mengapa PSI-Masjumi Gandrung pada Makar?* (n.p.: n.pub., n.d.). This document, only slightly altered, was later sold to the public in a slick paperback full of photographs and news clippings compiled by Marzuki Arifin, *Peristiwa 15 Januari 1974* (Jakarta: Publishing House Indonesia, 1974).

tempts to divide the nation, by the Dutch and subsequently by Indonesians; in another example of guilt by historical association, the obvious federalist option for the world's largest and culturally most diverse archipelagic nation was still unthinkable. Similarly, the white paper discredited the decentralizing alternative by linking it to the actions of the PSI in the 1950's, blaming the party for having tried at that time to turn the regions against the center by spreading the calumny that the republic was controlled by Javanese. Through his anonymous writer(s), the abangan general behind the paper dismissed as "PSI political agitation" the idea that the position of the center vis-à-vis the regions should not be too strong. Officers in my samples in 1968–1969 were not more inclined than civilians to place the center's interest above the regions'. But they were more prone to expect deference to authority and trust in leaders—and, in particular, more so than civilian intellectuals in the Development Group, several of whom were arrested in 1974 on suspicion of involvement in the January violence. In the wake of that affair, the minister of home affairs, also an army general, pushed through Parliament a bill cancelling any faint hopes the provinces might have had of being able to choose their own governors.

The third limitation relates to structures of information and accountability. In 1969, I found the elite to have a highly personal image of leadership; institutionalized feedback was irrelevant. The moral of the story about Abubakar and the widow boiling stones told to me by the PNI politician was not that structures—organizations, media—should have existed through which the widow could articulate her plight but, on the contrary, that Abubakar should have intuited it directly through psychic identification with the common people.

The story denied the need for structures of upward criticism to correct a leader's performance. Another, told to me by a high-ranking officer in the Department of Defense and Security, denied the need for structures of downward accountability as well. One night in 1969, in his home in the fashionable Menteng section of Jakarta, this man recounted how he had found in the American movie "David and Bathsheba" the model of the ideal leader. King David had served his people well by defeating the Philistines; but he had ordered one of his men into the fray, the man had been

killed, and David had married the widow. Some people whispered
that the king had purposely ordered the man to his destruction in
order to take her; some even thought that the king should be put
to death for his action. And there were inauspicious signs: drought
began killing the Jews' sheep in great numbers. On the other hand,
David had overcome the Philistines, and he was young, handsome,
and widely liked. An assembly of the people was held to judge the
king's conduct. David himself presided—as king, commander, and
judge combined. The prosecutor began the session by asking
David what should be done with a man who had taken another
man's wife. "Let him be put to death in accordance with our law,"
David answered without hesitating, and asked, "Who is this man?"
The prosecutor wept as he answered, "You are, my lord." King
David admitted having broken the law. But he said that since he
was king the only one who could judge him—that is, who was
higher than he—was God.[37] He would ask God's forgiveness. He
would undergo the ordeal of the box: if he touched it and died,
God had sentenced him to death; if he lived, God had forgiven
him. The king prayed, beseeching God; he sang and played his
harp. Hearing his music, birds fell at his feet; hearing his prayers,
angels wept. Finally, he touched the box. And at that instant a
great thunder sounded and life-giving rain poured down. He had
been forgiven. King David had triumphed . . . while in a dark
movie theater in a European country, tears of sympathy welled up
in my informant's eyes.

The story's meanings and contemporary parallels are easily
drawn. Service against the Philistines was equivalent to service in
the revolution and against fanatic Muslims and communists. King
David's triple role suggested ABRI's dual function in security and
politics and the fusion of powers in an executive answerable not
to Parliament but to God. My informant stressed that, after all,
David was really a good man, attractive and popular. It was only

37. Compare the remarks of Jakarta's governor—as noted, a marine general—to an audience in Bukittinggi, West Sumatra, defending himself from
the charge that by legalizing gambling to raise public revenue he had violated Muslim precepts: "Look here, if there are among you some who ac-
cuse me of sinning: you don't have the right to sit in judgment of me. The
one who has the right to judge me is God, because the matter of sin is a
matter between me and God, not between me and you" (*Haluan Minggu*,
July 20, 1969).

proper that God should forgive him, for his mistake shrank to insignificance alongside his bravery, talent, and service to his nation. My informant's notion of leadership was utterly astructural, personal, and charismatic in that word's original sense of someone graced by God. To sum up these limitations of elite political culture: the practice of finding scapegoats and the refighting of old battles inhibit system learning and postpone effective response to new kinds of conflict in altered circumstances; centralization raises the scale of the damage that conflicts can produce; and personalized, structurally unaccountable authority undermines the possibility of long-run, institutionalized solutions by preventing consensus on procedures.

Indonesia's elite does not merely reproduce the wary parochialisms of a culturally riven polity, nor is it a smoothly cosmopolitan outpost of the world culture. Society has not split apart the state, nor has the state yet fully integrated Indonesian society. Reality is a constantly changing situation between these extremes. The Dutch in the twentieth century were a magnet pulling the elite toward a cosmopolitan identity. Dutch success rested on two policies: socialization and isolation. In Western-style schools, promising native sons learned to prize the ideal of the loyal priyayi serving the bureaucratic clockwork and to disregard the counterideals of Islamic and leftist forces. Men like Purwoko were the result. The small size of the colonial elite also facilitated its integration, but not the integration of society; colonial unity derived more from the borders around the Indies than from social interaction inside them.

The net effect of the occupation, the revolution, and postindependence politics was to open, enlarge, and differentiate the elite and to move it away from the cosmopolitian end of the spectrum. The Usmans of Indonesia took their turn on the historical stage. More representative, the elite became less unified. Society recaptured the state; indeed, in the civil conflicts of the 1950's Indonesia nearly split up into several states. The hothouse conditions of the Indies had allowed the Dutch to nurture an elite political culture in the image of the metropole. After independence, Indonesian politicians did not enjoy that luxury; they had to try to fashion a new political culture in their own disparate images while trying simultaneously to utilize and survive the crises of cultural politics. Sukarno showed a consummate talent for cultural balancing in politics, but he allowed the economy to deteriorate. Guided Democracy was based on the acceleration of rhetoric against all obstacles, until in 1965 reality finally overtook the myth.

The legacy of this shift from a powerful but insulated and unrepresentative colonial order to a series of weaker but more open and representative postcolonial ones can be seen in the contrasts spelled out in this book between the bureaucratic and legislative institutions and between cultural majorities and minorities. That the New Order under Suharto has reversed the pendulum's direction is beyond doubt: the coercive weight of the military is swinging the system back toward the colonial model of an administrative state. But army rule will not reinstate that era—any more than priyayi nostalgia can. Among the preconditions of Dutch success in encapsulating the Indies earlier in the century were a pace of social change still slow enough to be subject to central control, population pressures not yet heavy enough to buckle traditional arrangements for sharing poverty, and a network of communications still simple enough that rulers could interpret the world culture selectively to their charges and inhibit (though not prevent) the spread of "unrealistic" expectations.

None of these conditions holds to nearly the same degree today. But neither is a fundamental, thoroughgoing revolution in sight. On the contrary, as the benefits of economic growth and imported technology accrue to the regime, its staying power may increase. The long-run prospect in Indonesia is instead for the elite's continued uneasy shifting between the extremes of cosmopolitan autocracy and authoritarian populism.

Within these limits, however, there are many uncertainties in the short run. One is the possibility that cultural and class issues will mesh, that previously cross-cutting cleavages will become aligned. In 1973–1974, unbalanced economic growth and Golkar's anti-Muslim gestures nearly drove two otherwise unlikely allies, urban students and rural kiyais, into the same corner. Muslim leaders are mainly middle-class entrepreneurs and landowners, like Usman, and thus might seem unwilling participants in any swing to populism. But they, especially lower-middle-class hajis and Muslim youths, are susceptible to the view that generals and priyayis are collaborating with non-Muslims—Westerners, Japanese, and local Chinese—against the ummat. Sarekat Islam cannot be resurrected.

But future official measures against the ummat, or actions interpreted as such, could elicit a violent reaction; and a crisis implicating imperialism and social injustice could activate a range of potential opposition groups, including student gadflies, abangan nationalists, and the urban underclass.

The likelihood that all these disparate groups will coalesce to overthrow the government is remote; that grievances widely shared among two or more of them could encourage a usurper in uniform to make the attempt is not. That may have already happened once, in January 1974. Least hypothetical of all is the prospect that, whatever the future holds, millions upon millions of human beings, in whose name this elite and its successors will continue to act, will continue to live in poverty and dependence.

PURWOKO AND
USMAN REVISITED

I left Jakarta in December 1969. Subsequent events, as summarized in the conclusion to this book, consolidated the administrative state. Muslim parties were forced into one body, denied the right to operate in the name of religion, and defeated in a national election. The drive for economic growth under the First Five-Year Plan replaced Sukarno's cultural balancing as the hallmark of government. Muslim amour propre, when it threatened to upset political stabiliy in the reaction against the marriage bill, was compromised back into quiescence. No sooner had this crisis been surmounted than another arose: in the violence of January 1974 in Jakarta an incipient class rift, itself a byproduct of unbalanced economic growth, threatened to split the regime. I returned to Indonesia four days before these riots occurred. Watching the repressive aftermath, I could not help wondering about the effects of these trends and events on the men I had interviewed five years before. A book must end, but life continues, and it is hard for an author to leave well enough alone.

I stayed in Indonesia until mid-1975. Although living outside Jakarta and engaged in other research, I visited the capital often enough to ask after most of my forty informants. Unlike the administrators, about half of whom were still employed in the core (departmental) bureaucracy (the rest having retired or taken other jobs), only five persons or one-fourth of the legislative sample were still in Parliament in 1974–1975. Golkar's stunning victory over the parties in 1971 had confirmed the greater insecurity of a political compared to an administrative career, a difference I had used, among others, to explain the greater optimism of the bureaucrats in 1969. The legislative sample remained as strikingly hetero-geneous and parochial as before. Whereas most of the men who were no longer part of the core bureaucracy still held government jobs, mainly in Jakarta or abroad, the former legislators continued to work in a variety of positions in the private as well as the public sector, in the provinces as well as the capital. Nor had the cosmo-politan advantage of the bureaucrats lessened. In 1974–1975, to my knowledge, five of the twenty members of the administrative sample were living outside Indonesia (including three who had been made ambassadors); not one of the men in the DPR was. Lastly, turnover among military men had been much less than among civilians. Six or two-thirds of the nine officers were working in the core bureaucracy or in Parliament compared to under one-third of the civilians. It was still an advantage to be an officer in Indonesia's elite.

I could not reinterview all forty men; they were in too many different places and I had too little time. Instead I decided to single out Usman and Purwoko once again. I had focused on them before because they were polar types—Purwoko, the cosmopolitan aban-gan bureaucrat, and Usman, the parochial santri politician. Had subsequent events moved them closer together or farther apart? Insofar as the regime had successfully depoliticized cultural cleav-ages and the two men had accordingly turned back into the Java-nese culture of their childhoods—a place in remembered time and space where the terms santri and abangan had not yet acquired the divisive political meanings that occupation, revolution, and independence would bring—Usman and Purwoko might have re-approached one another. But the strengthening of the secular ad-ministrative state could have had the opposite effect, alienating the santri politician as it incorporated the abangan priyayi and ranging them on opposite sides of the issue of technocratically induced progress. As for the income-skewing side effects of that progress, in the expanding gap between the village in each man's past and the capital city that lay, by comparison, in the nation's future, where did he stand?

Usman, I soon learned, had lost his seat in Parliament to a Golkar candidate in 1971; I reinterviewed him in 1974 in Jakarta. But Purwoko had gone to Europe. Not until 1975, on my way back to America from Indonesia, was I able to reinterview him.

My impression after these meetings was how little the two men had changed and how much they still differed from each other. Usman had acquired a watch but remained as casual as ever about time. Purwoko wore stronger glasses but was as observant as I remembered him. When, after repeated trips to his office, I finally found Usman in, we talked leisurely and at length. My first telephone call reached Purwoko at his desk, but he regretted that he could only clear a small space in his busy schedule to meet me that afternoon. So perfect was the match between this impression registered in 1974–1975—Usman relaxed and easygoing, Purwoko busy and efficient—and the image I had kept from our goodbyes in 1969 that I felt almost as if I were watching a movie that had been stopped in mid-reel and, years later, started up again.

But important changes had occurred. Purwoko had moved into the European heartland of world culture, leaving Jakarta, let alone his village, far behind. Surrounded by his fruit trees on the semi-urban periphery of Jakarta, Usman had laid plans in the opposite direction: toward retirement in a rural setting not far from his birthplace. The two men's lives had not converged or run parallel since 1969. They had moved even farther apart. In this postscript I want to show how and why and to speculate on the consequences.

Years earlier, a competition had been held in Purwoko's department to fill several coveted overseas posts. Candidates, among them Purwoko, had been tested for general knowledge, fluency in English, and psychological stability. Purwoko passed all three tests and showed a better command of English than any other candidate. He was promised the plum among the posts: an assignment in a major Western country. But a controversy broke out, the department changed ministers, and the promise was never met. A high official later recommended Purwoko for another overseas post, less prestigious than the first, but this prospect also vanished when, because of another political conflict, the official himself was transferred to the job. In these experiences Purwoko found bitter confirmation of his view of politics as undermining rational order and the reward of merit.

Later still, an official who had obtained one of the sought-after posts, in Europe, invited Purwoko to join him and work for him. Purwoko accepted, went off to Europe, and, in time, brought over his wife and several of their children. Purwoko enrolled the children in the best available schools, planning to send them back to Indonesia as graduates ready for higher studies and good careers. By 1975, one of his children was an engineer with an oil company, another had a medical practice, and another had returned to Java to begin work on an advanced degree.

In Europe, Purwoko's income was higher than it had ever been, and the longer he stayed, the more he saved. Although he expected to return to Indonesia eventually, in 1975 he had no plans to move. The circumstance under which he told me he might go back— "when the Indonesian economy improves"—was vague enough to justify prolonging his residence abroad indefinitely. When he did speak of returning someday, after his children had completed their European education, he talked of buying the government house in Jakarta where he used to live and of enjoying visits there from his children on Lebaran holidays just as his own father had in the village. As for retiring to that village himself, a wish Purwoko had expressed six years before, I heard no more of that.

The countryside still figured in Usman's future. He spoke unsentimentally about his birthplace, calling it a "dead village" where neglect, erosion, silting, and proximity to the sea gave the local population nothing but "thirst in the dry season, floods in the wet." He would not retire to that cycle of misery. Instead he had picked out a model community inland, where soils were excellent and a man could prosper. Usman's plans for this move matched in precision those he had made to travel to the pesantren with his soccer mates in the 1930's. He wanted to shepherd the three most promising of his children through higher education in Jakarta; that would take around five years. Meanwhile he would move in stages southeast toward his ultimate destination, buying and selling land to finance the education of his younger children. Finally, he would reach the village of his choice and retire there, happy in the knowledge that he had been able to finance his own and his children's futures. So ran Usman's scenario.

These plans to rejoin rural life afforded escape from what Usman had seen Jakarta become. "This government has development fever," he told me, interpreting the Indonesian word for development (*pembangunan*) to mean physical construction. "They'll build anything, just to build. Buildings have gone up all over the city. [With his hands he mimed the springing up of multistory structures.] But ordinary people have been ignored or left out." He shrugged. He saw the violence in Bandung and Jakarta in August 1973 and January 1974, respectively, as spontaneous upheavals by poor people, who had not benefited from development, against foreigners and Indonesian Chinese, who had. Above all he blamed the cosmopolitan intellectuals and technocrats for raising the gross national product (though he did not use the term) at the cost of the continued misery of the majority.

Usman gave examples. He owned some fifty bicycle rickshaws; unskilled young men drove them and paid him a fixed daily rent out of passengers' fees. But slow-moving pedicabs inhibited the flow of motor traffic, offered passengers little protection from accidents, and reminded city officials that Jakarta was not fully modern. (Usman himself had no car; the one he had owned had proved "harder to keep up than a second wife.") The government had already banned the rickshaws from much of the city and envisioned their disappearance altogether in favor of motorized public transport. Usman said he would willingly sell his pedicabs and buy buses instead. —But one bus costs more than 5,000,000 rupiahs (over $12,000) and you have to have at least fifty buses before the city will allocate routes to you and allow you to operate. Who but the Chinese can afford that kind of money? I certainly can't. I'm ready to exchange my rickshaws for taxis. But will the government lend me credits to do this and help train my drivers to drive cars? I doubt it. Once I went to a meeting of city officials concerned with transportation. I pleaded with them to help me find work for my drivers. I told the meeting: We fought the Dutch for our independence, but what did we get for it? [Usman's implication: unemployment.] I even invoked the name of Allah. But it had no effect. The Governor has decided Jakarta must be a modern metropolis. And so it will be.— He shrugged again.

That metropolis was already on Usman's doorstep. Land values were high and rising, buoyed by rumors of future development. Under official pressures, Usman had already sold, for a profit, most of the 5,000 square meters or so he used to own. On some of his former land, near his house, an assembly plant was being readied to produce tools. Just to the south stood a paint factory. Next to it the noisy looms of a textile company, built with Chinese capital from Hong Kong, were running around the clock. Farther south, past a women's prison, a motorcycle repair shop welcomed customers. I asked the Chinese couple who owned and ran the shop how long they had been there and how business was; four months, they answered, and business was good. A year ago most of the area had been ricefields; motorcycles were rare. When the influx of industry began to lift the price of land, many peasants sold off their fields and bought Japanese motorbikes. These were involved in enough accidents and breakdowns to justify opening the repair shop. Just south of the shop I noticed another 3,500 square meters up for sale. Not far away, Usman told me, a house was being built to order for a foreign employee of the World Bank at a reputed price of 25 million rupiahs (about $60,000), a figure the Bank was reportedly happy to pay in light of the even higher going rate for real estate downtown.

Usman was a smart businessman. Land speculation would help make his and his family's futures secure. When pedicabs were finally banned, he would sell his or shift them to a town where they were still legal. He would profit from the boom by moving with it south and east, staying just far enough ahead of it to take advantage of rising land values before moving on, step by step, toward the village where he would retire. Yet while benefiting from economic growth, he deplored its impact on the community around him.

The inhabitants who had given local life its stability and distinctive style were leaving, just as Usman would. —In these new government houses [Usman gestured as we walked past an example], priyayis live. They don't mix with the local people. They don't attend our mosque. They don't give to the community. [Nor, from what I could tell, did they shop at Usman's little store, apparently preferring more fashionable goods downtown.] They go to work mornings and come back afternoons; we only see them through the windows of their automobiles. Prosperity there is, yes, but it's ruining the old neighborly ways. When a farmer sells his land, his sons use the money to buy blue jeans, cutting them off at the knee, sometimes even ripping them to the crotch, aping Western styles. You [meaning me] are polite, but these kids take over only the morally destructive parts of your culture.—

According to Usman: —Every community should have four things: a school, a clinic, a market, and a place to pray. With the income from land sales, we could build these facilities and keep them in repair. We could charge the wealthy more when they get sick, tax transactions at the market in order to improve it. Instead the money goes to the Chinese and the foreign firms. The community is being scattered; basic services like medical treatment are already only available outside it. Industry is coming in. Smoke and pollution will follow. I can already taste the difference in the air. At night the noise of jet planes keeps the newcomers awake, until they get used to it.— Jakarta's new international airport was not far away.

In 1975, a year after this conversation took place, one of those jets carried Purwoko and his wife on a two-week visit to Indonesia, their first since they had left the country for Europe five years before. Purwoko saw Jakarta from the windows first of the plane and then of the chauffeured automobile that drove him through the city. In his words, he was "deeply awed" by what he saw, especially the new multistory buildings that looked to him as if the governor, Ali Sadikin, had "created them by magic" in the time Purwoko had been away. As he was driven down the city's main artery, he marveled at the modernity of everything, even the traffic, which included fewer pedicabs pumped by sweating men in rags and more European-, American-, and Australian-made cars. As an Indonesian, he felt "truly proud to see so many signs of progress." As a cosmopolite, he saw his personal status reflected in them. For example, by his own report, the presence of two cars waiting for him at the airport impressed him greatly. He knew in his mind that this luxury was the unintentional result of poor coordination between his daughter and a former superior in the ministry, who had brought the vehicles independently to pick him up. Nevertheless in his heart, as he put it later, he enjoyed the feeling that his high standing called for such lavish attention.

Most status-ratifying of all was Purwoko's trip back to his birthplace. From the back seat of a rented car over the road leading to the mountain slope where he was born, Purwoko and his wife observed that the clothing worn in the villages they passed seemed clean and neat, perhaps newly bought. Wherever they stopped for refreshment they heard transistor radios; a few villages even sported television aerials. Purwoko described these sights to me enthusiastically as harbingers of a "mental revolution," an electronic expansion in the horizons of ordinary peasants to encompass the great capitals and events of the world. He was delighted to find that the automobile he had rented could be driven up the mountainside to his village, almost to his father's grave (the old man had died a few years earlier) over roads once only suitable for pedestrians, animals, and light traffic. In the village itself, bamboo and leaves, once standard house-building materials, had been replaced by cement and tiles. Purwoko had the feeling that people had willingly cooperated to develop their community by contributing labor and money to make the new roads and buildings. (In the 1970's in a nearby area, according to another firsthand report, obligatory unpaid labor on the roads was so common that peasants there spoke of a new "Japanese time," a reference to the predatory occupation of the Indies during World War II.)

In the village, when curious children surrounded his car, Purwoko joked with them and gave them money, though some were too shy to accept his coins. Soon adults began to gather, among whom he recognized several of his childhood friends. Rural life had given one of these acquaintances the appearance of great age, though he was in reality not much older than Purwoko; many of the man's teeth had fallen out and the rest, rotting, would shortly follow. In contrast, Purwoko later recalled, his own cared-for set felt pleasantly intact. Answering the man's questions, Purwoko told him of flying from a place called Europe in a jet plane. The man nodded as if he understood, but Purwoko was sure that he did not. Purwoko met the local authorities, ate with them. Later in the day he took one of his aunts, in her eighties, whose bedtime tales he had so enjoyed as a child, in the rented automobile up and over the mountain to see, for the first time in her life, the lake resort on the other side, where fancy hotels catered to foreign tourists. On the lake, he gave her a motorboat ride, another first for her. Recalling the day later, he spoke warmly of the villagers: "They treated me like a god." His tone suggested that they had been silly to do so but that he had enjoyed their deference. At sundown he and his wife left the village, driving to a hotel in the nearest city to spend the night.

Usman and Purwoko also held contrasting political opinions. Purwoko praised the Suharto government for achieving political stability, which had attracted foreign aid and investment, which had in turn contributed to economic growth. On his trip home, he had seen encouraging signs that at last, after the political excesses of the Sukarno regime, Indonesia was applying a rational model of development: economic growth planned by enlightened technocrats backed up by firm government. Foreign dependence and domestic inequality were acceptable costs in Indonesia's struggle to become modern. Nor did Purwoko doubt the nature of the goal: to approximate Western standards of living. His sole criticism of Indonesian political life rested on the same precept: that his country did not have enough of what the West did. —The newspapers here in [Western] Europe criticize freely; there is freedom of speech. I want Indonesia to be like that.— Purwoko's self-image as an intellectual supported this priority. Insofar as the students who triggered the riots of January 1974 in Jakarta were asking for civil liberties, Purwoko sympathized with them. Insofar as they were demanding distributive justice and opposing foreign penetration, he did not.

Usman's criticism of the government flowed from a different source: not sympathy for the individual but concern for the community. First and smallest was the community of people who depended on him for a living. When men came to him from the hinterland, having heard that he might help them find work in Jakarta, he housed and fed them. Some of these men ended up renting pedicabs from him; others he tried to channel into jobs selling iced drinks in the neighborhood or peddling kerosene door-to-door. A few of these job seekers were youngsters once under his command in the Army of Allah who had fallen on hard times; one was a reporter who had lost his job in the government crackdown after the violence of January 1974. In 1975, Usman was toying with the idea of trying to keep his drivers employed once pedicabs were banned by converting the vehicles into pushcarts to retail fresh bread and other luxuries to the neighborhood's wealthy newcomers.

The neighborhood was Usman's second, larger community, and in it he felt more constrained. He wanted to play a role in neighborhood affairs, but as a Muslim politician he was suspect in the eyes of local officials—priyayis, he called them—and they ignored his advice. Recently he had made two suggestions about how existing official subsidies could be used to improve the lot of the poor. He had proposed that the government buy cows for people to tend and

fatten for sale at a profit during Lebaran (when holiday demand
inflated prices); from the proceeds, the government would regain
the original price of the cow and split the profits equally with the
cowherds, permitting the purchase of more cows to repeat and expand the cycle. Usman had also urged the government to encourage, if not also finance, the organization of a furniture makers'
marketing cooperative that could sidestep the mainly Chinese
entrepreneurs who paid the carpenters low fixed wages and retailed
their handiwork for large profits. According to Usman, local officials had refused to consider either of these recommendations and
had treated his initiative as a challenge to their authority.

Recalling this experience triggered older memories for Usman:
—Government subsidies never reach the people intact; officials
who handle the money take their cut. It all goes back to the priyayis. In colonial times they were the ones who got Western educations, from the HIS on up to the university. Ordinary people were
lucky to get a few years in a Volksschool. The priyayis used their
schooling only for themselves, to improve their own positions, not
to help others. And they depended on the government; they looked
up to superiors, not down to the people. We santris had a very
different life; we were taught to stand on our own feet and to help
the poor.— As for the technocrats who sometimes visited the
neighborhood, Usman faulted them for enjoying the fruits of a kind
of development not unlike what the Dutch had sponsored in that
it left most people behind. At least some of the priyayis had taken
part in the revolution, but the technocrats were too young to
remember it, and how could anyone understand the people if he
had not once lived in their midst and fought on their behalf?

The broadest community in whose name Usman criticized the
government was the Muslim ummat, "the most backward community in Indonesia," in his words, "backward in all fields: economics, politics, everything." Usman said he felt Islam's position
had deteriorated since our last meeting in 1969. He detailed the
events that had made Muslims even more of a beleaguered political
minority than they had been then. He spoke of his unsuccessful
campaign in 1971 and complained of military intimidation of non-
Golkar candidates. He contrasted that experience with the earlier
legislative elections, in 1955, when candidates could expect motorcycle escorts and cheering crowds. He admitted that the contro-

versy over the marriage bill could have turned out worse for Islam, but he saw the compromise as a sign of military not Muslim influence. Above all, within the DPR, Islam was hopelessly outnumbered: "The priyayis control Parliament now." Finally, Usman saw Islam's low fortunes in mainly secular terms; he resented the rule of priyayis and technocrats not because they were insufficiently Islamic but because they cared too little for the lot of the common people. In the realm of religious belief and behavior, Usman's relaxed tolerance of abangan ways had not diminished.

From the abangan side, Purwoko shared this lack of purely religious animosity. In 1969, I had inferred from his rising interest in Javanese mysticism and wayang a likely veering back into childhood religion, away from his cosmopolitan world of work. On this score I was doubly unprepared for Purwoko in 1975, for he seemed no less secular than before and had acquired a brand new interest in Islam. In the 1960's, he had been active in a mystical organization whose members engaged in various exercises under the guidance of a guru. Some of the tests were demanding, as when he denied himself sleep, just as his father had done sitting on the pendapa or immersing himself neck-deep in a river. In the 1970's, deciding that his physical health and his efficiency at work took precedence, Purwoko dropped out of the organization. In the secular atmosphere of cosmopolitan Europe, the shift back to abangan values I had thought I saw in 1969 was fully reversed.

The man under whom Purwoko worked in Europe was a devout Muslim. Every Friday in a nearby mosque this man joined, and sometimes led, the congregational prayer. Purwoko went along, he said later, less from religious conviction—his abangan preference had always been to stay away from mosques—than because he felt that his boss wished him to. After a while, however, attendance became habitual. He grew more comfortable in the austere ambience of the mosque and more fluent in the details of prayer. Along with advancing age came a heightened need to balance material comfort with spiritual well-being, to begin preparing for the afterlife. When Purwoko's boss was replaced by an abangan official who did not join the Friday prayers, Purwoko continued to participate.

Purwoko still retained an interest in mysticism. Once more he told the story of the rooster's execution, which had presaged the death of Purwoko's brother, and if in 1969 he had placed this premonition in one of his father's dreams, by 1975 he had come to believe that the incident had actually occurred. In another childhood image, seen or dreamed, a soccer ball was being kicked high in the air—an augury of Purwoko's career success and his father's role in launching it. And even in 1975, Purwoko seemed less converted to Islam than aware of its usefulness in enhancing his status. For example, he said that he wanted to make the pilgrimage to Mecca, but his reason was to acquire that extra margin of respect in Indonesia to which a man who had made the journey was entitled. When his wife intervened at this point in our conversation to note that for the pilgrimage to be religiously valid the pilgrim must have pure, unselfish motives, Purwoko agreed speedily but without conviction.

Purwoko's preoccupation with status also surfaced in his discussion of the revolution, a topic he brought up himself. Apparently keen to demonstrate that he had been an important participant in those events, he spoke with considerably greater fervor on the subject than he had in 1969. This retrospectively enhanced role in the drama of independence, the dream reality of the rising soccer ball, the story of his trip back to the village, a proud remark that his daughter's wedding reception in Jakarta had been attended by some two thousand people including officials of foreign embassies and the Ford Foundation—these accounts all advertised Purwoko's high status.

Usman needed such reminders less. As a practicing patron in a community, he took his social status for granted. His response to the onslaught of rapid social change was straightforward: to take personal advantage of it (by speculating in land) and to defend his community (of pedicab drivers) from it as long as possible, until forced to retreat (southeastward back into village life). Even then, Usman would not end up in some idyllic haven untouched by economic growth, but in a booming rural area. For all his vehement criticism of Indonesia's development as planned and implemented by callous priyayis and technocrats, Usman would prosper because of it. And in any case, through all future eventualities, his anchoring membership in the community of Islam would never be in doubt.

As an Indonesian expatriate in Europe, Purwoko could not assume his social status. Worse, he could not measure it with one yardstick. Cultural relativity translated his own experience; no single cradle of meaning could serve as his grave. My error in 1969 was to believe that his point of departure—the abangan core culture of the Javanese—could become his destination, that he could in old age turn his life inward on itself in a comfortably closing circle of meaning, without loose ends. Instead, lacking a sole conviction, he had to experiment with several; without one standard, he needed proof of high status in more than one. Secular achievement (high education, intellectual sophistication, material success), access to technology (the airplane that brought him to Jakarta and the automobiles waiting there to meet him), service to the nation (the post facto enhancement of his part in the revolution), supernatural preselection (the rising soccer ball), religious merit (through Islam)—all these he used to underscore his own importance. The onset of old age, far from allowing him to recapture the remembered tranquillity of his childhood, had made urgent the need to embed his life in multiple frames of meaning—multiple because, always the eclectic, he knew that none was exclusively valid. The religious idea that all roads led to Rome, in the sense of God, had meant that any one of them was acceptable; intellectually Purwoko tolerated all faiths. But reinterpreted in secular terms, the same metaphor could be taken to mean that the only sure way of reaching Rome, in the sense of recognized high status in life, was to travel all those roads at once. Eclecticism as a strategy for success in this world could be merely exhausting.

My last meeting with Purwoko ended past midnight. Bone tired, in the nearest place open—an all-night bowling alley—I wrote up my notes and sought conclusions. The two men's paths had certainly not converged; in physical and social space they were at least as far apart as they had been five years before. Which one had more successfully resolved the personal dilemma of changing yet staying the same, or the social paradox of facilitating change by preserving continuity? All my answers sounded glib or, worse, arrogant. After a time, so did the question. Perhaps I knew Purwoko and Usman too well; perhaps I could never know them well enough. And yet I could not help but feel that Usman would personally win his rearguard skirmish with disorienting, disadvantaging social change, even as his communities were dispersed. To his death, he would know just who he was. About Purwoko, for all his material security and accomplishments, I was less sure. For behind his enthusiasm for progress, Indonesia's and his, lay ambivalent unease: a hunger for status intensified by doubts that he could ever finally prove its possession. If modernity had made the world ambiguous, culture relative, and judgments inconclusive, it had cast Purwoko in this same insubstantial image. And that was why, in 1975, while Usman confidently retreated from the urban future, I found Purwoko embracing it so uncertainly as—for better and worse—his own.

A NOTE ON METHODS

Aside from drawing the samples and writing the questionnaire, a crucial first step was to improve my skills as an interviewer. Accompanied by a close friend (Javanese) who knew me well enough to be able to criticize me freely, I selected and interviewed a senior bureaucrat (also Javanese) in one of the larger ministries. Afterward, my critic took my performance apart. He even corrected my posture. At one point, I had placed my right ankle atop my left knee, an unexceptionable position in America but crude in the eyes of my refined priyayi interviewee.

Access posed another problem. How should I introduce myself to one of the senior officials or politicians in the samples? How could I explain that I had chosen him purely at random? Would I not be telling him that I did not care about him as a person, that he was only a number to me? For elite individuals proud of their reputations and unaccustomed to survey research, would this not sound either mysterious or demeaning, or both?

I sought advice from the official whom I had first interviewed as a test and, in the meantime, come to know quite well. He told me that elite-level Indonesians, especially bureaucrats, would want to see formal bona fides with official-looking seals and signatures before consenting to be interviewed. I should collect as many authorizing documents as I could to present at the first meeting with an individual, and I should flatter my prospective informant by stressing his knowledge and position as reasons for selecting him.

To try out this advice, I picked another bureaucrat at random and approached him in this way, showing him credentials from American and Indonesian institutions and officials authorizing my research. He promptly took me for a VIP and suggested that I should talk to the minister, or at least to someone more senior than himself; if he had been chosen for his authority, others had even more than he, and they were people who could speak on behalf of the whole ministry—in what, on the basis of the credentials on his desk, he had decided would have to be a formal discussion.

On my way back to the drawing board, I turned to an Indonesian student friend for fresh advice. He laughed when I told him of the credentials fiasco and said that Indonesians were, on the contrary, informal people. Alongside and far more important than the web of formal authority in government were networks of personal friendship. The trick was to approach an informant through his own network of acquaintances. Letters of reference were best kept out of sight unless requested.

Another Indonesian friend knew a senior official in another department and was willing to let me use his name as an introduction. But as soon as I met the official and mentioned his friend's name, I knew it was not going to work. He was obviously wondering why his friend should want this foreigner to meet him. What was in this for the friend, and what for the foreigner? In the Indonesian phrase, was there a "shrimp behind the stone"—an ulterior motive?

After that, I realized that the shortest distance between two points was a straightforward line. I approached each of the forty men in the samples directly, explained briefly who I was, why I was there, and how I had chosen him to be interviewed. Some informants were not interested in the randomization procedure; to those who were, I explained it fully. (The easiest way to do so was by analogy with a lottery, although I could not risk this metaphor with pious Muslims.) The absence of third parties to the interview, whether in the form of official signatures on important-looking credentials or mutual acquaintances whose motives might be suspect, helped to create a relaxed atmosphere from the start. Several of the more influential men could take comfort in the knowledge that, unlike their usual petitioners, I was not there to obtain a favor—other than the favor of being allowed to listen to what life had been like under the Dutch, under the Japanese, and in independent Indonesia. Apart from improving my performance and yielding a workable approach, the rehearsals also acclimatized me to the interview situation.

The language of the interviews was Indonesian in every case save one in which my informant spoke English throughout. I started interviewing in September 1968 and ended in August 1969. With politicians, I spent an average of six and a half hours in an average of three and a half sessions with each man; with administrators, the average interview time per man was five and three-quarter hours in three sessions.

Slightly over half of the sessions with bureaucrats took place in their offices; with a few exceptions, the rest were held in their homes. A little more than half the sessions with legislators were held in their homes (including temporary lodgings), about a third in the rooms and corridors of Parliament, and the rest in other places. Among the exceptions and the other places were a high school in Bogor and the central square in Yogyakarta; otherwise, meetings were almost always in Jakarta.

Some interviews were easier than others. One Muslim politician steadfastly refused to schedule meetings in advance, preferring that we should talk only when we "spontaneously" ran into one another at Parliament; I spent a lot of time in the DPR coffee shop waiting to be spontaneous. In an echo of Purwoko's father's didactic white nights, sessions at the home of another politician almost always ran from 10 P.M. toward dawn, and once beyond it, because these, he believed, were the most propitious hours for talk about wayang, religion, and the Javanese past. Usually we were alone, but sometimes there were as many as five other people listening to or taking part in the conversation. When others were present, I did not raise sensitive questions; nor were these sessions counted as interview time. But I did not regret such gatherings; they helped move me into the circle of an informant's acquaintances, among whom I might get to know one or two well enough for them to supplement or correct my impressions of our mutual friend. I also spent time outside the interviews becoming familiar with an informant's life circumstances—attending a daughter's wedding, perhaps, or a congress of his organization.

I met most of my informants first in their offices or at Parliament, later at home, informality growing as we went along. The statements with which I asked them to agree or disagree were normally presented only at the very end of the relationship, when a bridge of rapport had been built that was strong enough to sustain completion of the unfamiliar, formal questionnaire.

During the training interviews, I also experimented with different methods of preserving what was said. One foreign scholar just completing research when I arrived urged me to use a tape recorder, arguing that each replay would reveal a fresh nuance in the conversation. I knew that a machine would also free me to interact more creatively with an informant, for I would not have to memorize or jot down what he was saying. But this same foreign scholar also told me that informants (whose words were being taped) tended to talk a lot about official slogans and symbols; it struck me that the reason might be a "for the record" formality introduced into the interview situation by an absorbent microphone and a relentlessly circling reel. My suspicion was confirmed when, shortly thereafter, an Indonesian who had been interviewed on tape by the scholar in question mentioned with a smile that of course it would have been quite imprudent to have been spontaneous or frank in the presence of a recording device. One reason for the freewheeling, unofficial character of most of my interviews is that I decided not to record them.[1]

The choice between pencil and memory was made on the spot. I never started out by taking notes, but it often became clear that an informant not only did not mind but actually preferred that I do so. For several it made the interview seem more scientific; for others it enhanced the importance of what they were saying. All of these men also knew (and some regretted) that their anonymity was guaranteed. When I did take notes, rather than attempting a verbatim record I wrote down symbols or abbreviations that would later trigger, by association, my memory of a given part of an

---

1. Robert D. Putnam recommends the recording of elite interviews for subsequent coding as a compromise between intuitive appreciation and intersubjective validity, but his method would seem useful only in the case of individuals for whom a tape recorder is not a disconcerting or contaminating intrusion. His claim that few respondents will say things without a tape recorder that they would conceal with it, which he finds "the most convincing argument" for its use, is surely related to the short average length of his interviews (seventy-five minutes in only one session). Frankness is a function of trust, and trust takes time—especially in a multicultural society with a recent history of bloodshed and repression. See Putnam's "Studying Elite Political Culture: The Case of 'Ideology,'" *American Political Science Review*, 65 (Sept. 1971), 653, and *The Beliefs of Politicians: Ideology, Conflict, and Democracy in Britain and Italy* (New Haven: Yale University Press, 1973), pp. 20–21.

interview. Whether or not I took notes during the session, I wrote it up as soon as I could afterward.

I did not structure the interviews according to a set schedule. Informants were usually least reluctant to talk about their childhoods, and this became a natural starting point. The main thing was to gain and keep rapport. Sometimes the smallest things mattered. My enjoyment of locally made clove cigarettes led in one case to a discussion of the merits of different brands that established a bond of shared interest from the first meeting. In another, my lucky guess that a particular wayang figure was in fact Parikesit, grandson of Arjuna and destined to rule over the contested kingdom of Astina (thus an analog for Suharto), created an invaluable first tie. With practicing Muslims, making quietly clear that I had some understanding of Islam achieved the same end.

I also tried to control my "presentation of self," in Erving Goffman's phrase,[2] so as not to bias the encounter unwittingly. Informants reacted not only to my posture but to my clothes, my transportation, my address, and my religion. White shirts, I discovered, were less unsettling than brightly colored ones; my mode of transport should not be too far beneath my informant's circumstances; my address should not be too lower class and my landlady preferably not Chinese. (By chance, not design, I lived between upper-class Menteng and lower-class Senen, which was ambiguous enough, and my landlady was Sundanese.) When asked my religion I replied Unitarian, which was at least unfamiliar enough to make me hard to pigeonhole.

I do not think that in seeking close relationships I fell victim to overrapport. Without trying to see the world as my informants did, from within their own frames of reference and through their own eyes and those of their acquaintances, I could not have understood them. The questionnaire was a far more "objective" (standardized) stimulus than my personality, but had I relied on that alone my research would have been incomplete. True, when informants have become friends, one does not badger them lightly; that was my own choice, and if that is a cost of rapport, so be it. But with-

2. See his book, *The Presentation of Self in Everyday Life* (Garden City: Doubleday Anchor Books, 1959), an interpretation of public behavior as dramaturgy.

out the mutual liking and trust that I tried in this way to protect, these men would not have been nearly so willing, frank, or comprehensive in their recollections as they were.[3]

As for the questionnaire, I wrote a first draft in Indonesian and showed it to various Indonesian friends, primarily academics, for their advice. Items were thrown out or reworded and new ones inserted. The resulting second draft I submitted to a panel of five Indonesians—a writer, a journalist, a secretary, and two professors —well qualified to distinguish nuances and usage in the Indonesian language. Two were Javanese, one Sundanese, one Banjarese, and one Minahassan (from Sulawesi); two were female, three male. Separately, each panel member was asked to criticize the draft and to choose among alternative wordings of a statement that version most easily understood and closest to the orientation presumed to underlie it. From this advice a third draft emerged, which I pretested on 188 first-year students in the Faculty of Medicine at the University of Indonesia in Jakarta in July 1968. Of fifty-five items, eleven were dropped and several others reworded, either because students queried them in the space for comments provided at the end of the questionnaire, or because they did not answer these statements consistently in relation to other statements articulating the same orientation.[4] The resulting final draft was administered to the samples.

Thirty-six of the forty sample members completed the questionnaire. The four who did not represented no particular group: they were two legislators and two bureaucrats; three civilians and one officer; two Javanese and two non-Javanese; one pious Muslim, two nominal Muslims, and one non-Muslim. One was arrested before I could show him the questionnaire, one left Jakarta, and one found the choice among predetermined answers (Agree . . . Disagree) too constraining. The fourth man, although voluble and frank in conversation, was unwilling to commit his opinions to paper; he had opened our first meeting by asking suspiciously if I

3. For a parallel view on the question of rapport versus "objectivity," see Robert A. Stebbins, "The Unstructured Research Interview as Incipient Interpersonal Relationship," *Sociology and Social Research,* 56 (Jan. 1972), 164–179.

4. For the statistical test used, see William J. Goode and Paul K. Hatt, *Methods in Social Research* (New York: McGraw-Hill, 1952), pp. 275–276.

were a journalist, for, he said, he never talked to the press. He was also extremely powerful. I decided not to risk an otherwise fruitful relationship by pressing the questionnaire upon him.

Response set—reaction to the way statements are presented rather than to what they mean—was a problem. Four informants Agreed with both of two items intentionally reversed to check sensitivity to content: "It's impossible for a man to decide his own fate" and "A man's fate is decided entirely by that man himself." Another Agreed with 79 per cent of all 43 statements to which he responded. That is, 5 out of 36 respondents, or 14 per cent, may have been more sensitive to the format of the questionnaire than to the content of at least some of its items. Nor were these five men randomly distributed through the samples. Four were legislators, only one a bureaucrat. (Purwoko and Usman were not among them.) Their median age in 1968 was fifty-one, compared to forty-seven for the thirty-one men who did not show signs of response set. Only one of the five (the administrator) had a higher education. Finally, three were PNI politicians. In short, they tended to lie toward the less cosmopolitan end of the spectrum. Response set appeared to be a characteristic of older, less educated,[5] especially PNI politicians.

The oral commentary elicited to accompany the informants' choice of answer categories proved invaluable in the case of these five men. For it was clear that they were sensitive to the content of some or many statements, interpreting them correctly and expressing considered and often critical opinions about them. Rather than reject these individuals' answers, I excluded from the analysis all statements about which there was reasonable doubt concerning the content-sensitivity of one or more of the men in question. Although several items thus dropped were probably answered sensitively by most or all of the rest of the sample members, their loss seemed an acceptable cost. I considered a one-statement scale of a given orientation preferable to a scale of many statements whose

5. Henry A. Landsberger and Antonio Saavedra, "Response Set in Developing Countries," *Public Opinion Quarterly*, 31 (1967), 214–229, identified education as the critical variable determining response set; they found the greatest content insensitivity among workers who had not graduated from secondary school. However, all the men in my samples had at least a secondary education.

meaningfulness in expressing that orientation was suspect. This process of selection reduced the original list of forty-three statements to the fourteen presented in chapter 5 (Tables 9–15).

The average or absolute interitem correlations given in Tables 9, 10, and 13 for the three multi-item scales were developed using all thirty-six completed questionnaires. Despite oral interview evidence to the contrary, there remained a possibility that the five least obviously content-sensitive informants had approved of these statements because of response set—assent being the path of least resistance—and thereby artificially raised the average correlations within each scale. To check this possibility, average or absolute interitem correlations for these scales were also calculated excluding the five men. In fact, omitting the five individuals slightly increased the average correlation in the case of two scales (perceived anomie: $\overline{X} = .53$ with the five, .55 without; support for deference: $\overline{X} = .44$ with, .46 without); the hypothesis of inflated consistency because of response set for these orientations could be rejected. On the scale of perceived conflict, however, the exclusion did significantly reduce the size of the correlation ($\overline{X} = .45$ with, .33 without). To give a more realistic (conservative) picture of internal scale consistency, the correlations in Table 17 were computed without these five respondents. Even so, the resulting figures are, relatively, quite large compared to the distribution of all possible correlations between items in the forty-three-item questionnaire, as the lower half of the table demonstrates.

I encouraged my informants to comment freely on the statements in the questionnaire while they filled it in. This technique of using closed-end questions to trigger open-ended discussion proved highly successful. It flattered respondents in that they were asked not merely to check off their views mechanically in someone else's format but also to expound upon them in their own words. By the same token, it reduced for them the strangeness of the experience. And, as already noted, it enabled me later to select for further analysis only those items most obviously in line with the orientations I intended them to tap. Last but not least, it released an invaluable flood of impressionistic oral evidence. In this way a quantitative tool can be used to raise the quality of an otherwise unstructured interview.

Table 17. Interitem scale correlations

Perceived anomie	Support for deference to authority	Perceived conflict
Item 19 x 31 = .66	Item 2 x 37 = .59	Item 17 x 33 = .33
Item 27 x 31 = .57	Item 23 x 37 = .50	
Item 22 x 31 = .56	Item 2 x 23 = .47	
Item 22 x 27 = .56	Item 23 x 42 = .46	
Item 19 x 27 = .50	Item 37 x 42 = .46	
Item 19 x 22 = .46	Item 2 x 42 = .30	

Range of correlations	Percentage of all possible correlations (100% = 903)	Percentage of all scale correlations (100% = 13)
.000 through .299	83.1	–
.300 through .399	10.6	15.4
.400 through .499	4.2	30.8
.500 through .599	1.8	46.2
.600 through .699	.3	7.7
	100.0	100.1

GLOSSARY

Words in *Italics* are defined elsewhere in the glossary.

abangan: Describes a nominally Muslim Javanese in whose religious outlook and behavior Hindu, Buddhist, animist, and Islamic elements are mixed or coexist

Hizbullah: Army of Allah, a loosely organized Muslim military force active during the revolution

ilmu firasah: Muslim art of judging a man's character through his appearance

Jawa Hokokai: Java People's Service Association, a Japanese-sponsored mass organization (1944–1945)

jihad: Islamic holy war

kalima syahadat: Arabic formula—"There is no God but Allah; Muhammad is His Prophet"—whose utterance signifies membership in the *ummat*

kiyai: Teacher in the Islamic tradition, especially a teacher of *santris* in a *pesantren*

kraton: Javanese royal palace

Lebaran: Day that ends the Muslim fasting month

Mataram: Inland Javanese kingdom in the sixteenth to nineteenth centuries

merdeka: Free—used by nationalists during the revolution as a cry for Indonesian independence ("Indonesia merdeka!")

pamong praja: Central, territorial, and mainly Javanese administrative corps

patih: In the colonial period, a Javanese official one rank beneath a regent

pendapa: Large roofed area, open on three sides, extending from the front of a classical Javanese house

peringgitan: Front room in a classical Javanese house

pesantren: Communal center of traditional Muslim learning on Java (literally, a place for *santris*)

priyayi: Describes a member of the Javanese bureaucratic class

puasa: Muslim fast, observed during the month of *Ramadan*

Ramadan: Muslim fasting month

santri: Describes a pious or practicing Javanese Muslim, or a pupil in a *pesantren*

sara: Term, popular in the 1970's, representing four particularly explosive divisions in cultural politics: between ethnic groups (s for suku), religions (a for agama), races (r for ras), and other groups (a for antar golongan)

Sarekat Islam: Islamic Union, the colony's first mass nationalist movement, established in 1911

selamatan: Religiously syncretic ritual, involving prayer and the sharing of food, common among *abangan* Javanese

syahid: Muslim felled in the act of *jihad* and therefore guaranteed a place in paradise

takbir: "Allahu akbar!" (Allah is incomparably greater!), spoken by a good Muslim on occasions central to his life and that of the *ummat*

tapa: Ascesis in the *abangan* tradition

ummat: Community—here used to mean the community of Islam (ummat Islam)

Volksraad: People's Council, the colonial legislature (1918–1942)

Volksschool: People's School, a simplified, vernacular-language, colonial primary school for indigenes

wayang kulit: Ritual theater in the *abangan* tradition, in which a puppeteer manipulates flat carved leather figures, whose shadows are cast on a white screen, speaks their voices, and leads the accompanying Javanese orchestra in a performance of a play normally lasting one night

BIBLIOGRAPHY

Theory, Method, Comparison, and Reference

Abueva, Jose V. "Social Backgrounds and Recruitment of Legislators and Administrators in the Philippines." *Philippine Journal of Public Administration,* 9 (January 1975), 10–29.

Alford, Robert R. *Bureaucracy and Participation: Political Cultures in Four Wisconsin Cities.* Chicago: Rand McNally, 1969.

Almond, Gabriel A., and Sidney Verba. *The Civic Culture: Political Attitudes and Democracy in Five Nations.* Princeton: Princeton University Press, 1963.

Bachtiar, Harsja W. "The Religion of Java: A Commentary." *Madjalah Ilmu-ilmu Sastra Indonesia,* 5, 1 (January 1973), 85–118.

Benda, Harry J. "Democracy in Indonesia." *Journal of Asian Studies,* 23 (1963–1964), 449–456.

Billah, M. M. "Beberapa Masalah Metodologis di Seputar Pengusahaan Penelitian Lapangan." *Cakrawala,* 6 (March–April 1974), 407–456.

Cruikshank, Bruce. "Abangan, Santri, and Prijaji: A Critique." *Journal of Southeast Asian Studies,* 3 (March 1972), 39–43.

Deutsch, Morton, and Robert M. Krauss. *Theories in Social Psychology.* New York: Basic Books, 1965.

Feith, Herbert. "History, Theory, and Indonesian Politics." *Journal of Asian Studies,* 24 (1964–1965), 305–312.

Finifter, Ada W. "Dimensions of Political Alienation." *American Political Science Review,* 64 (June 1970), 389–410.

Geertz, Clifford. *Islam Observed: Religious Development in Morocco and Indonesia.* New Haven: Yale University Press, 1968.

——. *The Religion of Java.* New York: Free Press, 1960.

——. Review of *Politics, Personality, and Nation Building,* by Lucian W. Pye. *Economic Development and Cultural Change,* 12 (1964), 205–209.

Gibb, H. A. R., and J. H. Kramers, eds. *Shorter Encyclopaedia of Islam*. Leiden: Brill, 1953.

Goffman, Erving. *The Presentation of Self in Everyday Life*. Garden City: Doubleday Anchor Books, 1959.

Goode, William J., and Paul K. Hatt. *Methods in Social Research*. New York: McGraw-Hill, 1952.

Hardjowirogo. *Sedjarah Wajang Purwa*. Reprint. Jakarta: Balai Pustaka, 1968.

Heine-Geldern, Robert. *Conceptions of State and Kingship in Southeast Asia*. Reprint. Ithaca: Cornell University Southeast Asia Program, 1956.

Hopkins, Raymond F. *Political Roles in a New State: Tanzania's First Decade*. New Haven: Yale University Press, 1971.

Indonesia. "Djumlah Pegawai Negeri/ABRI/Sipil ABRI/Pensiunan dan Pegawai Daerah Otonom Pada Achir Th. 1967 KBN/DSPP." Mimeographed, Jakarta, 24 April 1968.

———. Biro Pusat Statistik. *Penduduk Indonesia, Sensus Penduduk 1971*, Seri D. Jakarta: Biro Pusat Statistik, 1975.

———. Biro Pusat Statistik. *Statistik Indonesia 1970 & 1971*. Jakarta: Biro Pusat Statistik, 1972.

———. Dewan Perwakilan Rakyat. *Risalah Perundingan 1950/1951*. Jakarta: Pertjetakan Negara, n.d.

———. Dewan Perwakilan Rakyat Gotong Royong. "Daftar Nama dan Alamat Anggota-anggota DPR-GR." Mimeographed, Jakarta, 1 March 1968.

———. Dewan Perwakilan Rakyat Gotong Royong. *Risalah Resmi* [uncorrected], 1968–1969. Mimeographed, Jakarta [1968–1969].

———. Sekretariat Kabinet Ampera. "Daftar Nama-nama Pedjabat Alamat & Telepon." Mimeographed, Jakarta, 1 December 1967.

Japanese Military Government on Java. *Orang Indonesia Jang Terkemoeka di Djawa*. Jakarta: Gunseikanbu, 1944.

Jaspan, M. A. *Daftar Sementara dari Sukubangsa-bangsa di Indonesia*. Yogyakarta: Gadjah Mada University, Social Research Committee, 1958.

Kavanagh, Dennis. *Political Culture*. London: Macmillan, 1972.

Koran. *The Koran Interpreted*, translated by Arthur J. Arberry. 2 vols. London: George Allen and Unwin, 1955.

———. *The Meaning of the Glorious Koran: An Explanatory Translation*, translated by Mohammad Marmaduke Pickthall. New York: Mentor Book, New American Library, n.d.

———. *Tafsir Qüran*, translated by Zainuddin Hamidy and Fachruddin. Reprint. Jakarta: Widjaya, 1963.

Kothari, Shanti, and Roy Ramashray. *Relations between Politicians and*

Administrators at the District Level. New Delhi: Indian Institute of Public Administration, 1969.

Landsberger, Henry A., and Antonio Saavedra. "Response Set in Developing Countries." *Public Opinion Quarterly,* 31 (1967), 214–229.

Lebar, Frank M., ed. and comp. *Ethnic Groups of Insular Southeast Asia.* New Haven: Human Relations Area Files Press, 1972.

Lerner, Daniel. *The Passing of Traditional Society: Modernizing the Middle East.* New York: Free Press, 1958.

Melanson, Philip H., and Lauriston R. King. "Theory in Comparative Politics: A Critical Appraisal." *Comparative Political Studies,* 4 (July 1971), 205–231.

Merkl, P., and J. E. Moore. "Beamtentum oder parteien: Rivalisierende eliten des modernisierungsprozesses." *Politische Vierteljahresschrift,* 11 (December 1970), 607–622.

Netherlands Indies. Central Statistical Bureau. *Indisch Verslag,* II. Batavia: Landsdrukkerij, 1941.

Olorunsola, Victor Adeola. "The Relationship between Bureaucratic and Political Leadership in the Nigerian Polity." Ph.D. dissertation, Indiana University, 1967.

Parlaungan, comp. *Hasil Rakjat Memilih Tokoh-tokoh Parlemen.* Jakarta: Gita, 1956.

Portocarrero, Cesar A., and Everett M. Rogers. "Empathy: Lubricant of Modernization." In *Modernization among Peasants: The Impact of Communication,* by Everett M. Rogers in association with Lynne Svenning, pp. 195–218. New York: Holt, Rinehart and Winston, 1969.

Putnam, Robert D. *The Beliefs of Politicians: Ideology, Conflict, and Democracy in Britain and Italy.* New Haven: Yale University Press, 1973.

———. "Studying Elite Political Culture: The Case of 'Ideology.' " *American Political Science Review,* 65 (September 1971), 651–681.

Pye, Lucian W. *Aspects of Political Development.* Boston: Little, Brown, 1966.

———. *Politics, Personality, and Nation Building: Burma's Search for Identity.* Cambridge, Mass.: MIT Press, 1962.

———. *The Spirit of Chinese Politics: A Psychocultural Study.* Cambridge, Mass.: MIT Press, 1968.

Rokkan, Stein. Review of *The Civic Culture,* by Gabriel A. Almond and Sidney Verba. *American Political Science Review,* 58 (1964), 676–679.

Saleh, K. Wantjik, comp. *Himpunan Peraturan dan Undang-Undang tentang Perkawinan.* Jakarta: Ichtiar Baru-Van Hoeve, 1974.

Sastroamidjojo, A. Seno. *Renungan tentang Pertundjukan Wajang Kulit.* Jakarta: Kinta, 1964.

Scott, James C. *Political Ideology in Malaysia: Reality and the Beliefs of an Elite.* New Haven: Yale University Press, 1968.

Searing, Donald D. "The Comparative Study of Elite Socialization." *Comparative Political Studies,* 1 (1969), 471–500.

Shaw, Malcolm. "Introduction: Legislatures in Comparative Perspective." *International Journal of Politics,* 1 (1971–1972), 291–298.

Sinar Harapan [Jakarta], 3–6 September 1973. [Text of the draft law on marriage.]

Soesastro, M. Hadi, ed. *Indonesia dan Dunia Internasional 1973: Ringkasan Peristiwa.* Jakarta: Yayasan Proklamasi, Centre for Strategic and International Studies, 1973.

Solomon, Richard. *Mao's Revolution and the Chinese Political Culture.* Berkeley: University of California Press, 1971.

Sosrodihardjo, Soedjito. "Religious Life in Java." *Monografi Sosiologi Indonesia dan Hukum Adat,* Special Issue (1963), pp. 17–30.

Stebbins, Robert A. "The Unstructured Research Interview as Incipient Interpersonal Relationship." *Sociology and Social Research,* 56 (January 1972), 164–179.

Surabaja Post [Surabaya], 10–12 April 1975. [Text of the decree implementing the marriage law.]

Yamin, Muhammad, comp. and ed. *Naskah-persiapan Undang-undang Dasar 1945,* I. [Jakarta]: Jajasan Prapantja, 1959.

History

Anderson, B. R. O'G. "Japan: 'The Light of Asia.' " In *Southeast Asia in World War II: Four Essays,* edited by Josef Silverstein, pp. 13–50. New Haven: Yale University Southeast Asia Studies, 1966.

———. *Java in a Time of Revolution: Occupation and Resistance 1944–1946.* Ithaca: Cornell University Press, 1972.

———. "The Pemuda Revolution: Indonesian Politics 1945–1946." Ph.D. dissertation, Cornell University, 1967.

———. *Some Aspects of Indonesian Politics under the Japanese Occupation: 1944–1945.* Ithaca: Cornell University Modern Indonesia Project, 1961.

Anshary, Muhammad Isa. "Rasa Tanggoeng Djawab." *Asia Raya* [Jakarta], 17 July 1945.

———. "Tjinta Tanah Air." *Indonesia Merdeka* [Jakarta], 25 June 1945.

Benda, Harry J. *The Crescent and the Rising Sun: Indonesian Islam under the Japanese Occupation.* The Hague: Van Hoeve, 1958.

———. "Decolonization in Indonesia: The Problem of Continuity and Change." *American Historical Review,* 70 (July 1965), 1058–1073.

——. "Modern Indonesia under the Historian's Looking Glass." In *Japan's Future in Southeast Asia*. Kyoto: Kyoto University Center for Southeast Asian Studies, 1966.

——. "The Pattern of Administrative Reforms in the Closing Years of Dutch Rule in Indonesia." *Journal of Asian Studies*, 25 (August 1966), 589–605.

——, et al., comps. and trans. *Japanese Military Administration in Indonesia: Selected Documents*. New Haven: Yale University Southeast Asia Studies, 1965.

Berg, C. C. "Indonesia." In *Whither Islam? A Survey of Modern Movements in the Muslim World*, edited by H. A. R. Gibb, pp. 237–311. London: Gollancz, 1932.

Blumberger, J. Th. Petrus. *De Nationalistische beweging in Nederlandsch-Indië*. Haarlem: Tjeenk Willink, 1931.

Boland, B. J. *The Struggle of Islam in Modern Indonesia*. The Hague: Martinus Nijhoff, 1971.

Bousquet, G. H. *La politique musulmane et coloniale des Pays-Bas*. Paris: Paul Hartmann, 1939.

Brugmans, I. J., et al. *Nederlandsch-Indië onder Japanse bezetting: Gegevens en documenten over de jaren 1942–1945*. Franeker: Wever, 1960.

Dahm, Bernard. *Sukarno and the Struggle for Indonesian Independence*. Ithaca: Cornell University Press, 1969.

Djajadiningrat, Achmad. *Kenang-kenangan Pangeran Aria Djajadiningrat*, translated by Balai Pustaka. Batavia: Kolff-Buning, 1936.

——. "Vorst en volk." *Djawa*, Mangkoenagoro-nummer 4 (1924), 62–63.

Djojohadikusumo, Margono. *Herinneringen uit 3 tijdperken*. Amsterdam: Nabrink, 1970.

Emmerson, Donald K. "Thoughts on 'Remembered History' as a Subject of Study, with Reference to Indonesia's Revolution." *Review of Indonesian and Malayan Affairs*, 8, 1 (January–June 1974), 3–6.

Feith, Herbert. *The Decline of Constitutional Democracy in Indonesia*. Ithaca: Cornell University Press, 1962.

——. *The Indonesian Elections of 1955*. Ithaca: Cornell University Modern Indonesia Project, 1957.

Frederick, William H. Introduction to *The Putera Reports: Problems in Wartime Cooperation*, by Mohammad Hatta, translated by William H. Frederick. Ithaca: Cornell University Modern Indonesia Project, 1971.

Furnivall, J. S. *Netherlands India: A Study of Plural Economy*. Cambridge, Eng.: Cambridge University Press, 1944.

Hasjim, K. H. A. Wahid. "Sekitar Pembentukan Kementerian Agama

R.I.S." Reprinted in *Sedjarah Hidup K. H. A. Wahid Hasjim dan Karangan Tersiar,* compiled by H. Aboebakar, pp. 856–859. Jakarta: Panitya Buku Peringatan, 1957.

Indonesia. Departemen Agama. *Peranan Departemen Agama dalam Revolusi dan Pembangunan Bangsa.* Bandung: Departemen Agama, 1965.

Kahin, George McT. *Nationalism and Revolution in Indonesia.* Ithaca: Cornell University Press, 1952.

Kanahele, George S. "The Japanese Occupation of Indonesia: Prelude to Independence." Ph.D. dissertation, Cornell University, 1967.

Kartodirdjo, Sartono. "Bureaucracy and Aristocracy: The Indonesian Experience in the XIXth Century." *Archipel,* 7 (1974), 151–168.

———. *The Peasants' Revolt of Banten in 1888: Its Conditions, Course and Sequel.* The Hague: Martinus Nijhoff, 1966.

Kat Angelino, A. D. A. de. *Colonial Policy,* II. Edited and translated by G. J. Reiner in collaboration with the author. Chicago: University of Chicago Press, 1931.

Latuharhary, J. "The Development of the Position of the Regents on Java." Typescript, Jakarta, 1 June 1943. Wason film 905, reel 3, Cornell University.

Lev, Daniel S. *The Transition to Guided Democracy: Indonesian Politics, 1957–1959.* Ithaca: Cornell University Modern Indonesia Project, 1966.

McVey, Ruth T. *The Rise of Indonesian Communism.* Ithaca: Cornell University Press, 1965.

Moertono, Soemarsaid. *State and Statecraft in Old Java: A Study of the Later Mataram Period, 16th to 19th Century.* Ithaca: Cornell University Modern Indonesia Project, 1968.

Mook, H. J. van. *The Stakes of Democracy in South-East Asia.* London: George Allen and Unwin, 1950.

Nakamura, Mitsuo. "General Imamura and the Early Period of Japanese Occupation." *Indonesia,* 10 (October 1970), 1–26.

Netherlands. Information Service. *Zeven jaar Republik Indonesia.* The Hague: Information Service Indonesia [1952].

Netherlands Indies. Bureau for Decentralization. "De Regeling van de verkiezingen voor den Volksraad." *Koloniale Studien,* Extra politiek nummer 1 (October 1917), 162–168.

Noer, Deliar. "Masjumi: Its Organization, Ideology, and Political Role in Indonesia." M.A. thesis, Cornell University, 1960.

Pigeaud, G. Th. *Java in the 14th Century: A Study in Cultural History* [The Nagarakertagama], IV. 3d ed. The Hague: Martinus Nijhoff, 1962.

Pluvier, J. M. *Overzicht van de ontwikkeling der nationalistische beweging in Indonesië in de jaren 1930 tot 1942.* The Hague: Van Hoeve, 1953.

Pringgodigdo, A. K. *Sedjarah Pergerakan Rakjat Indonesia.* Reprint. [Jakarta]: Dian Rakjat, 1967.

Reid, Anthony J. S. *Indonesian National Revolution 1945–1950.* Hawthorn, Vic.: Longman, 1974.

———. "The Japanese Occupation and Rival Indonesian Elites: Northern Sumatra in 1942." *Journal of Asian Studies,* 35 (November 1975), 49–61.

Schrieke, B. *Indonesian Sociological Studies,* Part II: *Ruler and Realm in Early Java.* The Hague: Van Hoeve, 1967.

———. "Native Society in the Transformation Period." In *The Effect of Western Influence on Native Civilizations in the Malay Archipelago,* edited by B. Schrieke, translated by H. J. Bridge, pp. 237–247. Batavia: Kolff, 1929.

Sihombing, O. D. P. *Pemuda Indonesia Menantang Fasisme Djepang.* Jakarta: Sinar Djaya [1962].

Soebekti. *Sketsa Revolusi Indonesia 1940–1945.* Surabaya: GRIP, 1966.

Stutterheim, William F. *Studies in Indonesian Archaeology.* The Hague: Martinus Nijhoff, 1956.

Sutherland, Heather. "Notes on Java's Regent Families." *Indonesia,* 16 (October 1973), 113–148, and 17 (April 1974), 1–42.

———. "Pangreh Pradja: Java's Indigenous Administrative Corps and Its Role in the Last Decades of Dutch Colonial Rule." Ph.D. dissertation, Yale University, 1973.

———. "The Priyayi." *Indonesia,* 19 (April 1975), 57–77.

Sutter, John O. *Indonesianisasi: Politics in a Changing Economy, 1944–1955,* IV. Ithaca: Cornell University Southeast Asia Program, 1959.

Vandenbosch, Amry. *The Dutch East Indies: Its Government, Problems, and Politics.* 2d ed. Berkeley: University of California Press, 1941.

Van Niel, Robert. *The Emergence of the Modern Indonesian Elite.* The Hague: Van Hoeve, 1960.

Vlekke, Bernard H. M. *Nusantara: A History of Indonesia.* Rev. ed. Chicago: Quadrangle Books, 1960.

Wal, S. L. van der. *De Volksraad en de staatkundige ontwikkeling van Nederlands-Indië.* 2 vols. Groningen: Wolters, 1964–1965.

Yamin, Muhammad, comp. *Lukisan Sedjarah.* Jakarta: Djambatan [1956].

Polity, Economy, and Society

Ali, Mustakim. "Isi R.U.U. Perkawinan Melanggar dan Memperkosa U.U.D. '45 dan Pancasila." *Abadi* [Jakarta], 24 October 1973.

Anderson, B. R. O'G. "The Idea of Power in Javanese Culture." In *Culture and Politics in Indonesia,* edited by Claire Holt, pp. 1–69. Ithaca: Cornell University Press, 1972.

Anwar, Sjamsu. "Apollo, Islam & Ummat Islam." *Indonesia Raya* [Jakarta], 12 and 19 August 1969.

Arifin, Marzuki, comp. *Peristiwa 15 Januari 1974.* Jakarta: Publishing House Indonesia, 1974.

Arndt, H. W. "Development and Equality: The Indonesian Case." *World Development,* 3, 2–3 (February–March 1975), 77–90.

Asjari, Samudja. "Kedudukan Kjai Dalam Pondok Pesantren." M.A. thesis, Gadjah Mada University, 1967.

Bakry, Hasbullah. *Pengaturan Undang-Undang Perkawinan Ummat Islam.* Jakarta: Bulan Bintang, 1970.

Bruner, Edward M. "The Expression of Ethnicity in Indonesia." In *Urban Ethnicity,* edited by Abner Cohen, pp. 251–280. London: Tavistock, 1974.

Castles, Lance. "The Ethnic Profile of Djakarta." *Indonesia,* 1 (April 1967), 153–204.

——. *Religion, Politics, and Economic Behavior in Java: The Kudus Cigarette Industry.* New Haven: Yale University Southeast Asia Studies, 1967.

Collier, William L., et al. "Choice of Technique in Rice Milling." *Bulletin of Indonesian Economic Studies,* 10, 1 (March 1974), 106–120.

——. "The Limits of Involution: Tebasan, HYV's, and Rural Change in Java." Mimeographed, Agro-Economic Survey of Indonesia, November 1973.

Deuster, Paul R. "Rural Consequences of Indonesian Inflation: A Case Study of the Jogjakarta Region." Ph.D. dissertation, University of Wisconsin, 1971.

Emmerson, Donald K. "The Bureaucracy in Political Context: Weakness in Strength." In *Communication and Power in Indonesia,* edited by Karl D. Jackson and Lucian W. Pye, forthcoming.

——. "Bureaucratic Alienation in Indonesia: 'The Director General's Dilemma.'" In *Political Participation in Modern Indonesia,* edited by R. William Liddle, pp. 58–115. New Haven: Yale University Southeast Asia Studies, 1973.

——. "Exploring Elite Political Culture in Indonesia: Community and Change." Ph.D. dissertation, Yale University, 1972.

——. "Gambling and Development: The Case of Djakarta's 'Flower Organization.' " *Asia,* 27 (Autumn 1972), 19–36.

——. "Students and the Establishment in Indonesia: The Status-Generation Gap." In *Population, Politics and the Future of Southern Asia,* edited by W. Howard Wriggins and James F. Guyot, pp. 259–295. New York: Columbia University Press, 1973.

Feith, Herbert. Review of *Showcase State,* edited by Rex Mortimer. *Bulletin of Indonesian Economic Studies,* 10, 2 (July 1974), 114–118.

——. "Suharto's Search for a Political Format." *Indonesia,* 6 (October 1968), 88–105.

——, and Lance Castles, eds. *Indonesian Political Thinking 1945–1965.* Ithaca: Cornell University Press, 1970.

Franke, Richard W. "The Green Revolution in a Javanese Village." Ph.D. dissertation, Harvard University, 1972.

——. "Miracle Seeds and Shattered Dreams." *Natural History,* 83, 1 (January 1974), 10–18 and 84–88.

Geertz, Clifford. "The Javanese Kijaji: The Changing Role of a Cultural Broker." *Comparative Studies in Society and History,* 2 (1960), 228–249.

——. "The Javanese Village." In *Local, Ethnic, and National Loyalties in Village Indonesia,* edited by G. William Skinner, pp. 34–41. New Haven: Yale University Southeast Asia Studies, 1959.

——. *The Social History of an Indonesian Town.* Cambridge, Mass.: MIT Press, 1965.

Geertz, Hildred. "Indonesian Cultures and Communities." In *Indonesia,* edited by Ruth T. McVey, pp. 24–96. Rev. ed. New Haven: Yale University Southeast Asia Studies, 1967.

Hamka [Haji Abdul Malik Karim Amrullah]. "Dari Hati ke Hati: RUU Perkawinan yang Menggoncangkan." *Harian Kami* [Jakarta], 24 August 1973.

——. *Pandangan Hidup Muslim.* Reprint. Jakarta: Bulan Bintang, 1966.

Hanna, Willard A. "Indonesian Projections and the Arithmetic of Anxiety." *American Universities Field Staff Reports,* Southeast Asia Series, 22, 3 (March 1974).

Harjono, Anwar. "Ada 'Jurang' Dalam RUU Perkawinan." *Harian Kami* [Jakarta], 28 August 1973.

——. "The Future of Islamic Law in Indonesia." *South East Asia Journal of Theology,* 14, 2 (1973), 56–60.

——. "Undang-undang Perkawinan: Sebuah Tanggapan." *Abadi* [Jakarta], 14 January 1974.

Hindley, Donald. "Alirans and the Fall of the Old Order." *Indonesia,* 9 (April 1970), 23–66.

———. "Indonesia 1971: Pantjasila Democracy and the Second Parliamentary Elections." *Asian Survey,* 12 (January 1972), 56–68.

Iongh, Rudy C. de. "Indonesia's New Five-Year Development Plan, 1969–1973." *Review of Indonesian and Malayan Affairs,* 2, 1 (January–March 1968), 8–18.

Jafizham, T. "Rancangan Undang2 Perkawinan." *Abadi* [Jakarta], 31 August 1973.

Jay, Robert R. *Religion and Politics in Rural Central Java.* New Haven: Yale University Southeast Asia Studies, 1963.

King, Dwight Y., and Peter D. Weldon. "Income Distribution and Levels of Living in Java, 1963–1970." Mimeographed, Jakarta, January 1975.

Koentjaraningrat. "The Javanese of South Central Java." In *Social Structure in Southeast Asia,* edited by George Peter Murdock, pp. 89–115. Chicago: Quadrangle Books, 1960.

———. "Tjelapar: A Village in South Central Java." In *Villages in Indonesia,* edited by Koentjaraningrat, pp. 244–280. Ithaca: Cornell University Press, 1967.

Lee, Oey Hong, ed. *Indonesia after the 1971 Elections.* London: Oxford University Press for the University of Hull, 1974.

Lembaga Penelitian Ilmu-ilmu Sosial. "From Peasant to Farmer: Suatu Perkembangan yang Memperluas Gejala Proletarisasi di Daerah Pedesaan (Sawah) di Jawa Tengah." *Cakrawala,* 6 (March–April 1974), 493–503.

Lev, Daniel S. *Islamic Courts in Indonesia: A Study in the Political Bases of Legal Institutions.* Berkeley: University of California Press, 1972.

Liddle, R. William. *Ethnicity, Party, and National Integration: An Indonesian Case Study.* New Haven: Yale University Press, 1970.

———. "Evolution from Above: National Leadership and Local Development in Indonesia." *Journal of Asian Studies,* 32 (1973), 287–309.

McVey, Ruth T. "Nationalism, Islam, and Marxism: The Management of Ideological Conflict in Indonesia." In *Nationalism, Islam and Marxism,* by Sukarno, translated by Karel H. Warouw and Peter D. Weldon, pp. 1–33. Ithaca: Cornell University Modern Indonesia Project, 1970.

Mengapa PSI-Masjumi Gandrung pada Makar? N.p.: n. pub., n.d.

Mertodipuro, Sumantri. "The Astabrata: The Eight Duties of a King." *Indonesian Observer* [Jakarta], 27 October 1967.

Mintaredja, H. M. S. *Renungan Pembaharuan Pemikiran Masjarakat Islam dan Politik di Indonesia.* Jakarta: Permata, 1971.

Montgomery, Roger. "Employment and Unemployment in Jogjakarta." Ph.D. dissertation, Cornell University, 1973.

Mortimer, Rex, ed. *Showcase State: The Illusion of Indonesia's "Accelerated Modernization."* Sydney: Angus and Robertson, 1973.

Palmier, Leslie. *Social Status and Power in Java.* London, Athlone Press, 1960.

Papanek, G. F. Review of *Showcase State,* edited by Rex Mortimer. *Bulletin of Indonesian Economic Studies,* 10, 2 (July 1974), 119–125.

Penny, D. H., and M. Singarimbun. *Population and Poverty in Rural Java: Some Economic Arithmetic from Sriharjo.* Ithaca: Cornell University Department of Agricultural Economics, 1973.

Prasadja, A. Buddy. *Pembangunan Desa dan Masalah Kepemimpinannja: Suatu Penelitian di Desa Gegesik, Kabupaten Tjirebon, Djawa Barat.* Bogor: Lembaga Penelitian Sosiologi Pedesaan, Institut Pertanian Bogor, 1974.

Rasjidi, H. M. *Kasus R.U.U. Perkawinan dalam Hubungan Islam dan Kristen.* Jakarta: Bulan Bintang, 1974.

Samson, Allan A. "Army and Islam in Indonesia." *Pacific Affairs,* 44 (Winter 1971–1972), 545–565.

——. "Islam in Indonesian Politics." *Asian Survey,* 8 (December 1968), 1001–1017.

Siegel, James T. *The Rope of God.* Berkeley: University of California Press, 1969.

Simatupang, T. B. "The Situation and Challenge of the Christian Mission in Indonesia Today." *South East Asian Journal of Theology,* 10, 4 (April 1969), 10–27.

Soemardi, Soelaeman. "Regional Politicians and Administrators in West Java (1956): Social Backgrounds and Career Patterns." M.A. thesis, Cornell University, 1961.

S. T. A. [Sutan Takdir Alisjahbana]. "Didikan Barat dan Didikan Pesantren: Menoedjoe ke Masjarakat jang Dynamisch." *Poedjangga Baroe,* 3 (December 1935), 180–184.

Sukarno. *Negara Harus BerTuhan.* Jakarta: Departemen Agama, 1964.

——. "Trias Politica." Speech to the National Planning Council (DEPERNAS), 13 August 1960.

Thomas, K. D., and J. Panglaykim. "Indonesia's Development Cabinet, Background to Current Problems and the Five Year Plan." *Asian Survey,* 9 (April 1969), 223–238.

Timmer, Peter C. Reply to William L. Collier, et al., "Choice of

Technique in Rice Milling." *Bulletin of Indonesian Economic Studies,* 10, 1 (March 1974), 121–126.

Wahid, Abdurrahman. "Pesantren sebagai Subkultur." In *Pesantren dan Pembaharuan,* edited by M. Dawam Rahardjo, pp. 39–60. Jakarta: Lembaga Penelitian, Pendidikan dan Penerangan Ekonomi dan Sosial, 1974.

Ward, K. E. *The Foundation of the Partai Muslimin Indonesia.* Ithaca: Cornell University Modern Indonesia Project, 1970.

Wertheim, W. F. "From Aliran towards Class Struggle in the Countryside of Java." Published in *Pacific Viewpoint,* 10, 2 (1969), 1–17.

Willner, Ann Ruth. *The Neotraditional Accommodation to Political Independence: The Case of Indonesia.* Princeton: Princeton University Center of International Studies, 1966. Revised and republished in *Cases in Comparative Politics: Asia,* edited by Lucian W. Pye, pp. 242–306. Boston: Little, Brown, 1970.

Wirjosukarto, Amir Hamzah. *Pembaharuan Pendidikan dan Pengadjaran Islam jang Diselenggarakan oleh Pergerakan Muhammadijah dari Kota Jogjakarta.* Yogyakarta: Penjelenggara Publicasi Pembaharuan Pendidikan/Pengadjaran Islam [1962].

Yuti [Sayuti Melik]. "Parlementaria (I)." *Suara Karya* [Jakarta], 15 January 1974.

Fiction

Rusli, Marah. *Sitti Nurbaja.* Reprint. Jakarta: Balai Pustaka, 1965.

Toer, Pramoedya Ananta. *Ditepi Kali Bekasi.* Reprint. Jakarta: Jajasan Kebudajaan Sadar, 1962.

———. "Gado-Gado." In *Pertjikan Revolusi,* by Pramoedya Ananta Toer, pp. 11–79. Reprint. Jakarta: Balai Pustaka, 1957.

———. *Keluarga Gerilja.* Reprint. Jakarta: Nusantara, 1962.

———. "Kemudian Lahirlah Dia." In *Tjerita Dari Blora,* by Pramoedya Ananta Toer, pp. 89–113. Jakarta: Balai Pustaka, 1952. Edited and translated by A. Brotherton as "Born Before the Dawn." *The Atlantic Monthly,* June 1956, 114–116.

Newsjournals

(Except for *Haluan Minggu* [Padang], all of these serials are or were published in Jakarta.)

Abadi.

Angkatan Bersendjata.

Asia Raya.

Berita Buana.

Berita Yudha.

Haluan Minggu.
Harian Kami.
Indonesia Raya.
Jakarta Times.
Kompas.
Nusantara.
Pedoman.
Sinar Harapan.
Suara Karya.
Tempo.
Warta Berita.

INDEX

Abangan: "beliefs" as legal alternative to Islam, 237-238, 242-245; defined, 21, 23-24; political organization, 22, 40-42, 60, 99; priyayi and, 24, 64, 99, 141; santri and, as coextensive, 106, 142-146, 173-174; santri and, as elite labels, 101-103; santri and, in politics, 21-24, 173-174, 193, 217, 237-239; santri and, views of wayang, 34, 83, 144-146; see also Elite: abangan military, and Islam; Elite: Javanese in; Javanese; Joint Secretariat for Beliefs; Kawula-gusti; Priyayi: abangan and; Purwoko; and Wayang kulit
ABRI, see Armed forces
Abubakar, story of, 204-205
Administrators, see Elite, bureaucratic
Alisjahbana, Sutan Takdir, 100
Ambonese, 152, 183
Angkatan Bersenjata Republik Indonesia (ABRI), see Armed forces
Animism, 24
"Anomic piety," 180
Anomie, perceived, 29-30, 175-185; defined, 29, 176
Armed forces (Angkatan Bersenjata Republik Indonesia, ABRI): bureaucratic representation of, 118-120; "dual function" of, 166, 237, 255; influence of, 119-120, 122; institutional penetration by, 132, 163-166, 173; legislative representation of, 121-122; recruitment into, 132; regional rebellions and, 42; see also Army; Coup, aftermath of 1965 attempted; Department of Defense and Security; Elite: abangan military, and Islam; and Elite: officers in
Army: anticommunist role of, 22, 78, 126, 161-162, 250; bureaucratic role of, 110-111, 120, 163-165; division within, 245-247, 258; in Parliament, 121, 166, 241-244
Army of Allah (Hizbullah), 92-93, 95-97, 267
Association of Native Administrative Employees (PPBB), 44, 48
Authority: appreciation of, and order, 94, 108-109, 158, 160-162, 164-165; support for deference toward, 28-30, 198-206;

support for deference toward, defined, 199; tendency to personalize, 204-205, 218, 254-256
Authority, central: regional poverty and, 189, 211-213; support for, 28-29, 210-218; support for, defined, 211; see also Decentralization, prospects for

Badan Koordinasi Intelijens Negara (BAKIN), see State Intelligence Coordinating Body
Badan Penyelidik Kemerdekaan Indonesia (BPKI), see Body for the Investigation of Indonesian Independence
BAKIN, see State Intelligence Coordinating Body
Balinese, 21, 34; in sample, 43, 137
Bandung, 74-76, 226-227, 231
Banjarese in sample, 137
Batak in sample, 137
Benda, Harry J., 34-35
Bima, 33, 65-66
Body for the Investigation of Indonesian Independence (BPKI), 55-57, 59
BPKI, see Body for the Investigation of Indonesian Independence
Broad Outlines of State Policy, 238-239, 244
Buddhism, 24, 237
Buddhists: marriage law and, 245; number of, 21
Bureaucracy: criticisms of, 170-171; dominance of, 26, 41-62 (passim), 105, 125, 167-170, 222, 231, 244, 250-252, 267-269; history of, 32-41; politicization of, 41-42, 77-78, 164-165, 170, 261; rank and status in, 118-119; size of, 117-118; see also Armed forces; Army; Authority, central; Colonial rule; Department entries; Elite, bureaucratic; Institutional hypothesis; Institutional identification; Pamong praja; and Priyayi

Catholic Party, 122, 228-229, 234-236, 239-240
Catholics, number of, 21
Center of the People's Strength (Putera), 52

INDONESIA'S ELITE

Designed by R. E. Rosenbaum.
Composed by York Composition Company, Inc.,
in 10 point Linotype Times Roman, 2 points leaded,
with display lines in monotype Deepdene.
Printed letterpress from type by York Composition Company
on Warren's Number 66 text, 50 pound basis.
Bound by John H. Dekker & Sons, Inc.
in Joanna book cloth
and stamped in All Purpose foil.

Library of Congress Cataloging in Publication Data

Emmerson, Donald K
    Indonesia's elite.

    Bibliography: p.
    Includes index.
    1. Elite (Social sciences)—Indonesia.   2. Indonesia—Politics and gov-
ernment—1966–   3. Indonesia—Social conditions. I. Title.
JQ776.E44   301.5'92'09598   75-36525
ISBN 0-8014-0917-9

DATE DUE

MAR 1 1 2002			
GAYLORD			PRINTED IN U.S.A.